N
Remembered

Jane Shaw

Nahanni Remembered

A. C. Lewis

NeWest Press
Edmonton

Canadian Cataloguing in Publication Data

Lewis, A. C. (Alfred Crandell), 1914–
Nahanni remembered

(NorthWest passages; 2)
ISBN 1–896300–18–9

1. Lewis, A. C. (Alfred Crandell), 1914– Journeys–
Northwest Territories–South Nahanni River Valley. 2. South
Nahanni River Valley (N.W.T.)–Description and travel. 3.
Trapping–Northwest Territories–South Nahanni River Valley.
I. Title. II. Series.
FC4195.S69L48 1997   971.9'3   C97–910587–0
F1100.S6L48 1997
Editor for the Press: Diane Bessai
Cover and book design: John Luckhurst /GDL

COMMITTED
TO THE
DEVELOPMENT
OF CULTURE
AND
THE ARTS

ALBERTA
Lotteries

The Alberta
Foundation
for the Arts

Alberta
COMMUNITY DEVELOPMENT

THE CANADA COUNCIL | LE CONSEIL DES ARTS
FOR THE ARTS | DU CANADA
SINCE 1957 | DEPUIS 1957

NeWest Press gratefully acknowledges the support received for its publishing program from The Canada Council's Block Grants program and The Alberta Foundation for the Arts.

The cover and chapter page graphic is reproduced from *Picturesque Canada* Volume 1 1882.

Printed and bound in Canada

NeWest

NeWest Publishers Limited
#201, 8540 – 109 Street
Edmonton, Alberta T6G 1E6

In Memory of Fran

Contents

Foreword – 1

Prologue – 3

1   The Trip In – 10

2   Moose Hunt – 25

3   Out on the Line – 45

4   Cold Siwash Nights – 66

5   Wolverine and Wolf – 82

6   Beaver and Caribou – 95

7   Waiting for Breakup – 105

8   Bears and Berries – 115

9   Dall's Sheep and Other Encounters – 126

10   Goodbye to Rabbitkettle – 139

11   Trouble on the River – 158

12   Dead Men's Valley – 182

13   The Portage Trail – 201

14   Gold Is Where You Find It – 213

15   Epilogue – 232

Foreword

I finished this book just as I was reaching my eighty-first birthday. Procrastination had stilled my pen for so long. It was Bill Mason, well-known nature film-maker, author, and white water canoeist, who helped me break the lengthy spell of indecision. I first met Mason in 1985 in Victoria at the Newcombe Auditorium, where he was showing his movie, *Cry of the Wild*. I was surprised to learn that he was the father of Paul, the guide on our Nahanni canoe trip just nine months before. When I recounted my sojourn in the Nahanni of 1937, he said, "You should write a book about that." Encouragement from a person of Mason's standing would renew anyone's inspiration, especially since the only published record was a brief and somewhat inexact sketch by Dick Turner in his 1975 reminiscence, *Nahanni*. Mason's suggestion, plus a mountain of patience displayed by my late wife, Fran, finally led to the completion of *Nahanni Remembered*. Our good neighbour of many years, Debbie Parsons, typed the manuscript.

Down through the years the Nahanni has claimed the lives of many men, including those, for reasons of space, not mentioned in this book. And I often think of them all as individuals, and of how they may have died. I'm not sure why I do this. Perhaps it is because I know I could so easily have been among them.

I am too old now to follow the mountain trails or ford the valley streams of yesterday. And in these twilight years often I find myself living in the past, retracing those long-ago footprints with all their memories.

A.C.L.

Travelling the Nahanni

Note: * name reflects usage at time of travels

▲ Camp

Inge Wilson / Mostly Maps

Prologue

The South Nahanni is totally a mountain river. Its headwaters flow from the height of land between the Yukon and Northwest Territories to its confluence with the Liard at Nahanni Butte, a distance of approximately 340 miles (550 km).

I was just out of high school in 1932 when I first heard about this wilderness waterway. Earlier reports stated that gold had been discovered "somewhere" on one of the numerous creeks flowing into one of the main tributaries of the Nahanni—presumably the Flat River. And in glowing terms it was strongly implied that if one could survive the treacherous waters of this wild Nahanni and reach these creeks, there was gold to be found—and lots of it.

Over the years I have been asked occasionally what brought me into the Nahanni in the first place, and it's still assumed that it must have been that elusive, yellow metal. Nothing could have been further from the truth. It was mainly chance—with the help of the Great Depression—that brought about my sojourn of 1937 in the Nahanni with one of the finest men I have ever known. His name was Harry Vandaele.

Harry's parents and mine had come from the United States to take up homesteads in Alberta during the same year, 1903. Our farms were three miles apart, and there was always a close friendship between our families. Harry was seven years my senior, and as a young boy I regarded him as my idol.

He left the farm at nineteen to reside in Calgary, where he worked in a service station. In 1934, during the height of the Depression, he and a fellow worker, Milt Campbell, decided to go into the Nahanni country to try to find that gold. They went North by way of Dawson Creek and Fort St. John, B.C. and thence with a winter freight-hauling outfit to Fort Nelson, B.C. After open water, using their canoe and outboard motors, they proceeded down the Fort Nelson and Liard rivers to the mouth of the Nahanni. They then had to navigate roughly 200 miles (320 km) of upstream water to reach their destination—Bennett Creek, a tributary of Flat River. Immediately after the ice cleared out of the Nahanni they made this upstream trip with no trouble.

Prospecting for gold on this creek that summer, they returned to Edmonton late in the fall. They followed the same procedure in 1935, but found no gold. In 1936 they again went North to wash for gold, this time on the Liard River, taking Harry's brother Joe in with them. Their new attempt at washing "fine" gold out of the sand was also unsuccessful. That fall Harry and Milt remained in the North while Joe returned home to the farm.

Meanwhile, the Mackenzie rather than the Nahanni had been much on my mind. I had been reading about this great river and set my heart on going to Fort Simpson some day to see it. From Joe I learned that casual labour was paid five dollars per day at Simpson and other places along the river, when work became available. This was the catalyst I needed. I decided to take my chances, a decision that prompted me to seek a boxcar out of Edmonton on a frigid late January morning of 1937—little realizing that the South Nahanni, not the Mackenzie, would be my final destination that winter.

As I walked eastward on 127th Avenue towards the CNR yards at Calder, a cruel southeast wind biting my face, I could see two workmen busy shunting freight cars back and forth, to make up the mixed train for its scheduled 500-mile (800 km) run to Dawson Creek, B.C. This happened to be my destination also, so I intended to be on that train when it departed. I planned to follow the same general route North from end of steel that Harry and Milt had taken in 1934, proceeding to Fort Nelson by the winter freight route to await breakup. Then I would seek boat passage down the Fort Nelson and Liard rivers, going beyond the mouth of the Nahanni to Fort Simpson on the Mackenzie.

Twice I felt my face beginning to freeze, and I'd stop to turn my back to the wind. I was trying to determine how long it would be before the train would roll, but I couldn't even see the head locomotive anywhere; it was likely still in the roundhouse. Well, there was no sense torturing myself any longer. Stooped over against this bloody wind and lugging my heavy packboard over my shoulders, I had to find an empty boxcar—and the sooner the better.

The frigid weather did produce a degree of compensation in my situation: I didn't have to worry about the CN railroad "bull" interfering with my plans. On this sort of morning, he would be back in the roundhouse, drinking coffee with the boys.

I was walking along the pathway adjacent to the main line, when a surprised brakeman suddenly appeared from between two of the boxcars. "Where in hell are you headed for, fella?"

"Westlock," I lied.

"You're crazy!" he said. "Westlock is fifty miles away. You will freeze before we get there!"

"Just tell me where I can find an empty boxcar; that's all I need," I said.

The brakeman took note of the heavy dunnage bag strapped to the packboard. He shot me a long look, then gestured to the rear of the train. "There's four empty grain cars down the line. You can take your pick." And without further comment he proceeded up to the head end of the train.

I finally found an unsealed car and slid the door open, heaved in my pack, and climbed aboard. Ages later, I heard two short whistle blasts, then car-couplings clanging, followed by a sudden lurch of my car as the train slowly rolled forward.

After the train was well out of the Calder yards, I opened the sliding door about a foot to let in some light. Having trouble keeping my feet warm, I began pacing back and forth from one end of the boxcar to the other. I kept this tedious routine up for a couple of hours or more. And the scenery never changed: four gloomy walls and a blank sky. It was a dull way to put in time, not conducive to productive thought, especially when at times I almost lost my balance from the continual swaying of the car as its wheels clattered over a track badly in need of repair—a common condition of railroads in these Depression years.

But the locale did serve to bring back memories—memories of more enjoyable freight train rides through parts of Alberta and B.C. in May and June of 1932. I and a friend had decided to seek greener pastures, using the freights as our mode of travel. We were both eighteen years of age with no experience in a venture of this sort, and we had to learn the various intricacies of riding boxcars, step by step. But after we discovered we could outrun the railroad cops, there really wasn't much to it.

But I knew this winter trip to Dawson Creek would be different. This ride was going to be one of sheer endurance. I had a legitimate reason for travelling hobo-style in thirty below zero weather: the cost was nil; an empty boxcar requires no ticket.

All my earthly possessions were with me, here in my dunnage bag. And I didn't need an accountant to total the inventory. The bag contained a vital outfitting of extra clothing, plus several other items essential to a sojourn in the North. The only articles of indifferent importance were a small pocket dictionary and a folding camera that had been given to me as a going-away gift. Also in my bag was my summer eiderdown—actually too light for winter use, but I wasn't about to spend eighty dollars for one of those Arctic Three-Star beauties that were prominently displayed at Uncle Ben's Exchange in Edmonton.

My total possessions? Well—not entirely: inside my woollen underwear was a hidden pocket containing $240. I had thirty dollars more in my leather wallet. Why, I was rich! Then why had I not purchased a ticket that would have allowed me to ride in comfort in the passenger coach? I had considered this alternative the day before I left home—and then I remembered something that was too hard to forget: it had taken me five years of extremely high-paid farm work to accumulate this small fortune. Five years! At this rate I would be an old man before I became financially stable. No, when I could afford it (if ever) I would ride first class.

At 9 p.m. that evening—almost twelve hours after leaving Edmonton, the train finally arrived at McLennan, a divisional point on the Peace River run. I was cold and hungry. And tired. I was not familiar with this new exercise of walking while riding, especially when the terrain was a swaying platform that synchronized its movement to coincide with the number of times the brakes were applied.

Several times I found myself colliding with the end walls of the car.

I knew that another crew would be coming aboard at McLennan, and so I shouldered the packboard and made my way to a nearby restaurant and bought a meal. Presently, in walked the brakeman I had met in the Calder yards. He stared at me, incredulously, and shook his head. "I thought you were supposed to be going to Westlock?" he said—more an exclamation than a question.

"I'm headed for Dawson Creek," I said. "I have a job offered me there," I lied again. "I thought you might prevent me from boarding the train at Calder if you knew I was going that far in this cold weather."

"Well chap, you will be a corpse before morning if you intend to spend the night in that boxcar. Listen! I'll do what I can; the train will pull out about 10:30 p.m. There will be another crew on board to Dawson. I'll tell the relief brakeman to look in on you. Which car are you in?" I told him, and thanked him for his concern. I thought that here was a chap I could learn to like.

Sometime during the early hours of the morning I heard brakes screeching and the train slowed to a stop. We seemed to be in the middle of nowhere, as far as I could make out through the grey darkness. Presently a man, swinging a lantern, came up to the car door where I was standing. It was the new brakeman. He handed me a thermos of coffee. He explained that we would be stopped for about fifteen minutes to sidetrack a carload of railway equipment for the track repairmen.

When he came back a little later to pick up the thermos, he exclaimed, "Cee—rist it's cold! I'll tell yuh one thing: if there's any of those brass monkeys climbing around out there in the trees tonight, they sure as hell are gonna git their testicles froze off before morning, I can promise yuh that." I couldn't resist a chuckle. I had often heard this favourite cold weather expression back home, but never uttered in such an explicit manner.

Later that morning, we were stopped for two hours at the town of Grand Prairie, Alberta, while the train crew and yardmen added and subtracted various cars of freight, as well as making repairs of some sort near the head of the train. It had been a long night and I was hungry. Up on the main street I spotted a small cafe. I walked in and sat down on one of the stools at the counter. On the wall behind the counter there was a sign in large capital letters: PANCAKES. ALL YOU CAN EAT. 20¢. Now this was language I could understand. Shortly, the cook came in from the kitchen and asked, "What will it be for you, young fella?" I said I'd have the pancakes. He likely didn't need to ask; he had seen me eyeing the sign, and I must have looked as if I hadn't eaten in a week.

While I was waiting, my mind became occupied with a complex calculation as to how many pancakes I could consume at this sitting. I realized that it would depend upon how big the flapjacks were. The number was never finalized, because as time ticked by, the cook finally exclaimed, "Look fella, that's it! There ain't no more batter left."

Late in the afternoon, I could see two grain elevators rising above the hills as we neared Dawson Creek. I was glad this trip was nearly over. Up on the main street, I registered at what appeared to be a prominent hotel. The bathroom was down the hall from my room, and it was a heavenly feeling to have a wash and thaw myself out. I had supper at the town's main restaurant—or so I was told. The meal was low on meat and heavy on partially boiled beans. I expressed my dislike for the victuals offered, and the cook didn't enjoy my complaint. But I was more than reasonable; I did pay for the meal, not the cheapest one on the menu by any means.

Later, upstairs in my room, there was a rap on the door. It was the hotel clerk, who handed me a telegram just delivered by a messenger from the railway station. It was from my brother Bill at Innisfail, Alberta. It read:

CAN ARRANGE YOU FLY INTO NAHANNI TO JOIN HARRY VANDAELE AT RABBITKETTLE RIVER STOP WIRE ANSWER AT ONCE STOP BILL

I reached for my tobacco pouch, rolled a smoke, and sat down in an old wicker armchair to try to concentrate on this unexpected message. It left so many questions unanswered. I knew that Harry Vandaele was trapping at George Dalziel's base camp near the Rabbitkettle River (a tributary of the South Nahanni River). I had learned that much from Harry's brother, Joe, in the late fall of 1936. This was all. What the arrangements were between Harry and Dalziel I didn't know. Presumably, Harry was trapping on shares with

Dal, popularly known as The Flying Trapper, who had a registered trapline.

I found myself wondering about Harry's partner, Milt Campbell. Where was he? And why wasn't he with Harry? Any speculations that may have come to mind would have been pure guesswork on my part. I didn't even know the exact location of the Rabbitkettle—except that its confluence with the Nahanni was somewhere above Virginia Falls. And where would I fit into this proposed picture? Probably my brother didn't know for sure when he sent the telegram.

What I did know was that I had no trapping experience, except for gophers back on the farm; that I'd read of all those men who went into the Nahanni and never came out; that I had no experience with a bad river, and couldn't even swim.

But the primary question—which naturally perturbed me—was what the plane flight would cost from Edmonton to wherever Dalziel's camp was situated. I wasn't that naive; there was no way a flight of this magnitude could be arranged unless it involved the contents of that hidden pocket in my underwear. After thirty-seven hours since leaving Edmonton, I decided to sleep on it.

Chance helped me to reach a decision the next morning. I happened to meet a fellow in the lobby who had just made the two-day trip from Fort St. John by team and sleigh. If I decided to stay with my original plan, I could ride back to the Fort with him. Yes, he was well acquainted with Joe Clarke, the freight-hauler I had expected to find in Dawson Creek. But he told me that Clarke had already left for Fort Nelson three days before. This changed the entire situation. I was now not sure of what might lie ahead in the way of winter employment. And so I immediately wired my brother that I was returning at once, and would meet him in Edmonton at the Leland Hotel. My impulsive nature asserted itself that morning; I decided to splurge. I bought a passenger ticket back to Edmonton.

The Trip In

Back in Edmonton by 5 p.m. the next day, I sought out my brother Bill in his room at the Leland. To my surprise he was accompanied by a medium-built man in his early thirties who turned out to be George Dalziel, The Flying Trapper himself.

I had heard more than one story about this man. A few of them were firsthand from Harry Vandaele himself, who had the opportunity on several occasions of meeting the man at the mouth of the Nahanni and also at Fort Simpson. It was Dal who had flown Harry into the Rabbitkettle just this past autumn. Harry's partner, Milt Campbell, was trapping elsewhere.

Dalziel was tough, his own best teacher. His ability in the air was in direct proportion to his ability in this bush. This was the man who had snowshoed from Lower Post on the Liard River to Fort Norman on the Mackenzie River. Nearly 400 miles (645 km) as the crow flies! And Dal sure as hell never followed any crow. Through mountains, swamps, river valleys, and plateaus, he made the winter journey with rifle, axe, and two pack dogs. One of the dogs—a bitch—had her young pup with her. And the pup completed the journey. In the beginning of the Thirties this must have been a formidable undertaking for any man, no matter how experienced he may have been.

For an hour or more, we discussed my forthcoming trip and how it had come about. Joe Vandaele was concerned about his brother being alone for the rest of the winter at the Rabbitkettle. Bill, knowing I had enough money for the plane in my secret pocket—and was on my way North in any case—had suggested me as the solution.

"A Mackenzie Air Service plane is leaving tomorrow afternoon to Fort Simpson," Dalziel explained. "If you are all set to go, we can arrange for you to be on that flight. The fare will be $200."

The amount did not exceed my expectations. But my chief concern was how Harry Vandaele and I would be coming out of the Nahanni in the spring, after breakup. I presumed that Dal would be flying us out to the mouth of the Nahanni after open water near the end of May—or shortly after.

"I'm afraid that may not be possible," Dal said. "My plane is here in Edmonton and will be out of commission for some time. There are repairs needed—and other matters to be taken care of—before I'm flying again. But you and Harry won't have any trouble coming down the river, after the beaver hunt. You can build a raft. Better still, you can put a platform on my set of pontoons; they're up there at the Rabbitkettle camp. You could float down on them."

So everything had been worked out to everyone's satisfaction—including mine—a young, green, totally inexperienced kid, just recently dry behind the ears, although very impulsive by nature. However, I did wonder why it would take four months for Dal to have his plane repaired, but I didn't delve into the matter. He had said that there were "other matters to be taken care of," which would take time, I assumed.

And so with the important aspects of my journey discussed and resolved, Dal rose to go, saying he would meet us the next day at 11 a.m. in the MAS office located in the Macdonald Hotel. Then, as an afterthought, he asked, "Have you got a rifle?"

I said that I would purchase one in the morning at Uncle Ben's Exchange.

"Make sure you do!" Dal said, with noticeable emphasis. "You will also need a mosquito bar."

This was an item I had completely forgotten. There was no time to waste. My brother and I were at Uncle Ben's when it opened next morning. I bought a used .30-.30 calibre Winchester rifle, four boxes of cartridges, eighty rounds of ammunition, and forty feet of three-eighths-inch Manila rope. The store was sold out of mosquito bars. A standard article no trapper or prospector would ever think of forgetting, was tobacco. I bought seven, half-pound tins of fine-cut Turret. I knew Harry also smoked. Perhaps my most important purchase was a light-weight Hudson's Bay axe. I also needed a pair of snowshoes, but Uncle Ben advised me to purchase these at the Bay store at Fort Simpson. They had a better selection for individual needs, he explained.

Uncle Ben was quite amused when he saw me cut open the hidden pocket in my underwear. I don't suppose he had ever ridden a freight train. I wasn't so amused when I noted I was down to less than a dozen dollars, which forced me to borrow thirty from my brother—something I was reluctant to do.

Over at the Macdonald, I paid for the flight at the agent's counter. He was careful to check the weight of my dunnage bag, a practice that I noted was never overlooked on any subsequent flight during my time in the North.

A few minutes later, Dalziel arrived and engaged in conversation with a tall, slim man, who was to be the pilot on the flight. His name was Stan McMillan, who had already become one of the veteran bush pilots of the North. On a sheet of hotel stationery, Dal quickly drew a sketch of the Nahanni River, showing the exact location of Harry's camp at the Rabbitkettle—or so I gathered from bits of their conversation. Then turning abruptly to me, he said, "Let's have a look at your rifle." I handed him the Winchester. Dal quickly worked the lever-action a couple of times, then sighted down the barrel. "It's okay," he commented. "Make sure that ice doesn't plug up the barrel in cold weather. Leave your rifle outside in cold weather while in camp." (He was alluding to the problem of condensation.) Then he reached into a pocket of his overcoat and withdrew a bottle of Governor General rum and handed it to me. "Here, stuff this in your dunnage bag. It's for you and Harry. Oh yes—here's a list of groceries you fellows will need before the winter is out. I've left a notation for the Bay manager at Simpson to put the bill on my account." With that he turned to leave. We shook hands and he was gone. Dalziel struck me as a man in a hurry—a man who knew where he was going—and how to get there. A man of action and little talk.

Early that afternoon, the pilot and mechanic, myself and two other passengers were driven out to Cooking Lake (a few miles southeast of Edmonton) in the MAS van. Another mechanic, who had been doing repairs to one of the skis, already had the plane warmed up and waiting when we arrived. We quickly stowed our duffel and climbed aboard the Norseman. In a matter of minutes we were airborne.

As we gained altitude, I saw the patchwork quilt view of the white, snow-covered fields below. In half an hour we were over a vast expanse of mixed conifer and aspen forest. Farther north the forest became increasingly interspersed with large areas of swamp and muskeg, partially covered with stunted spruce.

This was my first flight. I kept my eyes glued to the small window, trying to memorize this aerial world which was passing too swiftly beneath me. Five days ago I was travelling no class, as an unshiny knight of the rails; today I was soaring with the elite of the North. The only thing lacking on the plane was proper seating accommodation. We three passengers simply hunkered down on our dunnage bags with our backs propped up against the fuselage.

It was nearing dusk when McMillan brought the plane down on the Clearwater River, near its confluence with the Athabaska. We taxied into the snye (a small channel of the river between an island and the mainland), adjacent to the old Hudson's Bay post at Fort McMurray. Leaving the mechanic to adjust the canvas tarp over the plane's engine, McMillan hoisted the mail sack over his shoulder and we followed him up the steep bank, then across the main road to the New Franklin Hotel.

Henry Moberly, of the Hudson's Bay Company, had founded McMurray in 1870. In those days it was conceived for one reason only: fur. But in 1937, this village of several hundred people—a blending of Indians, Metis, and whites—was motivated by other business inducements as well. McMurray was now the gateway to all water navigation north to the Beaufort Sea. And it also served as the main base of operations into the far North for two fledgling airlines: The Mackenzie Air Service and Canadian Airways.

There was another business just beginning to sprout wings: down the road, two miles east of McMurray, at the end of steel at Waterways, was a small oil plant—a pilot plant experimenting with ways and means of extracting the oil from the tar sands along the Athabaska River. Everyone knew there was a lot of oil in this part of the country. It was there for all to see—a black and brown, molasses-type tar, oozing out of the banks of the river. But the oil had to be taken out of the sand by some means, and this was the problem. An expensive problem. Conventional oil from the wells in Alberta was far cheaper to produce (and still is). But in 1937 no one knew—or even dreamed—that this industry would reach such giant proportions fifty years later.

All travellers proceeding into the North stayed at the New Franklin Hotel. It was so popular it even had an annex nearby. At 6 p.m. we all filed into the spacious dining room for supper. At the time I was twenty-two years of age and had acquired a healthy interest in girls. While eating my meal, it was only natural that the greater part of my attention was diverted to the attractive young waitress who was serving the tables. I was trying to think of a way to strike up a conversation with her, when two parka-clad men entered the dining room and sat down at the table reserved for the bush pilots. This gave me the opportunity I was looking for. I asked the waitress if she knew these men. "They're both pilots; they fly for MAS," she said. "The one with the mustache is Bob Randall. The other is Archie McMullen. You must have flown in with McMillan. And where might you be off to?"

"I'm going up the South Nahanni River to join an old friend."

"And will you be seeing the Virginia Falls?"

"I hope to," I said. Each succeeding cup of coffee brought the waitress back to my table. I drank a lot of java that evening.

Breakfast was at 6:30 the next morning, and as I turned to go, the waitress said, "I hope you find some of that gold in Dead Men's Valley—or wherever it's supposed to be. And be careful of that river!" As we shook hands, I thought I detected a trace of apprehension in her voice—as if she was thinking: "Well, we likely won't see this chap again." I gathered she also read the newspapers, with all their sinister stories of the area.

At daybreak we took off on the 140-mile (225-km) flight to Fort Chipewyan, situated on the rocky, north shore of Lake Athabaska. Here at the old Fort, we stopped just long enough to toss the mailbag out on the ice and receive the ongoing mail from the Hudson's Bay store.

In that brief interval I recalled a bit of history connected with this famous Fort. It was near the south shore of this lake that in 1778 Peter Pond of the North West Company established the first fur post on waters leading to the Beaufort Sea. And from this same area, in 1789, Alexander Mackenzie set out on his journey down the great river that bears his name. A feeling of wonderment came over me as I thought about that long-ago day when this explorer paddled into the unknown to find a route to the Pacific Ocean—which he did later, in 1793.

But my train of thought was soon broken by a sudden revving of the plane's engine, sending us down the marked runway in a cloud of swirling snow. In a few, short moments the cluster of Indian cabins and red-roofed buildings of the Hudson's Bay Company were rapidly fading away in the distance.

Our next stop was at Fort Smith, a comparatively large settlement extending along the south shore of the Slave River, at the sixtieth parallel. Here we had dinner, and afterwards considerable time was spent waiting for the clerk to sort out the mail in the tiny post office, a simple task that should have been taken care of while we were eating dinner. McMillan was annoyed by the delay and told the clerk to "hurry it up. I've only got so much daylight left between here and Simpson; I can't fly in the dark." The weather was also bothering our pilot. The sky had clouded over and there was a premonition of impending snowfall in the air. One could sense it—although the weather report from Simpson was clear. Finally we were airborne again, flying over the Slave River to Fort Resolution, the destination of my fellow passengers.

Since leaving Edmonton, I had found these two men very uncommunicative. They were sociable only to the necessary degree; my attempts towards congenial conversation, as to who was going where, were met with vague answers. They did ask me where I was bound, and I didn't think I was giving away any secrets when I told them. And so I never learned where they were from or why they were going to Resolution. (The following September I was to see one of these chaps in Yellowknife; he was a closed-mouthed mining executive.)

Alone now in the cabin, I could observe the scenery on either side of the plane. But it wasn't of any benefit, for as the afternoon wore on, the weather deteriorated. It became difficult to make out the shoreline of Great Slave Lake on our left, and to my right, all I saw was a vast expanse of white—one of the largest areas of snow-covered ice in all of Canada.

When we landed at Fort Providence, a group of Indians was waiting down on the ice at the foot of the trail leading up to the settlement. While the mailbags were being exchanged, one of the Indians climbed into the cabin and sat down alongside me. He seemed congenial—eager to make friends. We weren't stopped longer than five minutes, so I don't remember much about Fort Providence.

Height reduces the size of all objects below in direct proportion to one's altitude, and so I didn't realize the magnitude of the Mackenzie River as we flew over the white expanse of "The Great One," as it was often referred to in the North. Vision was also blurred by the rapid increase of snowfall, so that it became difficult to define an outline of anything. I was beginning to wish we had stayed at Providence.

But flying in a snowstorm didn't seem to bother my Indian friend at all. He turned to me and remarked, "Dis plane—she sure beats walkin', eh?"

I allowed as how it did but that I didn't like the weather conditions. "A pilot has to be able to see where he's flying."

"Dat don' bodder me none; dat's up to him," he pointed to McMillan. "Snow, she stop by an' by, mabbee."

I spent a few moments digesting this chap's philosophy, and decided his attitude was reasonable. It was the pilot's responsibility to keep the plane in the air. And it likely would stop snowing, sooner or later.

Now, when I looked up forward into the cockpit I saw the snow beating against the plane's windshield. Suddenly one wing dipped and McMillan brought the Norseman down to treetop level near the north shore of the river. Through the snow flurry the olive-green forest rushed dimly past us. I could almost feel the ice on the river under my feet. There was no room for error here, but neither the mechanic nor pilot seemed to be perturbed. I think the Indian could sense that I was a shade uneasy. He leaned over and said, "Suppose engine quit, we ain't got far down." Well, he was right about that. With such an ultra-positive outlook on life, I could imagine this fellow living to a ripe old age—with any luck at all.

But the plane droned on, hugging the tree-lined shore, and for good reason: at eye-level with the line of timber, it was easier to follow the bends in the river. And if the storm increased, the pilot would simply "set her down" on the ice.

I was disappointed in the weather. I had read so much about the Mackenzie River and had actually seen so little. And in a few minutes we would reach its confluence with the Liard. This river, almost as large as the Mackenzie, comes in on the left, about a mile (1.6 km) above the Fort. But the snow-laden dusk effectively blotted out this great tributary, and I saw nothing of it.

Our pilot knew where we were, for soon the plane began gaining altitude, then veered abruptly to our left in a wide 180-degree turn, then slowly the engine's power receded, trees flashing by on our right. I felt the skis touch the ice in a swirl of snow. We had landed in the snye that ran past the west side of the wooded island at Fort Simpson.

As we stepped down from the cabin, I was surprised to see a team and sleigh approaching on a trail which led out of a grove of poplar trees. Horses yet . . . and I thought I had left the farm. A tall, broad-shouldered, mountain-sized man stopped the team alongside the plane, and we began loading the mail and bags into the sleigh box. McMillan came over and introduced us. "Mr. Lewis, this is Tiny Gifford, the unofficial mayor of Fort Simpson. You will likely be staying at his place tonight." We shook hands, then drove off to the village, leaving the pilot and mechanic behind to prepare the Norseman for the morning's flight. Amos, the Indian, left us to join his family, who lived on the south end of the island.

After the team was taken care of, Tiny stoked up the fire in the big Ontario heater in the log living room of his "humble abode," as he put it, then read the letter that Dalziel had given me in Edmonton.

"So you're heading up the Nahanni to join your friend. I know Harry Vandaele well. He's quite a guy. He will be glad to see you. We will talk about that country later; you would best go over to the Bay and purchase that list of supplies that Dal gave you, while I rustle some supper. It will save time in the morning."

Over at the Bay store, I bought three pairs of Indian, moose hide moccasins, a mosquito bar, and a pair of trail-set snowshoes. This left me financially unstable once again.

When I handed Dalziel's grocery list to the manager, he perused it for a moment, then said, "These food items are not sufficient for two men over the remainder of the winter. You chaps would have to live almost entirely off the land—which you could do, of course—providing the moose and caribou are plentiful, but if things go wrong, you are not leaving yourselves much to fall back on. And things do go wrong in that Nahanni country. I know."

"Listen!" I said. "When I pay for tonight's lodging I will be stone broke; I do not have the money to make extra purchases."

The manager could see I was unfamiliar with the way business was transacted in the North. Whites and natives alike purchased supplies in the fall and paid for the goods in the spring when they brought their furs into the posts. It was the way trading was done.

"You have no problem," he explained. "You can settle the account in the spring. The quantity of some of these items should be enlarged."

"No," I replied. "I don't buy on credit; I never have. I pay as I go." And that was that.

The manager just shrugged his shoulders and filled the order:

5 lbs. tea	10 lbs. sugar
2 tins baking powder	6 boxes matches
3 lbs. salt	24 candles
4 lbs. lard	10 lbs. rolled oats
10 lbs. tinned butter	4 - 24 lbs. sacks flour
5 lbs. dried prunes	

Tiny Gifford had a sumptuous supper waiting when I returned; fried moose steak, Fort Simpson grown potatoes, and raisin pie. And his cold-weather coffee was strong.

Later Tiny reminisced about his many years in the North. Several years back, his knees had given out and he was forced to leave the bush and settle down here at Simpson. "I'm a sort of part-time farmer now; I grow potatoes here on the island and take them downriver in the fall to the various posts. I had two milk cows once, but I finally sold them to the Roman Catholic mission. Eight tits, morning and night, were eight too many for me." And Tiny sounded off with a roar of laughter that almost shook the cabin.

"The winter months are my busiest," he added. "Hauling firewood across the river is a big job. I keep the Royal Canadian Signals and the hospital supplied. I also look after the mail, here, and service the planes as they come in and go out. And there's always something for me and my horses to do. My horses mean everything to me."

"How far is it across the Mackenzie at Simpson?" I asked.

"It's more than a mile. The sleigh trail, over which I haul the wood, is double that. That's because it dodges around a hundred big ice-blocks, caused by the rough freeze-up we had last fall. But nevertheless, she's a big stream."

During the rest of the evening, we discussed my forthcoming trip into the Nahanni. I'm sure Tiny realized that he was talking to a young chap who could use some timely advice, so he proceeded to touch upon the more important aspects of the venture.

"Never take any chances on that river, my boy!" he began. "There are places on that Nahanni which never freeze over. Watch out for overflow. Remember: you only go through the ice once. And be careful of fire; it's your worst enemy. If your cabin or tent burns down, ten chances to one you're as good as dead! By the way—have you a mosquito bar?"

"I bought one this evening," I said.

"Well, you will need it. I have several here; I'll give you an extra one for Harry. You never can tell . . . I see you have a new set of snowshoes. You won't go far without them."

"I've never worn a pair of snowshoes," I admitted. "I'm a little concerned about how long it will take me to learn to use them."

"You needn't be. Here's what you do: as soon as you arrive at Harry's camp, take a walk into the timber through the deep snow— and it will be deep! It will be an extremely short walk. Then come back and put those shoes on. You will learn as fast as a newborn calf learns to suck its mother."

Tiny made a cup of tea. It was time to turn in, for tomorrow would be a busy day—for me at least.

As I was preparing to climb into one of the bunks in his two-room cabin, Tiny thought of something that might be of some benefit either to Harry or me when we were out on our trapline. He knew that Harry had only two dogs. His long experience told him that when I arrived in camp, we would each have one, or one of us would have none.

"I have a four foot toboggan that you can take with you. You will find that out on the trapline it beats packing a heavy load on your shoulders. You're welcome to it."

So this was Tiny Gifford—a big, happy, jovial extrovert, if ever I met one—a man who overflowed with exuberance, one who possessed the rare ability to impart a large portion of these qualities to anyone who came in contact with him.

Next morning we were up long before dawn, to observe a sky filled with stars. This was all to the good, for I knew that McMillan would not attempt the flight into the mountains under uncertain weather conditions. After a hurried breakfast, we harnessed the horses, and loaded my supplies into the sleigh box, along with a drum of aviation fuel. When we arrived Stan and the mechanic were already down on the snye, fixing one of the struts on the plane. They had been working by lantern light.

We had just wrestled the forty-five gallon drum of gas into the plane when a dog team trotted down the trail from the Fort. In the toboggan was Mrs. Daisy Mulholland, wife of the freetrader at the mouth of the Nahanni, an Indian settlement then also called Nahanni Village, now known as Nahanni Butte. She had recently recovered from an appendectomy and would be returning to the settlement with us. Dressed in all the accouterments of a Northern resident—heavy, woollen ski-pants, bright red parka, and wearing the most brilliantly beaded pair of mukluks, I'm sure, that ever graced this part of the North, Mrs. Mulholland cut an impressive figure. We arranged a place for her among the dunnage bags and other supplies as best we could.

Repairing the strut had delayed our take-off, and I could see that Stan was anxious to "put this bird in the air," as he put it. As soon as the canvas tarp was removed from the engine, he began turning the motor over. Tiny Gifford bid me goodbye and gave me one last piece of advice: "Watch those wild Indians up there at the Rabbitkettle. They skin white people alive, and tan their hides into moccasins!" Then came his roar of laughter. He then added, "The raisin pie in your grub box is for Harry. Give him my regards." I boarded the plane and waved to him through the window.

Within minutes we had reached the junction of the two rivers, and as we flew south over the Liard, I couldn't detect much difference in their size. They were both huge expanses of meandering ice and snow. We covered the ninety miles (145 km) to the mouth of the Nahanni in less than an hour, and Stan banked the Norseman to the right and landed near the north shore, just below the Indian village.

Jack Mulholland, the freetrader, and Milt Campbell (Harry's partner of the past three summers) were waiting on the riverbank as our plane landed. Milt was just as surprised to see me as I was to meet him here. It was only a coincidence, however. He had snowshoed the day before, down from the mouth of a small river called the Netla, a tributary of the Liard upriver about twelve miles distant, to purchase supplies.

There wasn't much time for explanations as to why I happened to be going into the Rabbitkettle. Milt enquired about my provisions and he seemed to think they were adequate. I told him about Dalziel's plane being out of service and that Harry and I would be rafting out, come open water in the spring. Milt seemed confused about this news. I gathered that he thought coming down the Nahanni on a raft was a bit risky. But Mrs. Mulholland interrupted our conversation by insisting that Stan and the mechanic and I come up to their cabin for coffee. This we did, leaving Milt and Jack down at the plane to unload the drum of fuel and Mrs. Mulholland's numerous pieces of baggage.

During that brief interval up at their cabin, it never occurred to me that I might be enjoying the costliest cup of coffee that I would ever drink during the rest of my life.

Back at the plane, Jack Mulholland asked me to be on the lookout for any sign of his brother Joe and his partner, Bill Eppler. I had known about the two missing men since last October. Dalziel had flown them in to Rabbitkettle Lake to trap during the winter of '35/'36. The men had been missing since the early summer of '36. Since Rabbitkettle Lake was only a few miles from Harry's camp, Jack naturally thought we might discover some clues about the men's disappearance.

The Norseman droned on, high over the Mackenzie Mountains, into the northwest. Far below, the South Nahanni turned and twisted, a white, silent serpent, tracing its ancient water course all the way from the Yukon boundary, down to the mighty Liard. We had been flying over an open area and there were several ribbons of white channels branching away from the parent stream, only to join it again a mile or more along its ancient path downstream. As we flew overhead at that moment I thought the river's course was ancient. What I didn't then realize was that this river kept changing its channels from year to year. I didn't realize the *power of water*, especially during the spring floods. From my view above, I wondered how a riverman could know which channel to take among all those islands. This area of the river, I learned later, was locally known as The Splits. It certainly was a logical name.

Suddenly the mountains closed in against the river, and I could see a deep gap between two steep walls. This must be one of the canyons that Harry had often talked about, back on the farm. In less time than it takes to eat a light lunch, the western inlet of the canyon opened into a wide area where the mountains had retreated on either side of the river. The mechanic turned in his seat and touched my arm. "That's Dead Men's Valley below," he pointed through the plane's windshield.

So this was where the two McLeod brothers died in 1905! This was the valley, popularly known as "Headless Valley," that spawned the Nahanni Legend, a legend told and retold in a dozen different versions of mysterious death by decapitation and lost gold. Well, one thing was certain: down below us—somewhere on the north bank of this river, there lay the graves of those two men—their bleached bones resting there since they were discovered in 1907 or 1908.

But in a few moments my attention was drawn to another canyon beginning at the upper end of this valley. The ribbon of white twisted and turned through mile after mile, finding a pathway through these mountains, as it had down through an aeon of time. I was wishing I were making this flight during the summer; now most of the detail was subdued by the mantle of white. Amazingly, I was later to learn, this winding river existed aeons before the mountains, so that the sweeping curves of the canyons were forged by the Nahanni's powerful resistance to the rising rock.

And soon another valley appeared, leading into the mountains to the southwest. Out of it came another waterway on our left. This was the Flat River, the largest tributary of the South Nahanni. It was up this river that Harry and Milt had prospected during the summers of

'34 and '35. And it was to the creeks of this river earlier gold seekers went, hell bent, trying to find that elusive metal, gold, spurred on by one campfire rumour after another.

Minutes later, the mechanic again drew my attention to a spot on the river, off to our right: a plume of fog appeared to be rising off an ice-shrouded pillar of rock (if it was a rock). "There's the Virginia Falls!" he called out loudly above the drone of the plane.

The Virginia Falls! The Big Drop! The Eighth Wonder! I meant to see those Falls, come springtime. But this famous place vanished as quickly as a wink. The problem with this mode of travel is that the scenes change in a matter of seconds—faster than one's mind could grasp their full significance. Too much to see in so little time. But as the Indian said: "It sure beats walkin'."

Back in the hotel in Edmonton, Dalziel had said that Harry's camp was about eighty miles (130 km) up the river from the Falls. And sure enough, in less than an hour, I saw McMillan point to a valley stretching into the southwest. And then I caught a quick glimpse of a smallish river on our left, another white ribbon joining the Nahanni, the Rabbitkettle River.

The mechanic was peering over Stan's shoulder, trying to spot something. "There's the tent down there!" I heard him say to Stan.

The tent? Dalziel never said anything about a tent. I was expecting to see a cabin.

The plane quickly began to lose power, as McMillan brought the Norseman around in a complete turn, facing downriver near the right bank. Suddenly there it was: a tiny, grey canvas tent, with only the gable portion showing above the snow.

Stan stopped the plane a few yards from Harry's water hole out on the river. Leaving the mechanic to unload my gear, the pilot and I made our way up to the tent. There was a pencilled note written on a piece of birch bark lying on the roughly-constructed pole table. The message read:

Will be back Feb 5th. Harry.

It was now February 2. Apparently Harry expected Dalziel would be flying in near the end of the month, and had left the note for him.

Up on Harry's cache, I found five lynx and seven marten pelts stored in a gunny sack. Stan took the fur down to the plane, with instructions from Dalziel to leave it with the Bay manager at Fort

Simpson. The fur would be a lot safer at the Bay than up here in the Mackenzie Mountains.

There was no time to lose. Bush pilots are always racing against time in the North. I shook hands with the two flyers, and from the cockpit, they waved goodbye.

I stood there in the snow, watching the Norseman rising off the river—watching it until it was nothing more than a tiny speck in the cold, blue sky to the east. All that remained of contact with civilization had vanished, leaving only two parallel ski tracks in the snow, ending abruptly a quarter of a mile down the river.

Moose Hunt

My thoughts now turned to the little mound of supplies lying there in the snow. Something didn't seem right about its size. It looked so small. . . .

I reached for my tobacco pouch in my hip pocket, rolled a smoke, lit it—then paused for a moment or two. There was something wrong! Badly wrong! The gunny sack containing the four, twenty-four pound sacks of flour was missing! It just wasn't there! I stared at the mound in disbelief. And there was this other packsack! Now who the hell did it belong to?

Well, I couldn't stand here in the snow forever; my feet were getting cold. The first thing was to get my belongings up to the tent. Gifford's little toboggan made the job much easier, I soon discovered. Then I needed to light a fire in Harry's tiny stove—brew some tea—then exercise some control over my jumbled thoughts, before these thoughts took control over me. Then perhaps I could try to determine how this mistake had happened.

Harry's spacious abode consisted of an eight by ten foot (2.4 by 3 m) tent that was set over a rectangular framework of small poplar logs. This framework was about thirty inches (seventy-six centimetres) in height. On one side of the tent, he had built a narrow table, also constructed of poplar poles. On the back wall of the tent, was a shelf built from an old packing crate. My eye caught the picture of Harry's girlfriend. It was set in a crude wooden frame, upright on the shelf. I had grown up with her and her folks, back where the family farmed near ours in Alberta. Harry's Three-Star eiderdown was lying on a mat of spruce boughs laid out on the dirt floor. In a corner near the front of the tent was his tiny stove. It was the smallest stove I had ever seen in my life (then or since). It consisted of two, four-gallon petrol tins jammed together, with a small door at one end to take the wood, and a round hole cut in the top at the other to accommodate the stove pipe.

Harry's furniture consisted of a block of wood that had been sawn from a dry spruce tree. This "chair" was about fourteen inches in diameter and perhaps a bit longer in length. It blended into its surroundings perfectly.

Harry had left birch bark and kindling near the stove and I soon had snow melting in my tea billy, a small cast-iron pot with a hoop-shaped handle that can be hung over the open campfire. After a second cup of tea, I finally decided what may have happened to the flour. I distinctly recalled seeing Gifford loading the gunny sack into the plane at Fort Simpson. This fact was clear enough in my mind. The mistake must have been made while we were stopped at the mouth of the Nahanni. Jack Mulholland must have inadvertently unloaded the flour, thinking that his wife had purchased it at the Bay. Milt Campbell knew I had the flour—or assumed so—because I had shown him the grocery list. Well, what difference did it make how it happened? The most important item on the list was missing.

And where was I when this happened? Why, I was busy; I was drinking coffee with the flyers in Mulholland's cabin. And why wasn't I down there by the plane, watching over my supplies? Well, it was just a simple oversight, really. A mere triviality—nothing to make such a fuss about.

Sure, I could spend the rest of the day, making up excuses to cover up my stupidity. But I knew I'd have to live with the result. What really bothered me, was how I was going to explain the flour situation to Harry. I couldn't. And I knew it.

I had another bother, another concern almost as troublesome as the flour. A further example of my mental deficiency was lying there on the dirt floor: the packsack that did not belong to me. I opened it.

Its contents consisted of two dresses, three blouses, four pairs of panties, one pair of silk stockings and two pairs of grey cotton ones, and two brassieres. There were also two lipstick capsules. The most interesting article in the collection was a pair of bright blue woollen bloomers (blue was my favourite colour). Apparently Mrs. Mulholland had been drinking coffee also. But that didn't lessen my responsibility. Not in the least.

"What a helluva way to begin a sojourn in the Nahanni," I brooded. Well, after a certain length of time, there comes a point when a man can feel so low and dejected that he just says to himself: "To hell with it! It's happened."

I rolled another cigarette and poured myself a third cup of tea.

I glanced at Harry's note again, and suddenly a hair-raising thought entered my mind: what if Harry doesn't arrive on the 5th? What if he had an accident out on his trapline and didn't come back? Period. Just what would I do?

I had no knowledge of this vast country, except what I had seen from the air, and what little Harry had told me back on the farm. Why, hell, I didn't even have a map of the Nahanni River, and neither did Harry in 1934.

I knew I had to put an end to these questions—this line of thought. Now!—before I let myself get out of hand. What would I do if he didn't appear? I would look for him. And if I couldn't find him, I would come back to this camp and stay put. There was no other alternative. I had an axe, a rifle and ammunition, and a fair idea about how to hunt. And who knows, after a lengthy period of time, I might even begin to use my head for other purposes than growing hair.

The main thing was to keep busy and tackle first the jobs of most importance. Of immediate concern were my supplies; they must be put up on the cache. McMillan and I had waded through more than three feet of snow to reach the cache (the path had snowed in from recent downfalls). What better time than now to introduce myself to my snowshoes?

My initial attempts were all abortive. This particular brand of footwear simply refused to cooperate, and I was becoming more than a little annoyed with their rebellious antics. Neither shoe wanted to have anything to do with the other. Their main objective was to sepa-rate—or so it seemed. Finally, after an hour of barely-controlled frustration, I managed to force each shoe to follow the other. But it wasn't an easy struggle.

Climbing up on Harry's cache was not a simple maneuver either, as I had previously discovered. His "ladder" consisted of a single item: a spruce pole about fourteen feet (four metres) long and nearly five inches (twelve centimetres) in diameter. There were notches cut along its length at regular intervals, providing a foothold for the feet as one made the climb to the platform.

A large tarp covered the entire cache, and the first item I saw as I folded it back was a coil of three-quarter inch Manila rope. At that moment I had no idea how important that rope would be in the months to come. Another important item caught my eye: a double-bitted axe—an indispensable article, to be sure. The rest of Harry's belongings were stored in gunny sacks, of which there were several extra ones neatly folded.

There wasn't much in the way of food; three pounds of tea, part of a hindquarter of caribou, and perhaps ten pounds of flour. There were a number of lynx legs in two of the sacks. I wondered about these. Was Harry using them for dog food? In a cardboard box I found two tins of tobacco, matches, and several boxes of small-calibre ammunition. I wasn't familiar with these cartridges, and had no idea of what rifle they fitted.

The tarp was placed so that it folded back on itself, the bottom half covering the pole floor of the cache. And what really drew my attention was the wooden stock of a rifle protruding out between the bottom part of the tarp and the pole floor. A peculiar place to store a rifle I thought.

I pulled out the gun, and what I saw was beyond belief! It was a 280 Ross, and it had a different shape than any rifle I had ever seen. Its barrel was split into two halves, right down its full length, from the breech to its muzzle. Both halves were bent outwards in the shape of a crossbow. Now what in hell was this all about? It soon was obvious: the gun had exploded when fired. Had ice accumulated in the barrel through condensation? This is what Dalziel had meant when he advised me to leave my rifle outside during the night.

But how could the holder of the gun escape from being hurt? Obviously Harry had. I carefully examined one of the boxes of ammunition again in the cardboard box. The identification read: .22

Hornet. I had never heard of a rifle by that name. The cartridge may have been suitable for bringing down a caribou, but it would have been a little light for moose. I was more than thankful I had my .30-.30.

Every essential article that Harry possessed—with the exception of his eiderdown—was up here on the cache. And this was where my meagre supplies were going to be right shortly. A fire in the tent could mean curtains for the both of us if the wrong articles were lost. A wolverine could mess things up in a hurry as well. The lowly porcupine had been known to chew the handle out of an axe. Out in these far-off mountains, there was no such thing as being too careful. There were no general stores operating in the Nahanni.

Down through the years, many people have asked me how a cache is properly built. A few years ago I built six miniature cabins, complete with outhouses and caches, and with the normal contents such as saws, axes, rifles, stoves, bunks—even down to the lowly sawhorse. I tried to make each item conform to scale. The cabins and caches were constructed of real logs cut from small willow saplings that grow here on the Pacific Coast. These cabins and contents were built by the same methods used in the Nahanni. The only exception was the outhouse; Harry owned the real thing, the great outdoors, and couldn't see the necessity of one of those.

Details of construction are as follows:

Two sound trees, roughly ten inches (twenty-five centimetres) in diameter are selected. They should be about five to six feet (1.5 to 2 m) apart and in reasonable proximity to the tent or cabin. Not less than ten feet (three metres) above ground, a triangular notch is cut in the side of each tree. These notches much be facing each other, and should not extend more than three inches (7.6 cm) into the heart of the tree at the point where the tree is still eight inches (twenty centimetres) in diameter. The reason is obvious. The exact size and position of the notches are indicated on the sketch.

A green spruce tree, roughly six inches (fifteen centimetres) in diameter is now selected, from which two cross pieces are cut and shaped with the axe, so as to conform to the shape and size of the tree notches. Each triangular-shaped cross piece is now driven halfway through its respective tree notch, until its ends are equidistant from the centre of the tree. If the notches are cut and lined up correctly, then the two "key" cross pieces will be parallel to each other. These pieces provide the support for the small logs that form the platform.

Beginning about three feet (about one metre) from ground, a sheet of tin must now be wrapped around each tree trunk to a height of seven feet (two metres). In other words, a four-foot sheet of tin would suffice. The sheet metal prevents wildlife—mainly mice and wolverines (and black bears) from reaching the platform. Without this metal protection, the cache is useless.

A ladder of some sort is obviously required in building a cache. A pole ladder can be made quickly with lengths of babiche (rawhide thongs) if wire or rope is not available. Using a "monkey pole" as Harry had been doing, is strictly for the monkeys. And it's an easy way to get hurt.

Although it was 2 p.m. by my pocket watch, the afternoon sun seemed unusually low in the southwest. Then I remembered that I wasn't in Alberta now: at this time of year the days are short in the North. There were other jobs to be done during the remaining daylight. The galvanized water bucket was empty, which prompted me to go down to the water hole, which was frozen over. It took me awhile to chop it out. The ice on the river was over three feet thick.

Making a spruce bough bed was next on the agenda. This job entailed the use of my snowshoes, and back among the evergreens, I discovered how deep the snow really was. Without those shoes, I don't think I'd ever have gotten back to the tent. Tiny Gifford was right: this was the way to learn to use these elongated inventions.

I spent the remaining daylight cutting firewood. Harry—bless his heart—had brought in an old-fashioned bucksaw—the original saw manufactured in North America, God knows when! But it worked. It later proved to be an indispensable tool. That saw and the little toboggan Tiny had given me, were two of our most valuable possessions.

Now for supper. It was simple. I sampled one of the lynx legs I had brought down from the cache. I cut up part of it into small pieces and boiled them in Harry's large billy pot. The meat tasted somewhat like wild rabbit, only worse. But who was I to complain? If I had taken the Bay manager's advice in Simpson, and used common sense, I could have been eating a steaming pot of rice this night. And for only a few dollars that, one way or another, could have been repaid in a few months. I realized I had carried frugality beyond its sensible limits. Well, I would learn the hard way, and in the meantime I would eat lynx legs.

February 2, 1937. My first day at the Rabbitkettle. It had been a long one; I needed sleep. I laid out my eiderdown on the spruce boughs and remembered nothing more until the next morning. I was half frozen. I should have used Harry's Three-Star, but I didn't want to enjoy any luxuries that I wouldn't be able to have later. The stove was tiny, but so was the space inside the tent, and by daybreak I was thawed out sufficiently to think about breakfast. I knew what I wanted—bacon and eggs—but the order never came. I settled for three cups of scalding hot tea and what remained of the boiled lynx legs from the night before.

The thing I had to do was find a moose. Pronto! I had no way of knowing if Harry had meat cached elsewhere. I had to assume he didn't. But I needed more practice on the snowshoes before I ventured too far away from camp.

There was a trail back of the tent, partially filled in with snow, which led into the deep spruce to the south. I put my axe in the packboard and decided to follow what proved to be a section of Harry's trapline. I couldn't believe the depth of snow in this area. In the places untouched by the wind, the trail resembled a miniature canyon. It was a good place to gain experience in the use of these stretched-out tennis rackets. But my control was improving. I soon learned to adjust the leather harness so that my feet were set farther forward on the shoes. This made it easier to bring the toe of each shoe out of the snow. I also learned to lengthen my stride, making all the difference in the world.

This was my first excursion on a genuine trapline—a neophyte's initiation into the fur-gathering business. About a mile up the line, I came upon the first fur-bearing animal I had ever seen in a trap— with the exception of several weasels that I had caught as a kid still in school. It was a female lynx and she was frozen to the point near death. She raised her head slightly, as I drew near, and looked towards me through a pair of glazed eyes. But I don't believe she was conscious of seeing anything; she was too far gone to make the slightest struggle. I quickly felled a small tree and put the animal out of her misery.

Late that afternoon when I returned to camp, I was still carrying a mental picture of that animal as she raised her head for the last time. It was a picture that seemed to bother me. That evening when I put the animal up on the cache, I brought a small portion of the caribou hindquarter down for my supper. I knew there was no way I could stomach lynx leg on this particular night.

The next day, I snowshoed down the river and found a track that crossed the river to the north bank. It wasn't a fresh track, but neither was it old. I wasn't an expert on animal tracks; I simply compared it to the tracks of another cloven-hoofed animal—the domestic cow. Yes, I knew about the cow. At least, this meant there was meat in the area. And I intended to find it. But on this evening, I had something more important on my mind than moose meat. Tomorrow I would stay in camp, for that was the day Harry was supposed to be back.

I was up before dawn the next morning, busy cutting wood on Harry's crude sawhorse. There is nothing like manual work to dispel bothersome thoughts. At mid-afternoon I was down on the river, opening up the water hole again. If the weather stayed this cold, it looked like this was going to be a daily chore.

Suddenly I heard a dog bark! Wolves don't bark; they howl. Then another dog barked! I looked up to see this strange figure standing there on the river bank. As he slowly came down the path, I recognized him: It was Robinson Crusoe! I couldn't possibly be mistaken. The big, black dog ran ahead, then abruptly stopped, and slowly wagged his tail. He knew that strangers were few and far between in this country. The other dog was leery. She stayed behind her master. Harry stared at me for a moment, then we shook hands. "Al! You're the last person I ever expected to see up here!"

"And this is the last place I ever dreamed I'd be!" I exclaimed. "We have a lot to talk about and you look cold. Let's go up to the tent."

I soon had a roaring fire burning, and tea was brewing in the billy by the time Harry had taken care of his dogs. I sat there on my bedroll, gazing in solemn wonderment at this fellow I once knew. And my mind drifted back to those happy-go-lucky days we spent on his dad's farm—three miles north of ours. I remembered that day in 1929, when Harry drove me down 8th Avenue in Calgary in his bright new Peerless automobile. That car was a black beauty. He was dressed in a blue pin-striped suit, and he wore the latest style hat over his pompadour haircut. He was a flashy-looking man in those days. I was a kid of fifteen then, just beginning high school. He was seven years my senior. But that was before the "Big Crash." Now here we were at the Rabbitkettle. And Calgary was a million miles away.

Harry was sitting on his "chair," hunched up over the little stove, trying to melt the ice out of his body, his calloused, grimy-looking hand reaching out for the cup of tea I had just poured. He took a couple of gulps and sat the tin cup back on the stove, then began removing his blackened, greasy parka, soiled by more than one siwash campfire. Off came his torn bib overalls. Underneath these, he was wearing the standard apparel of the North, a pair of woollen ski pants.

Several times I saw him eyeing my summer eiderdown. I knew what he was thinking: how the hell is he going to keep warm enough to sleep in that?

One part of Harry's dress drew my attention: his Indian moccasins. One of them was coming apart at the seams. I asked him if he had extra pairs. (I knew he had extra clothing up on the cache, but I hadn't examined it.)

"You had better believe I do!" he exclaimed. "Your footwear is your life in this country! How is your supply?"

"I have three other pairs," I said.

"Good! You will likely need them." He reached for the tea billy.

But it was the massive, matted haystack of hair, almost extending down to his shoulders, that had changed his appearance to such a degree. And his soot-filled beard and singed eyebrows told the story of his many nights sleeping with the siwash fires built alongside his spruce bough bed. One thing we had in common was our headgear: the brown beret. Everyone in the North wore them.

"Now tell me. Who flew you in? I heard the plane go over. Not long after I heard it go back out, and I knew it wasn't Dal." Harry was wanting to know all the latest news.

"I flew in with Stan McMillan of MAS. Dalziel's plane is grounded now, and will be until repairs are made." I then explained in detail how I came to be here, relating each evolvement in its proper order. I could see that Harry was having difficulty in grasping the implications of what I had explained.

33

"Do you mean that Dal will not be in after open water? It doesn't take that long to repair a plane."

"I distinctly asked him if he would be coming to fly us out. He said it wouldn't be possible. He spoke of repairs, and mentioned that there were other matters to be taken care of."

"Other matters—now I think I understand," Harry commented. I was waiting for him to explain but he didn't, and I didn't ask him to. I did have the feeling, however, that something was amiss, somewhere.

Then I remembered another part of the conversation that I had had with Dal. "By the way Harry, where are Dalziel's pontoons?"

"They're back of the cache, buried in about four feet of snow. Why do you ask?"

"Well, Dal said that we could put a log platform over his pontoons, and use them to float down the river after breakup."

Harry looked at me, strangely, for a long moment, then asked, "Was Dal serious when he made that suggestion?"

"I assumed he was," I said.

Harry couldn't resist a chuckle. "Why Dal must have been drinking when he proposed such a foolish stunt. He knows this river as well as anyone. That would be sheer suicide! No, we will leave his pontoons right where they are. And after the beaver hunt, we'll go out to the mouth of the Nahanni on a log raft. They are easy to build, and we sure as hell won't have any trouble finding logs in this country. No shortage of material. No problem."

Harry was about to pour himself another cup of tea, when I thought about the bottle of rum. "Hang on a second," I said. "At the rate you drink tea, we'll run out in short order. I happen to have a good substitute." I went up on the cache and brought down the bottle, and handed it to Harry. "Compliments of Dalziel!" I explained.

"Well glory be! And Governor General to boot. I'll be frazzled by the fickle fingers of fate! It's a bit late for New Year's, but we'll celebrate anyway." Harry reached for the tin cups. "Now just to show my appreciation, I'm going to pour you one, too." It turned out there wasn't much saving of tea; we had to use the Blue Ribbon as a mixer. Rum was rum in 1937.

We talked into the late afternoon about our folks back home. I finally decided I might as well get what was bothering me off my chest now, as later. I showed Dalziel's grocery list to Harry and said,

34

"I have something to tell you, and it's not going to be easy." Harry gave me a curious look. He could see that something was troubling me. Feigning an expression of sheer horror, he exclaimed, "Good God! Don't tell me you've gotten one of those Spruce View girls in trouble and you've come to the Rabbitkettle to hide! I would have expected better of you, my boy."

I managed a sickly laugh and said, "No, it's nothing of that nature." I then recounted in detail, the story of the missing flour. "I can't believe that I would be guilty of such a bloody blunder, but it's a fact."

Harry knew that I was upset. He was also aware of the implications of not having one of the primary food items over a period of several months. But like the guy he was, he simply shrugged his shoulders and said, "Don't worry about it, Al! These things happen. Flour is really a luxury in this country. Any kind of white grub—store food—for that matter." But in this instance I knew it couldn't be called a luxury when a Norseman plane had just flown into this country carrying only one passenger.

"By the way, Al, you have something more valuable to us than the flour."

"And what's that?"

"I saw your .30-.30 hanging on a tree out there. God knows, we can sure use it. I only have the Hornet."

"What in hell happened to your 280 Ross?"

Harry stared down at the stove, and poured himself another drink. "The damned gun blew up!" he exclaimed. "Pour yourself another, too. I get shaky every time I think about it." He gazed into his cup, and slowly shook his head, as though he still couldn't believe what had happened.

"I was lucky. Real lucky!" he said. "I was out on the far end of the line—about twenty miles east of here. There was a wolf in one of my traps, and he was very much alive. Nigger, the black dog, was behind me, with Liza bringing up the rear. I knew Nigger would jump the wolf if he had the chance, so I quickly unslung the rifle and fired. The next thing I knew, I was lying in the snow, flat on my back, gazing up at the sky. My nose was bleeding and my left arm was numb. I couldn't even wiggle my fingers. I managed to roll back on the trail, somehow, and finally got Nigger tied to a tree. I didn't need to worry about Liza; I knew she wouldn't tackle anything larger than a mouse.

Then I grabbed my axe in my right hand and felled a small jack pine. I made a club out of the butt end of the tree, and soon finished the wolf. It was then I noticed that I was also using my left arm. That was one helluva big relief.

"I tell you. I was scared shitless! I was terrified—from the top of my head, down to my toenails. It was the first and only time in my life I've ever known what honest-to-god fear was."

"When did it happen?"

"Just before New Year's."

"What was wrong with the rifle?" I asked.

"Ice in the barrel. No doubt about it," Harry stated, emphatically. "It was my fault; I knew better. I always made a point of keeping the rifle outside the tent, but just that once I forgot and brought it inside. One mistake is all it takes. The place for both axe and rifle is outside in the winter. In the summer, the situation is different; you have the bears to think about."

"It's almost a coincidence," I said. "Dalziel warned me, back in Edmonton, to always leave my .30-.30 outside in cold weather."

"I can thank my lucky stars I didn't find myself in real trouble," Harry continued. "And Nigger—with a heavy pack on his back— would have been a dead dog, if he had tackled that wolf."

I thought of what Tiny Gifford had told me about making that first mistake: "Remember—it might be your last."

I hadn't realized how long we had been talking until Harry announced that he was famished, and would I shinny up on the cache and bring down the caribou meat.

"I shall oblige—right pronto," I said. "But I should like to remind you that damned monkey pole could kill a man. Did you invent that weird ladder?"

"Now listen Alfred! You have been at my humble establishment less than three days, and already you are finding fault with my equipment. I must remind my long-time friend which way the Nahanni River flows." Feigning a dictatorial attitude, he pointed eastward towards the back of the tent. There was no mistaking his meaning, and so I said, "It's a long ways to go on snow shoes, so I guess I'll just keep on using the monkey pole." And we both laughed.

Harry may not have looked like the man I once knew, but he was still the same humorous guy, a man who did not let many negative thoughts enter his mind. He was always a positive thinker, and a more likable fellow, one could never hope to meet.

I also brought down Mrs. Mulholland's pack, along with another article I knew Harry would be interested in. I casually handed him the raisin pie and said, "Compliments of the day. Tiny Gifford."

Harry's eyes opened wider and wider, his expression resembling that of a convict who has just discovered his cell door is unlocked. He didn't utter a single word. He simply removed the pie from its plate. Then holding the pastry in his grimy hands, he proceeded to trace a 360-degree circle around the perimeter of the pie with his teeth. It was done in much the same manner as a beaver fells a tree, only faster. It didn't take him more than two minutes to reduce the diameter of that pie down to the size of a twenty-five-cent piece. I was mesmerized by the procedure. It was the extreme precision that he exercised during the operation that fascinated me.

I don't believe Harry realized he was eating his supper backwards, but if he did, I'm sure he couldn't have cared less. He was a hungry man, just off the trapline. But when I observed the amount of caribou meat he was consuming—and presumably with no foreseeable end, I thought it prudent to discuss our food situation. It turned out that Harry didn't have meat cached elsewhere. I expressed my regret again, on not having brought in more supplies.

"Don't worry about it, Al. We will both go hunting tomorrow. There is game here in the Rabbitkettle—and I'm not referring to rabbits. There seems to be damned few of them. We will cut moose tracks somewhere. There are moose yarded up north of here, but they are too far from camp. On a cold morning, you can hear them moving about in the deep timber. But they may be five or six miles from here. If need be, we will go after them. But the snow is close to four feet deep in the heavy timber; I don't look forward to that kind of exercise."

It seemed an appropriate time to add a measure of mirth to our first meeting together, and so I brought out Mrs. Mulholland's pack-sack. Harry examined the contents carefully, with mixed emotions— some of genuine concern, others of profound amusement. It wasn't something to joke about. There were items of clothing in that pack that Mrs. Mulholland would certainly need before winter was out.

"I never dreamed that I would see anything like this at the mouth of the Rabbitkettle," Harry said. "Tell you what we will do. We will divide every thing equally. You can have Daisy's panties, and I will take the brassieres and the lipstick. We shall take turns wearing the dresses."

"What about the bloomers?"

Harry's expression turned to one of serious and prolonged thought. "My boy! That will be a tough decision to make. These bloomers are woollen! They would be very warm on forthcoming nights out there on the line. We shall negotiate and settle it somehow. I wish to be fair, you know; I'm not hard to deal with." But we both knew this mix-up wasn't going to be a joke to Mrs. Mulholland.

Late that evening, while we were preparing for bed, I caught Harry glancing dubiously at my summer eiderdown. He also noticed that I wore my extra cardigan beneath my parka, and a second pair of heavy woollen socks over my feet. Time would tell: come the dawn, I would still be breathing, or terminated by the climate, for it was going to be a cold night.

I would have overslept that morning, had I not felt something skittering across my face. I sat up with a start. There was a rustle among the spruce boughs underneath the tarp. There were visitors present. Mice! At that moment, I didn't realize how many of these unwelcome visitors we would have before the winter was out.

Harry was still curled up in his Three-Star—dead to the world. It was mid-morning when we finished our caribou breakfast and departed from camp. Harry had decided to run his short two-mile trapline, south of the tent, and where he thought he might spot something in the way of moose meat. I should head downriver to a large muskeg situated about two miles to the east, on the north side of the river. Harry thought it a prime place for moose to feed. He said that he and Dalziel had found game there late the previous fall.

There was a strong breeze following me all the way down the river. This was not to my advantage. Any successful hunt had to be made against the wind, not with it. I would have to approach the muskeg from the east, putting me into the wind.

Near mid-afternoon, I found the muskeg. It appeared to cover a large area. I decided I'd traverse it towards the west, then follow the dense stand of timber along the river, back to camp. It would be dark by that time anyway.

Wind direction is the all-important thing to note when trying to locate game. This much I had learned in the foothills of Alberta, while still in my teens. A moose may not possess the keenest eyesight in the world, but there isn't anything wrong with its smeller. And they do have a large one. And they use it.

The muskeg, probably a quarter of a square mile in area, was dotted with small patches of black spruce. Small tamarack trees in bunched stands fringed its perimeter. There were many open areas, bordered by columns of red willows. It was a perfect feeding ground for moose, and in the spring I could imagine it would also be a prime nesting ground for the ducks, as these open spaces of marsh would become ponds of water when the ice and snow melted.

Visibility was fair over most of the area. I took plenty of time scanning the scene, but nothing moved. A dozen times I was almost sure I saw a moose partially hidden in the spruce patches. This was known as "wishful vision" by the hunters back home. Everyone admitted to being affected by it at one time or another.

I was trying to find a way through a tamarack island when I suddenly spotted a damaged sapling a few yards away. I went over to investigate and found that the wound was recent. There it was: a track! About two feet away. I had cut the track of a bull moose that had been feeding on the tips of these young trees. I could see where the branches had been snipped off.

I quickly bent down to examine the hoof prints with my bare hand. They were a calligraphic revelation of this animal's whereabouts, and it had to be a bull. The double toe-marks were large and rounded. A cow's imprint was narrower and the toes more pointed. Well, the sex didn't matter. It was the age of the track that counted. It was fresh. The imprints were sharp and well-defined, not glazed over with tiny snow crystals. There was even the odd tuft of snow falling into the tracks—a sure giveaway of their age. How long ago had this track been made? An hour? No. Perhaps fifteen minutes at most. I suddenly came alive!

I knew this animal hadn't winded me because its prints were spaced at normal length—like those of an animal feeding—shorter perhaps, in this depth of snow. Now this track translated into meat-on-the-table, and I intended to follow it until hell froze over—and longer if necessary.

The main thing was not to "jump" the bull. If I did I'd likely never have time to get off a decent shot. I knew that would not be much value to me. There was still an hour's daylight left. Well, I'd stick to this track—like baby dung to a damp diaper. That I would!

Near the edge of the muskeg, the track turned sharply into the heavy timber. I was now moving with the wind. There was only one thing to do. I began tracing a wide arc to my left, then back again toward the river, in the hope that I might cut the tracks again, with the wind in my favour.

I traced two more circles in this manner, each time crossing the bull's tracks, but no sightings. My strategy wasn't working, because I didn't realize what was happening. My maneuver could never have succeeded, because in keeping up to this moose, I had more than twice as far to travel. And his legs were twice as long as mine. Moose don't wear snowshoes either. I still might have stood a chance, had the moose decided in which direction he wanted to go.

But it was all irrelevant now. I noticed his strides were almost double the length they had been before. There were long leg furrows imprinted in the snow, a clear indication this fellow was moving out—and quick about it.

Well, that was that; he had gotten wind of me. To hell with it! My snowshoes were sinking six inches into the snow with every step, and I was getting fed up. It was late in the day, and I had to think about getting back to camp. The only reason I kept following the track was because it led to the south and finally to the river. I didn't want to be prowling around in the bush after dark.

Dusk was beginning to settle in, as I stood on the north bank, gazing out across the river. My eyes were having trouble following the track, but it didn't matter; daylight was running out on me. It wasn't completely a wasted effort. Bright and early tomorrow morning I'd hit that track again, and perhaps my luck would change.

I was rolling my first cigarette of the late afternoon when I saw a dark object standing near two trees on the south bank. The object slowly moved, then stopped between the trees. Even in the twilight there was no room for mistake. I was looking at the outline of a moose. I shook off my packboard and laid it down in the snow at the edge of the embankment. Off came my snowshoes, then using my pack as a gun-rest, I stretched myself out in the snow. Holding the sight well above the animal's back, I cocked the rifle and fired. Nothing happened. The moose never moved. Just as I was levering another cartridge into the chamber, the moose slowly ambled off into the timber.

As I recall that moment, my main objective in wasting ammunition was just to warn that moose that I would be back on its trail at break of day tomorrow. It was an impulsive move on my part and totally in keeping with my nature. It wasn't intended to be made with any degree of accuracy, because I hadn't even adjusted the distance scale on the rear sight. I hadn't even contemplated the distance across the river. I had a fair idea of the trajectory and velocity of a model 94 Winchester .30-.30 rifle, but as I recall, I simply regarded the distance as being beyond its range.

From my position on the high bank on the north shore, I could barely see the outline of the Rabbitkettle Valley in the southwest. I knew it would be pitch dark when I reached camp, but that didn't present a problem here on the river; I would pick up my midday snowshoe track and follow it back to the tent.

I soon found my trail across the river. It was only a stone's throw from where the moose had been standing, so I decided to climb the bank and have a look. There—between the two spruces—I saw a splash of blood. I made sure by flicking on my cigarette lighter and holding it over the stain in the snow. There was no doubt about it!

I moved forward into the dark gloom of the heavy forest—slowly—one step at a time, each shoe barely ahead of the other. Only a few yards ahead, I saw the moose lying down in a hollow. I saw his head turn towards me, but he never got up; a bullet through the neck stopped further movement.

Meat! Meat at my feet! And plenty of it.

There was no time to waste. I put my hunting knife to work, quickly bleeding the animal, then began the job of gutting the bull. My hands were damned near frozen, and I needed more light so I could see what the hell I was doing. A fire had to be built—a big one—as close to the kill as possible. Luck seemed to be following in my tracks this past hour. I found a small patch of dry spruce within carrying distance of the kill. What I needed was the big, double-bitted axe, but it was up on the cache, so I went to work with mine in a manner that would put a lumberjack to shame. The white ground cover provided some semblance of light, just barely enough to keep me from chopping into my feet during the tree-felling operation. This was the only benefit that more than three feet of snow provided. I now had to stamp out a canyon trail to the kill, to skid the logs out. I then stacked them lengthwise in a pile and built a roaring fire in the centre to let the flames do the extra axe-work. I thought of the Robert Service poem that I had often recited at the high school concerts in Innisfail, AB. But I wasn't trying to cremate anyone here at the Rabbitkettle; I just wanted some heat and light. In a few minutes the flames were casting a yellow glow over the area, and the spruce backstop began reflecting the light and heat over the kill. Now I could continue dealing with the moose.

I was having enough trouble trying to roll the old bull over on its side so that I could finish the cleaning job, when I heard help coming. I should have known; Harry had heard the shots and seen my fire as he crossed the river to examine a couple of traps just at dusk. First at the scene were the two dogs. It was comical to watch their antics: they were crouching down in the snow, only their heads showing. Then ever so slowly, both dogs would move forward inch by inch, Liza making sure that Nigger was in the lead. It was as if they fully expected the moose might rise to its feet and make an escape.

"This is one helluva time of day to kill a moose!" Harry exclaimed, as he stepped up to the firelight. "How come you didn't shoot him earlier?"

"I'll have you know I use my head when I hunt," I retorted. "I've spent considerable time and effort herding this animal closer to camp, so that we wouldn't have so far to pack the meat. Is that understandable?"

"Well bless my soul! I would never have thought of that. It's a brilliant piece of forethought, I must admit." Harry was examining the animal closely. "I declare! This old bull is the one that Noah brought over on the ark. I hope my friend has a good set of teeth."

"What makes you so sure about his age?"

"I can tell from experience. Here—I'll show you." Harry lifted up one of the bull's hind legs and pointed. "Notice those testicles; they're all shrivelled up—like two dried prunes. This critter is ancient! But don't misunderstand. I'm not complaining."

This little confab was typical of the many hilarious exchanges that we were to enjoy during the coming weeks. Never a dull moment did we have in each other's company. There were serious moments, but they were never dull. And on this evening, I'm sure that the age of this moose was the last thing on our minds. All we could visualize was steak on the plate.

There was no more time for idle banter. The fire had created a big gap in the centre of the pile, and it was clear we would require more wood before this job was finished. Harry suggested he attend to the butchering while I scouted for more fuel. I thought I had the better of this arrangement until I found myself tramping out further tunnels in the snow. But Harry didn't have a cinch by any stretch of the imagination, either. He was having trouble keeping his hands from freezing. My difficulty lay in locating dry timber in the dark, and getting it up to the fire.

By 7 p.m. Harry had finished the butchering job, but the meat still had to be taken into camp or hung up in the trees.

Harry, however, had thought of everything. Along with the dogs, he had brought the toboggan and my coil of three-eighths rope. "We will take home what we can tonight, and hang the rest of the meat up in a tree. It's the best we can do. We have to hope that a wolverine doesn't come along during the night."

"What about the wolves?" I asked. "I know they don't climb trees, but I was wondering about their numbers."

"There are plenty of them around. Wherever there are caribou, you will find wolves. If a loner happens by within a quarter of a mile, he or she will find the kill, and in less than an hour a half dozen will show up. Wolves have the best broadcasting system that I know of—except the coyotes."

"Are there any of those around?"

"I've never seen one here. Nor did Milt and I ever run into any when we were prospecting."

All was under control, as well as possible—except for one problem: whisky-jacks. There were dozens of these Canada jays, round balls of fluff and feathers, flitting back and forth through the yellow firelight, bold as brass. And they were hungry. What we needed was an extra tarp to cover the meat that we had hung in the spruce. "Extras translate into luxuries at the Rabbitkettle," Harry remarked. "Now that light rope of yours—I wouldn't call that a luxury—that's a necessity."

The dogs were excited as we loaded their panniers with the smaller parts of the meat; they knew the sooner back to camp, the sooner they'd be fed. Harry went on ahead with one hindquarter tied onto his packboard, which was a load in any man's country. The dogs followed behind, with me bringing up the rear with the other hindquarter on the toboggan.

Back in camp, the dogs—as always—were fed first. We then set about preparing "a banquet which will be the envy of the chef at the Palliser Hotel in Calgary," so stated Harry. Our meal consisted of moose heart and kidneys, followed by eight boiled prunes (I counted them out) each, topped off with lots of scalding tea.

For myself, at least, this was a day to be remembered.

Out on
the Line

By mid-morning the next day, we had the remainder of the meat safely up on the cache. Harry admitted the toboggan was an energy saver. To me—not being as strong as my partner—it was a godsend.

We had expected to find wolf tracks around the kill area that morning, but there were none. On our last trip, Harry set three number four traps around the offal and head of the moose. "You can bet those bastards will be here in the next day or so. One less wolf is one less wolf if we're lucky."

I gathered that Harry didn't like wolves.

Now that our food situation was taken care of, we could turn our attention to the main objective: fur. Harry's trapline extended approximately eighteen miles in both directions along the river from our camp. The line was laid out on either side of the river, and most of the trail wasn't more than a mile from either shoreline.

Dalziel had helped Harry route the line with several important considerations in mind. The main reason for this particular plan centred on a well-known fact: a man with only two dogs cannot cover more than fifteen miles a day on snowshoes—especially if the trail is partially snowed in, which is usually the case. Much time is spent taking care of the traps and making sure they are not frozen in. As Harry had had no experience in running a trapline, Dalziel had deemed it prudent to reduce the day's travel to twelve miles on the average.

Having the line plotted in this fashion meant that Harry would never be more than a day's travel from the home tent, should something unforeseen occur. It also meant that he would only be required to spend two nights in a siwash camp; on the third evening he would be at the tent. Then during the following three days he would run the other half of the line.

Yet it wasn't that simple. One flaw in the procedure was the fact that frozen animals had to be thawed out, which required a day—or more—in a tent, to take care of the pelting. In Harry's situation there were other hardships; the toughest job of all was back-packing a frozen animal such as a lynx or wolf. The dogs were limited to what could be put in their panniers, such as the trail equipment, food, and smaller fur-bearing animals. The average dog carries from twenty to thirty pounds in these double pouches.

A fully established trapper has a team of four or more dogs that pull a cariole (a toboggan with canvas or moose hide sides attached) which is at least six feet in length. Thus provided, he has ample power, and plenty of room to transport his equipment and daily fur catch to his outlying cabins. Cabins! The basic essential! Usually they are placed about fifteen miles apart—just a short daily run for the dogs. Cabins are not luxuries, they are necessities—if a trapper is to collect any amount of fur during the winter seasons.

But Harry wasn't an established trapper. He had spent three summers prospecting for gold in these Mackenzie Mountains, true enough, but his meagre knowledge of trapping had been gleaned over a period of two weeks, under the tutelage of an experienced trapper, Dalziel. I'm not sure that Harry had ever given the trapping profession a second thought. In any case, he hadn't been in the Territories the required length of time to obtain a license. Thus any trapping activity had to be conducted with someone who had a registered line.

Like so many others, Harry had resorted to trapping when he failed to locate the gold. "Perhaps we were too determined to find it, too reluctant to admit defeat. I've thought since that we were looking for something that was never there in the first place." This was the one and only comment that Harry ever made to me about the "gold myth" of the Flat River country.

So Harry was doing this thing the hard way: two dogs. One tent.

No cabins. And with the minimum amount of supplies. "There hadn't been much time last fall to build a cabin," he said. "It was the biggest mistake I ever made. I should have taken the time. I realize that, now. A tent is better than a siwash camp, but not by much.

There were a number of questions I wanted to ask my partner about this business of siwashing, but if I swallowed too much knowledge in too short a time there was a chance I might not be able to digest it all. I did have a vague idea of what the term meant, and in any event I would learn soon enough.

That afternoon, Harry outlined a simple plan of procedure for the days ahead: we would each run half the existing line. "That way we can cover the entire trapline in half the time I've been taking. I was only making one trip a week. The traps should all be inspected more often than that.

"Now I've given this careful thought. You can run the 'upriver' portion and I shall take the 'downriver' part. Since our tent is situated almost in the centre of the line, we will each have the same number of miles to patrol. Of course you will have the harder half of the line, but you are seven years younger, and it is only right that you should respect my age."

"I don't believe I get your logic. I am slightly puzzled," I said. "If we each have half the line to cover, how can mine be more difficult?"

"Simply because you will be going up the river, whereas I will be travelling downstream on my half. Water runs downhill, you know. Can't you see? It's only logical."

"Well, I realize water runs downhill," I replied, "but I still can't understand how you arrived at that conclusion. You are dead wrong! You will have a much tougher go of it, simply because you will be climbing all the way back to camp on your part."

Harry scratched his matted head of hair a moment or two before he replied, "By jove, you may be right. In that case, perhaps we should swap ends." We both laughed, and decided we would settle the matter after we had a billy of tea.

That evening, as I was reclining on my bedroll (we still only had the one "chair"), watching my partner stoking the fire, I suddenly exclaimed, "I was right, Harry—you do look like Robinson Crusoe!"

"Now is that a fact! I always thought I bore a slight resemblance to Clark Gable."

"Nope. You're a dead ringer for Crusoe."

"Well then, if I'm Crusoe, you must be my good man, Friday. Right?"

"Friday, I shall be," I said. And from then on, those were our new names while we were in the Nahanni. The only times we reverted to our given names were when the chips were down, and things were not well with us.

Later, while we were having supper, I heard a rustle among the spruce boughs beneath me, and a mouse suddenly appeared in front of my plate that I was holding on my lap.

"We could use a few cats up here at the Rabbitkettle, Crusoe. These bloody mice are getting bolder by the hour. This one just jumped up on my tarp. How do you put up with them?"

"It's not easy, Friday. They have an extensive breeding ground in that slough just back of the tent. There's a foot of dead grass underneath all that snow. It provides a perfect home for the local population. And in addition, I've had to contend with the visitors."

"Visitors?" I asked.

"Sure thing. I have mice here from the Yukon, even some from as far away as Alaska."

"How can you tell they are from Alaska?"

"That's easy; they have webbed feet. Their feet act as snowshoes. Our common, Rabbitkettle mice could never travel that far on ordinary feet." Harry obviously knew a thing or two about mice.

"They've made my life miserable all winter long," he continued. "I wouldn't mind if they paid for their lodging, but they share our beds, and we also provide the little buggers with free heat. It's the heat that attracts them here in the first place. But worst of all, they add insult to injury: the bastards shit in the flour, the oatmeal, the rice—you name it. And to show their appreciation for all this kindness I have shown them, what do they do?—they shit in the big, cast-iron skillet. That's my main grievance. Mice love grease. You get up in the morning; you're in a hurry; you don't have time to fart around cleaning fry pans. And there it is—the bottom covered with mouse turds. It's enough to make a man want to join the Foreign Legion."

"One would think the little beggars would show a little gratitude to their host. My problem has been trying to go to sleep, listening to them playing hide and seek among the spruce boughs," I said.

48

"Well, tonight I'll set the 'eliminator' up before we go to bed. That helps to a certain degree. Or perhaps I just imagine it does; I'm not sure. Perhaps it's like dipping water out of a swamped canoe with a teaspoon."

"What is an eliminator—if I may ask?"

"It's a simple device I use when these little turd-dispensers really get out of hand, and I lose my temper. If Friday will be so kind as to pour me another cup of tea, Crusoe shall explain the operation in detail."

Harry was a very observant man; he knew the tea billy was empty. And he also knew the water pail was empty. This meant that someone would have to make a trip down to the water hole. And surely Friday wouldn't refuse. Twenty minutes later, Harry had his tea, and I was sitting on my bedroll, waiting to hear about this mouse exterminator.

"It's the simplest thing to set up that you ever saw," Harry began. "I leave the water pail about one-third full and place it on the floor, close to the stove. I put a flat stick—which is sharpened at one end—into the dirt floor, and lean the opposite end up against the top of the pail, and tie it to the pail. The stick is pressed firmly into the ground, on a slant to the top of the pail. Then I stretch a length of snare wire across the top of the pail, from each end of the pail. Now I bait the wire with small pieces of moose or caribou suet. Mr. Mouse smells the bait. It scampers up the stick. At the top it stops to ponder the situation: the bait is four or five inches beyond its reach. . . . Faint heart doesn't fill the stomach. Mr. Mouse creeps out on the wire. Kerplunk! Population reduced by one. I'll show you tonight when we turn in."

"How many do you usually catch in an evening?"

"It depends on how cold it gets. On a mild night I've caught as many as six. But we don't have many mild nights in January. When it's cold, the water in the bucket freezes before midnight, and if it's half full, the mice simply jump out. I soon caught on, and put less water in the pail."

"And then what happened?" I was curious.

"A mouse would fall from the wire onto solid ice, then scramble continuously to reach the top of the pail. The noise created would scare the other mice away. So you see, the project was only a partial success. But I still use it; it gives me a personal satisfaction to know that I'm reducing their numbers to a certain extent."

"I do believe you should have this invention patented. How did you get the idea?"

"It wasn't mine. Dal showed me," Harry said. This was another example of the ingenuity of The Flying Trapper of The South Nahanni. I was to learn of others in the weeks to come.

But mice dung in the frying pan was a minor problem compared to the damage that a couple of mice could do to a fur pelt in the course of a single evening. They could easily ruin a pelt by pulling out tufts of fur from the skin. They used this fur to line their nests, prior to raising another batch of young—and another. Thus it was necessary to keep all pelts up on the cache, a chore that required extra time and effort. In a sizable cabin, heated with a proper stove, we would have had a measure of control over the mice. A cabin wouldn't solve the problem entirely, but it would cut the skinning chore down to half the time, or more, as Harry well knew. Frozen animals could be suspended from the rafters of a cabin and thawed out during the course of one evening. Moreover, a cabin banked with dirt up to the second round of logs, would be a deterrent to most of the mice population.

These discussions finally gave me a brain wave, and in my best copycat version of the "Crusoe mode" of elucidation, I said, "I know how we could get rid of the mice, and we would be able to make money doing it, by using a bit of imagination—except that we don't have any traps."

"Traps? What sort of traps are you talking about?"

"Mouse traps, of course. If we had enough of them, we could catch mice by the hundreds and pelt the buggers. Their skins must be worth something. The fur trade could perhaps make mouse gloves for the rich, European ladies."

"You're on the right track, Friday, my boy, but it's a risky business, and you have to have money to get started. And besides, it's been tried before. There used to be a market for mouse pelts, but not any more. When Henry VIII was king there was a big demand for them. The designers in Paris used to make fur brassieres out of them, but the demand finally fizzled out. The trouble was, only the women with small headlamps could afford them. The price of the brassiere was governed by the number of pelts it took to cover it. Which was understandable."

Of course. And there it was: for the umpteenth time I had tried to outwit this "old man of the island," and I had failed again.

As always on a Northern evening, winter or summer, when two, or a dozen, trappers congregate, the subject invariably turns to wolves. It never fails. And so it was with Harry and me, as we took turns shoving the small sticks of spruce into what passed for a stove, as we gradually reduced our Blue Ribbon tea supply, cup by cup. During these first days at the Rabbitkettle, I had seen the odd wolf track on the river, and now that I would be out on the trapline, I had a few pertinent questions that needed to be answered.

"Crusoe, I've heard and read more than a few stories about wolves."

"Who hasn't?" Harry interrupted.

"Now this is the fourth year you have been in the Nahanni. What's the lowdown on these animals? I've been told that the country is full of them. Have they given you much trouble?"

"I wouldn't say so. They have taken the odd marten out of a trap. How many, I'm not sure of, because marten will often chew themselves out of a trap when they are caught just above the paw.

"There are plenty of wolves here on the Nahanni. It's because of the abundance of caribou. Wolves follow the caribou. When the caribou migrate in the spring to the tundra, a number of wolves will follow. But not all of the caribou migrate; some stay behind. Many of the wolves do also. Milt and I saw wolves in the Flat River country each summer we were there prospecting. There were caribou along the creeks, too."

"Your brother Joe was with you fellows on the Liard last summer. Judging from what he had heard among the trappers he had met, he told me that he firmly believes wolves will attack a man. What is your opinion?"

"My brother Joe is very gullible. He's a good guy. And he's as honest as the day is long. But he's gullible. He reads too many outdoor magazines and he is too eager to listen to too many wolf stories. Last fall, at the mouth of the Nahanni, when he was waiting for Dalziel to fly him out to Edmonton, about a half dozen Liard trappers and myself were gathered at Jack Mulholland's cabin to bid Joe goodbye. It turned out that Dal didn't show up for some reason or other, and so we spent most of the afternoon drinking coffee, swapping jokes, and telling stories. Whenever the subject turned to wolves, Joe was all ears. Some of those tales—all true, so help me God—were pretty far out. But I could tell that Joe was swallowing each and every one. A lot of people are like that.

"Every trapper that I've met hates a wolf. They all do. It's understandable. Wolves are predators and so are we. We just happen to be in competition with each other. It's as simple as that. I'm not in love with wolves, either.

"As for a wolf attacking a man, I'd have to see it to believe it. They've never worried me in the least. Twice this winter, I've caught them following me when I've been on the river. I admit it gets a little scary, but they seem to be smart enough to keep their distance. They are not easy to trap. I've managed to catch three, including the one when my gun blew up. Dalziel hated wolves with a vengeance. He would shoot at a wolf a quarter of a mile away, but I never wasted any ammunition on them; their pelts aren't that valuable. But if one ever comes within range of my .22 Hornet, it will likely not suffer from old age. I can promise you that."

In camp, the next morning, Harry explained the main rudiments of the trapping of fur-bearing animals, as he had learned from Dalziel. He showed me several different sets to make for the lynx and marten, and the smaller animals such as mink and weasel. The latter was the only animal I'd ever caught.

"I'm almost as green at this trapping game as you are. We can only do the best we can." This was Harry's attitude, which was as good as any, in my estimation.

February 8th. My first day on the western part of our trapline. Harry's snowshoe trail was easy to follow, as there had been no new snow recently, nor wind. And it was well marked; the trees were blazed at frequent intervals.

The marten and lynx sets were also easy to locate. Even in three-plus feet of snow. Harry always put two axe blazes, one above the other, wherever he placed a trap. This was usually at the base of a tree, in the case of the marten sets. His lynx sets were usually in heavy stands of small jack pine on the higher ridges.

After leaving camp, the trail followed the river for about two miles until it reached the mouth of the Rabbitkettle. Then it veered to the left and ran along the south side of the tributary, and through the heavy timber. A few yards to my left, I saw a huge mound of rock—or at least it looked like a mammoth-sized, snow-covered boulder. Had there been less snow on the level, I probably would have investigated this strange-looking monolith that seemed out of place in its surroundings. It didn't seem to belong alongside the Rabbitkettle River. In any event, I would inquire about this queer-looking object, later.

I always knew when I was approaching a marten set: I would see a picture of a red tomato, attached to a tree, a foot or more above the snow surface. These pictures were the wrappers off the Royal City tomato tins. (Harry explained later that Dalziel always used them on his marten sets.) Marten are curious animals; a red object will always catch their attention. A few years later, at Yellowknife, a trapper told me that he often used a short length of red ribbon, placed directly above his sets.

A common marten set consists of a small enclosure built against the trunk of a tree. Short lengths of willow saplings are planted in the snow, in the form of two half circles. The tree forms a background, and an opening at the front provides an entrance. The bait, consisting of a small piece of rabbit or caribou meat, is placed on a stick that is leaned up against the tree (or otherwise fastened). Many trappers scent the bait with castoreum, an oily substance taken from the sexual glands of the beaver. This is a common practise used in trapping any fur-bearing animal. Harry and I, of course, did not have any such convenience. We placed the trap in the centre of the enclosure, and camouflaged it by sprinkling spruce needles over the entire set, inside the pen. These extra efforts take time, but are worth the trouble. We usually placed a small piece of paper-thin birch bark under the pan of the trap to keep it from freezing into the snow, should a spell of warm weather occur. This precaution, however, is mostly necessary in late fall or early spring.

Lynx are mainly caught by using the teepee set, so-called because of its resemblance to an Indian teepee, minus the covering. Small, slender poles are used for this set, and are placed in teepee fashion, with an opening left in the front. The bait is hung from the top of the cone.

The traps used for catching fur-bearing animals are numbered according to their size, and the number used depends upon the size and strength of the animal the trapper is endeavoring to catch. All traps have a chain attached to their spring. The other end of the chain is spiked to a drag log. Again, the size of the log depends on the size of the animal. If the trap is set in a "fixed" position, the animal may jerk its foot out of the trap. However, we always attached the small traps for mink and marten directly to the tree.

These basic details mentioned are only the barest rudiments of the trapping profession. My scant knowledge would not have been sufficient even to regard myself as a novice. And to be honest, what little I did learn about the trapping vocation while in the Nahanni, was not acquired through any great enthusiasm on my part.

I was following the trail along the narrow ridge that rose above the Rabbitkettle River, where the higher elevation provided a perfect view of its long valley rising into the southwest. I paused for a moment and rolled a cigarette. There were some solemn thoughts running through my mind, as I gazed into that valley that was flanked on either side by the high mountains. I was suddenly reminded of where I was, and why this country had acquired a grim reputation down through these past thirty years.

For somewhere up this valley—just thirteen months ago—two men had disappeared. Their names were Bill Eppler and Joe Mulholland, the brother of Jack Mulholland who had asked me to be on the watch for any clue as to what might have happened to the two men, since I was to be in that particular part of the country where they were last seen. There wasn't time at Jack's trading post that morning at the mouth of the Nahanni, to learn the particulars of the men's disappearance, but I had heard about the missing men from Harry's brother Joe. Dalziel had flown the two trappers in to Rabbitkettle Lake, which was situated about two miles west of where I was now standing. The flight had been made just after New Year's of 1936. When the two men didn't come out to the mouth of the Nahanni in the late spring after open water, as they had intended, a search was made for the men that fall. They were never found.

And now as I stood there in the deep silence, staring into that valley, I wondered about the secrets those mystic mountains might have hidden away. The Nahanni Mountains don't reveal their secrets easily, nor very often.

My many thoughts were interrupted by Liza nudging me, reminding me in her own manner that it was time to be on the move. When

Harry laid out our plans for trapping, he suggested that I take Liza with me. It was important that we each have a dog, "in more ways than one," was the way he put it. I had already gathered that Nigger was his favourite. As for me, I was perfectly satisfied with Liza.

At the bottom of the ridge, the trail dropped back northward towards the Nahanni River, into the white spruce, and through the trees, I caught sight of the river below. Here, underneath a canopy of evergreens—I came to Harry's noonday stop. Dry wood was waiting and my tea billy was soon boiling over a small fire. One can make a pot of tea in nothing flat—if dry wood is handy.

I didn't stop long. After the second cup, I replenished the wood supply, then Liza and I were off again on the trail. During that short afternoon, the trail was never more than a quarter of a mile from the river, always keeping to the heavy timber. There was a specific amount of territory to cover, and at the end of the day, I had a siwash camp to make. I hadn't had any experience in this particular art—nothing more than a basic idea of what that operation was all about.

At 4 p.m. I came to Harry's siwash camp. It didn't look like much of a place to spend a winter's night. But there was plenty of dry wood in the area, which was the important thing. I removed Liza's panniers and tied her toggle chain to a tree—just in case she had any ideas about returning to the home tent. Then I grabbed my axe and made the chips fly.

During these many years past, friends and relatives have been asking the same questions: Just what *is* a siwash camp? How do you go about constructing one? How long does it take? Do you really go to sleep at night when it's so cold? And what about the wolves? And the questions still come, and they never vary to any degree. Perhaps I should endeavour to define a siwash camp in detail.

It's a night camp where a man endeavours to keep from freezing to death in thirty below zero or colder. The greater his degree of proficiency in its construction, the greater his chance of survival will be, come the dawn.

Actually speaking, a siwash camp is a bedroom with the highest ceiling in the world—the starry sky above—and four walls consisting of the entire continent of North America. To the uninitiated it would appear that the sleeping quarters are already in existence, and one had only to remove his snowshoes and turn in for the night alongside some likely-looking tree. But there is a misconception to such an assumption. It's going to be a long, long night—and that's where the catch lies.

While it is still daylight, the trapper must fell at least one-half cord of wood, as close as possible to where he intends to make his bed. This is the fundamental part of the operation, and the part that requires experience: one must know the amount of daylight required to put the night's supply of wood where it belongs. This, of course, will depend on the circumstances. The ideal location for the night camp will be where the standing *dry* trees are near a canopy of green spruce or pine.

Having the fuel supply at hand, the trapper now removes his snowshoes, and using one of them as a shovel, he clears away the snow in an area adjacent to the shelter of the spruce, where the bed will be. Remember, the snow is three or more feet deep, and it must be removed to the bare ground, or water will come trickling under his tarp.

By this time darkness is setting in. The trapper drags each dry log through the snow to the cleared space and lays them parallel to each other in a long pile—as if he were loading them onto a sleigh. This is no job for a weakling, and it burns up a bit of energy after a day on the trapline.

Now it's time to make the bed. A mound of spruce boughs are cut from several smaller evergreens, and are placed in the form of a mat in the cleared area next to the fire logs. These branches are placed with the convex side *down*, with the tips of the branches curling *upward*. This is important: any collection of moisture from thawed ice or snow will be directed to the bottom of the mat.

It's time now to light the fire in the centre of the log pile. The next half hour is spent thawing out frozen moose meat (or caribou), for the man and for the dogs. Dogs should *never* be fed frozen meat. But they often are!

By the light of a blazing fire, the trapper can now relax over several tin cups of scalding tea while waiting for his supper to boil in the large cast-iron billy. He might even have a few wistful moments wondering what his girlfriend is up to back home. If he has no girlfriend, he always has his pack dog by his side to talk to.

Thus can be appreciated the amount of work involved in making a siwash camp. And much of this work must be done in partial darkness, which increases the chance of a night slip of the axe, the worst thing that might happen out on the trail. It's something that all men in the bush think about, or should. Each simple task takes time—melting snow to make water, for instance. One learns to dig down deep to find the older snow crystals in making a pot of tea.

And so, after finally eating his meat supper, the trapper has only *one* thing on his mind: sleep. He spreads part of his tarp over the bed mat, then folds the other half over himself, as his one and only cover. Then, with his axe and rifle within reach, but away from the fire, he promptly falls asleep.

How can he go to sleep so soon, under these conditions? He's tired, that's why. Dog-tired! That's the simple reason. But the night has just begun. In roughly two hours or less, the fire burns down in the centre of the pile, and the sleeper awakens—because he's beginning to freeze. He arises and pushes the ends of the logs together, and the fire flares up again. Back to bed he goes. Another two hours go by. The fire is down again. Up he gets, and there is more pushing of logs. This routine is repeated several times before the dawn rolls around.

Most of the long nights, I never waited for the dawn—after I knew where the traps were set. In the wee hours of the morning, I would say to myself, "To hell with it! I've had enough punishment." I would rise and boil my breakfast of moose meat, feed Liza a scrap or two (dogs should only be fed at night), and hit the trail.

On this first night out, I found myself in luck; it hadn't snowed since Harry had used this night camp, nor had there been any wind to speak of. Consequently I was spared the work of shovelling a ton of snow. And there was plenty of dry timber available. However, there was one important requisite missing at this camp: there was no background of heavily-branched evergreens to act as a reflector of the heat from the night fire. And this was the main reason I spent such a miserable night. But I did make one or two mistakes. Being totally inexperienced in this business, I had placed my bed too far away from the fire. I was over-cautious, afraid the tarp might catch fire.

My other problem was one of a physical nature—one that the doctors hadn't been able to solve, even when I reached my eighteenth birthday. From that time on, I solved the problem myself: I simply refrained from drinking liquids after 6 p.m. in the evening. But on this particular night, I had drunk too many cups of tea: I urinated in my pants while still asleep. A thing like this is bad enough in the middle of the summer, but at thirty below in an open bedroom it is a catastrophe!

I didn't spend much time the next morning breaking camp. Not long after daylight, the trail swung sharply to the right, leading down to the Nahanni River. I remembered Harry saying that I would be at the halfway mark when I reached this point. As we were crossing the river, I noticed that Liza had perked up considerably, and even showed a bit of interest in our outing. She knew where we were; we were heading in the direction of the home tent, where she wanted to be.

During the forenoon we were never far from the river, and at my mid-day tea break, I heard Liza growl. Out across the river, I saw two caribou heading westward, near the south shore. Liza's hearing was obviously better than mine. Early in the afternoon, the line veered off into high jack pine country, swiftly gaining altitude each foot we travelled. Although we were climbing steadily, I didn't find it abnormally tiring pulling the toboggan, mostly because it was lightly loaded and the trail was in fair condition.

On the steep inclines, however, I was having trouble handling my snowshoes properly. I hadn't as yet gained the knack of turning the shoes sideways at an angle, and always putting the same shoe above the other when negotiating steep places. There were times when I literally cursed those shoes. Twice I fell sideways into the snow, much to Liza's amusement. At least I caught her wagging her tail the second time I fell.

It was typical marten country here on the plateau. There was a beautiful female in the first set I came to, and farther up the line, a live male was still fighting the trap. Had I arrived an hour later, I would likely have found only part of a front leg in that trap. Grim business, this particular vocation, and one that I already had second thoughts about. But fur meant money, and I was Harry's partner now; it was imperative—and my duty—that I uphold my end of our relationship. He was the last man in the world I would want to let down.

I was afraid I might be taking up too much time examining and resetting the traps, making sure they were in working order, but it was only 3 p.m. by my watch when we reached Harry's second out-camp. Now I was beginning to understand his *modus operandi*. He had neatly solved the problem of dragging logs through the snow at this camp. He had simply placed his night bed in the centre of a stand of fire-killed timber, where he felled sufficient trees for the night, into one another, making a long pile, as one would do when cutting cordwood. The dry timber covered a large area, and he had only to move his night bed adjacent to his next pile on the succeeding trip around the trapline. This method saved much back-breaking work, but as at his first camp, the canopy of evergreens was missing. To my way of thinking, this was a mistake. Cattle and horses, in the dead of winter, will always seek shelter in the most heavily-limbed woods they can find because of the advantage of windbreak. The Indians make camp under the protection of green spruce or pine, as do most hunters I knew back home.

Harry was a strong man who took pride in being able to handle most any adversity that came his way. And he was just as tough as he was strong. But he had one fault: he was completely indifferent to his own comfort in the bush. (A fact I became aware of before winter was out.) To him, the less time spent in making a camp, the more time was available on the trapline. Hard physical work was a characteristic that he had inherited from his father and mother. This is an admirable trait in anyone, but it can be overdone. Both his overworked parents died young.

I stood there awhile, rolling a cigarette, pondering the situation. The wind, which had been steadily blowing in from the northwest, began increasing in volume. That settled the matter. Trying to make a decent night camp with no protection from the wind would be an exercise in futility in my book. I'd go on until I found a different site.

Another half-hour's travel brought us into a deep ravine, and up on the ridge above, I spotted several dead birch trees. There weren't many but I knew there was double the heat in a birch to that of a spruce of the same size. I'd conserve the fuel at hand and try to rustle a bit more beyond the ridge. I needed only to fell these trees into the ravine, and gravity would take care of most of the transportation work. Setting up camp in the ravine proved its worth. It was something of a relief to lie on my bed and listen to the wind whistling overhead. And so I managed to endure another cold night with a minimum of torture.

Early in the morning we were into short-height jackpine, thick as hair on a dog's back. It was ideal lynx range. Harry had made several sets, using number three traps, but all were empty. Near noon I stopped in a poplar grove and made tea. Liza lay there by the toboggan during the brief stop, looking annoyed by this unnecessary stop. She wanted to be home with Nigger.

By mid-afternoon we were back in the spruce forest again, near the north shore of the river. And in less than an hour we climbed the south bank to our "home" tent. There was still plenty of daylight to spare. I felt a great sense of relief, knowing that I could handle my part of the line.

Harry arrived in camp an hour later with a big tom lynx strapped on his packboard, and two marten in Nigger's panniers—a bit of money in these Depression days.

Harry seemed surprised that I had arrived in camp so early in the day, and wanted to know how I had enjoyed siwash camping.

"I've had better sleeping quarters, Crusoe," I said.

"Yes, it's not to be compared with staying at the Palliser Hotel in Calgary. But never mind, Friday, the worst of the winter will be over in a few weeks, I hope. I can tell you I put in some rough nights out there between the last few days of December and the first part of January."

"I can imagine you did," was all I could say.

"I had trouble with my back on several of the colder nights. It sort of scares the hell out of a person."

I didn't know what to reply to that. I was to have good reason to remember this conversation some twenty-two months later at Yellowknife, N.W.T., in the late fall of 1938, when Harry was forced to leave the North because of his bad back.

I set about making supper while Harry hung the frozen lynx under the ridgepole of the tent to thaw out. This was the problem with the tent; it didn't hold heat. It had been a time-waster to Harry, all winter long.

"I should have built a cabin last fall," Harry said.

"Having a larger stove to go with it, would be a useful addition also," I added. The words were no sooner spoken than I could have bitten off my tongue. Who the hell was I to comment or make suggestions? I was responsible for our flour situation, wasn't I? Henceforth, it might be prudent for me to keep certain observations to myself.

But the stove was a joke; there was no denying that. We must have spent a third of our time in camp, poking small pieces of wood into the tiny firebox. It was a never-ending job.

"Yes, there are numerous items missing around this camp, Friday, me lad. But it is not good to be too comfortable. We must understand that money is the root of all evil. It's a sin, you understand, to crave all these good things in life. Don't you realize that it is much more noble to give than to receive? That's the philosophy that I've always followed."

"I know you have, Crusoe," I retorted. "And I agree to a certain extent. But personally speaking, I wouldn't mind having a little something to give—just to find out how it felt. Now I shouldn't wish to live a sinful life everyday, but I don't see any harm in craving a plate of bacon and eggs for breakfast tomorrow morning."

"Well now, Friday, I would be willing to receive something of that nature. There are exceptions to everything."

This chore of thawing frozen animals was one aspect of the trapping game to which I hadn't given much thought, and now I was beginning to understand the conditions that Harry had been working under since arriving at the Rabbitkettle. "Doing it the hard way" had to be an understatement.

During supper, I asked Harry about the big mound of rock over by the Rabbitkettle River.

"A mound of rock?"

"Well, that's what it looked like to me. It's on the south side of the river."

"You must mean the hot springs," Harry replied. "Dal told me they were caused by an overflow of calcium from underground. He had taken some samples of the overflow to the government labs in Edmonton earlier in the summer. Dal and I went over there last fall to look around; we thought we might find some clue concerning Bill Eppler's and Joe Mulholland's disappearance."

"What do you think happened to those men?"

"Nobody knows, Friday, no one. Dal flew them in to Rabbitkettle Lake early in January of last year. They had gone in to trap marten and lynx. Apparently they were staying in a cabin that was already there, or one in that vicinity. They were supposed to come out to the mouth of the Nahanni in the spring, after open water. They never showed."

"Did they have a boat?" This was what was interesting me, because I knew we would be facing the river, come this June.

"They were going to put one together up there," Harry said. "Jack Mulholland told me that the boys took several yards of canvas with them to build a canvas canoe."

"What is your opinion of that idea?" I asked.

Harry carefully rolled a fat cigarette and said, "We were talking about skin boats and canvas canoes down on the Liard River, at Ole Lindberg's cabin last fall. Albert Faille was there. We asked him what he thought about using canvas to build a canoe. He said: 'I don't know anything about canvas, but I built a skin boat once—and only once. Either way, I think it would be a sure way of committing suicide on the Nahanni.' And when Faille talks about this river, you listen.

"No. I'd rather build a raft. You can't sink a log raft. I've heard of people building birch bark canoes, but the only kind Milt and I used on the Flat and the Nahanni were made in Peterborough, Ontario, as I remember. I know that the Indians often built skin boats using moose hide to cover the framework, but they knew when the river was safe; they were never in a hurry to take chances on bad water.

"I do know that Bill Eppler was an experienced man in the bush. He was also familiar with the Nahanni. Joe, of course, hadn't been in the North very long.

"Down at Fort Simpson, it was arranged that Dal fly into the Nahanni to see if he could locate the boys. I went with him on that flight, and that's how I came to be here at Dal's main camp.

"Their cabin had burnt down sometime during the winter, because there were two rounds of logs still showing, which meant that the fire must have occurred when there was a couple of feet of snow on the ground. I was busy making a new cache here and cutting wood. I never went with Dal on the search, so I didn't see the remains of the cabin."

"Did the boys have a cache?"

"Yes, Dal did say that the few articles remaining on the cache indicated that the men had left the site after the cabin had burned. But where to? That's the question."

"If they lost essential items such as clothing and bedrolls in the fire, they may have been forced to walk out of the country," I offered.

"Well I sure as hell wouldn't want to try it," Harry said. "If they attempted to walk out of here in the middle of the winter, I think they could have kissed themselves goodbye. It's about 200 miles from here to the Liard River. It's an impossibility without a good dog team and plenty of supplies. To try it would be like signing your own death warrant. No, I'd rather suppose they met trouble on the river, after open water. This, of course, would be assuming that the cabin burned in late April or thereabouts. But who knows?"

"But why would they not have left a message at the cabin site?" I asked. "One only has to blaze a tree and leave a short note. It can be written with charcoal if one hasn't a pencil. A person can even carve a note with his hunting knife. I've heard of tree-blazed notes being deciphered several years after they were written."

"That's the method always used in the North, Friday, but not all trappers or prospectors are in the habit of leaving messages. If they did, more causes of some Nahanni deaths would be known. I'll give you an example: Albert Faille. That man knows his way around in the bush, and he is fully aware of what can happen to a man. Sometimes he leaves messages at whichever cabin he happens to be in, and sometimes he doesn't. He's been in the Nahanni since 1927, and most of the time, nobody knows what part. Milt and I stayed at two of his cabins on the Flat River, but we never knew where he was. And so it is.

"We can speculate and postulate until the cows come home, and still be no closer to the truth as to what happened to Eppler and Mulholland."

I then mentioned about the advice Tiny Gifford had given me—about the danger of fire, and about trappers—experienced trappers—making mistakes.

"I'm sure they do, Friday. We all do. I made one—as you know—when my rifle blew up. We're all human."

It was time to change the subject, which Harry did with ease.

"I do believe our fire has gone out, Friday, me boy. Now if you would be so kind as to rectify the matter, I shall round up my deck of cards, and we will indulge in a game of 500 rummy—for no other reason, I might add, than to prove that I am a superior player—you understand."

"I understand. I've often wondered, Crusoe, how you ever found a beret large enough to go over your head. You must have had one specially made."

But it was Harry's way of steering our thoughts into a more cheerful channel. Tomorrow would be our day in camp, tending the fur, and catching up with the camp chores.

All was quiet in the little tent, as we sat there on our bedrolls, playing each card by the dim light of the flickering candle that we had placed on Harry's "chair."

Suddenly I thought I saw the bottom of the tent flaps move. Then a small head with two tufted ears poked itself through the flap. "Crusoe! There's a marten at our doorway." The head disappeared in an instant at the sound of my voice.

"Oh, I forgot to tell you, Friday. His name is Fritzie. He's a welcome visitor here. I've been laying out meat for him since the beginning of January. He's becoming quite tame. I've managed to coax him into the tent a couple of times. But he doesn't like noise. And he doesn't like to be watched. Try to ignore him. I'm sure he will accept you as a member of the household. I always leave some meat on one of the small stretcher boards just inside the tent for him. And of course, he gets all my dead mice. I've seen him snatch a mouse off the board, faster than the eye can see. He appreciates the handouts. He even visited me on New Year's Eve. Christ, it was cold that night! That's a fact!"

Knowing that a marten was in the habit of entering someone's tent when it was occupied, was something that had to be seen. I remembered that proverb: "Truth is stranger than fiction." And then again, I remembered that weasels often raised their young under the floor of farm houses in Alberta, simply because of the food supply: mice. And of course, the additional bonus of a heated maternity room. I wondered how many mice Fritzie had caught while Harry was away from the tent.

"Do you realize what you have done, Crusoe? You have made the discovery of the century! You will be rich! It will take some time—

but you will be rich. You will receive the Nobel Peace Prize for 1937."

Harry looked puzzled, which filled me with glee. I had bettered him this time.

"Don't you comprehend, Crusoe? You have discovered the world's greatest mouse-eliminator. It will render the mousetrap obsolete. Dal's invention will also be forgotten."

"How so, Friday?"

"Just think of it: all we have to do is find a mate for Fritzie. We can find out how to live-trap the marten. After that there is no end to the possibilities. Why, every farmer's wife in America will purchase one of our martens."

"Where do you get this 'we' stuff from, Friday? You've already admitted that Fritzie was my discovery. Now you want to horn in on it."

"I am totally shocked by your attitude; Crusoe—when I stop to think of all I did for you when we were on that island."

Cold Siwash Nights

On most days during the first part of February, the weather had been moderate. We hadn't had any new snow to any extent, and very little wind, except for that one night when I had camped in the ravine. As far as we were able to judge, it was never colder than thirty below. But of course, we didn't have a thermometer to verify our daily guesses. Understandably, however, the cold was always on our minds.

Considering that we were both amateurs in this business, we were satisfied with the catch to date. I had caught four marten and one lynx. Harry had had a couple of good runs: three lynx and three marten. If each pelt averaged fifteen dollars, it still added up to a bit of money. But fur prices had been fluctuating so often during the Depression years that we didn't have any idea of what they were at the moment.

But out on the line, a trapper's mind is always on the number rather than the price of each pelt. He will receive that information soon enough when he reaches Fort Simpson, come spring time.

Liza's attitude out on the line hadn't changed to any degree. Her formula for getting through each day was to exert the least amount of energy as possible. Apparently from the beginning, she had realized that I was a novice at this game and it didn't take her long to adjust her formula to take advantage of the circumstances. Her main tactic—among others—was to lag behind—slow the pace down, especially when leaving the home camp to run the line. After I finally became familiar with my snowshoes, I was in the habit of covering ground in the shortest time possible—from trap to trap. I had always been a fast walker. Liza didn't always agree with my speedy mode of travel. Finally after our third trip over the line, and overcome by frustration, I asked Harry if he had any answers to my problem.

"I sure do, Friday! Next time she pulls that caper, just tie the end of her ten-foot toggle chain to the bottom of your packboard. When you feel the chain tightening up, stop, turn around, grab the chain with both hands and heave ho! Just yank that bloody dog into the snow, to one side of the trail. Repeat that move about three times in rapid succession, and I guarantee she will get the message. Liza is not a dumb dog; she will con anybody she can."

On the next trip over the line, I gave Harry's motivator a tryout. It worked. I even improved upon it; I stepped up the pace after each time I jerked her off her feet. After that she kept close behind the toboggan. As Harry would say, "she forestood." Things went along quite smoothly out on the trail now that my dog and I had an understanding.

Harry also solved another problem I was having. It concerned my snowshoes. They were equipped with a leather harness that tended to freeze and harden in the cold weather. This caused painful abrasions on my ankles and heels. In camp one evening, he brought out a couple of yards of material, which he had purchased at the Bay store in Simpson. It resembled lantern wick in texture and colour, but was made of wider material. The new harness took only a few minutes to assemble, and remained pliable during the remainder of the winter. This prevented a problem that could later have proved serious if not attended to. Harry didn't say, but he likely received this tip from someone down at Nahanni village.

A particular observation I had made here at the Rabbitkettle was the absence of rabbit "runs" in the snow. They were always plentiful when I grew up in Alberta. Wherever there was bush, there were rabbits. Was this year a downward trend in their life cycle here in the Nahanni? Back home I had been told that the lowly cottontail has a seven-year increase in numbers, after which a disease peculiar to their species would substantially decrease their population. As a young boy

I used to snare the rabbits in their runs, then skin them and feed the carcasses to our chickens. Sometimes I would pretend I was a big-game hunter, living off the "wild wilderness": I would build a fire in the snow and roast the odd bunny. I don't remember enjoying the meat to any great degree.

But here in the North, I knew that the main diet of the lynx and marten was the rabbit. Few rabbits, few lynx and marten. As this was Harry's first trapping season, he didn't want to comment too strongly as to what extent the scarcity of rabbits would affect the fur population. He did remark that when the snow leaves the ground we would see rabbit runs "all over the place." So there must have been plenty of them in the country not too long ago.

One evening in camp, about mid-February, I had a suggestion to make. I had lost two marten on this last trip over the line. Each had been caught by one leg, and they had simply chewed themselves out of their trap.

"I don't see any need for me to spend the fourth day here in camp, Crusoe. You can tend to the pelts. If I spent the extra day out on the line, it would mean that my traps would be inspected that much sooner. It should cut down on the loss."

"It might," Harry said. "But I believe it would be a mistake. Nobody can spend every day on the trail. Physically, you could do it, Friday, but it wouldn't be long before you would be fed up. And then you would want to take a week off. If I were you I wouldn't try it."

So my idea was dropped. But it set me to wondering how many three-legged marten would die in these Northwest Territories this winter—without benefit to anyone. It was an unpleasant thought. Better to brew a cup of tea and have a Turret roll-your-own, and put certain things out of your mind.

And so the subject turned to coyotes—and where were they? I hadn't seen any tracks.

"Neither have I, Friday. I haven't seen one coyote since I've been in this country. There were none on the Flat River, that I know of."

"Why is that?"

"This is wolf country, Friday. The wolves would drive the coyotes out. It's a no-contest thing. The wolf is a much larger animal, its legs are much longer; it could easily outrun a coyote, especially in deep snow. And this is 'deep snow country,' as you know."

"I know," I said.

"I have heard that wolves and coyotes do exist together in the northern parts of some of our provinces. But only where the wolves are few and far between. This doesn't suggest that wolves will sooner or later eliminate the coyote. Far from it. I'll bet the coyotes will be around long after the wolves are gone."

"Why do you say that?" I asked.

"Because they're smarter, that's why. Coyotes use caution to the greatest degree, every time they hunt or search for food. They stay outside the range of trouble. Look at how long they have survived in Alberta, where every man and his brother have been hunting them down since the settlers first arrived."

I had to agree with Harry, because I knew what he was talking about. I too, had hunted coyotes in Alberta. In the early Hungry Thirties, the coyote pelts were worth about ten dollars in Calgary or Edmonton. There were a substantial number of coyotes in that province, and a few dollars could be obtained if one could catch them. Coyotes shunned traps like the plague. They knew more about traps than the trappers did.

Harry was busy stoking up the fire when I returned from the water hole with fresh water. "I do believe we're out of tea, Friday. It seems that my faithful helper has been letting his duties slip of late. Remember your promise: you offered to take care of the camp chores if I looked after the pelts."

"I'll shinny up that monkey pole, right this instant, your honour, and fetch some down. I shall see that it doesn't happen again," I retorted.

Up on the cache, I received a welcome surprise. I discovered seven pounds of tea in the grocery box. I knew that Dalziel had ordered five on the list. Did the Bay manager make a mistake? I thought not. When I told Harry about the find, he said, "I think the manager knew that a couple of extra pounds wouldn't do us any harm. I tell you one thing: it's hard to be without the Blue Ribbon. I know."

We played three games of 500 rummy before turning in for the night, and as usual, I lost all three. I tried to be a graceful loser, but there is a limit to anyone's endurance. "I might even consider burning that damned deck of cards," I thought.

During the third week of February, there was a gradual change in the weather, much to our liking. The days were getting longer, now, and noticeably warmer. But the change was also bringing more snow. Every new inch was steadily adding up to what became known as the year of the Big Snow in the Mackenzie Mountains.

What I noticed mostly, was a substantial increase in all animal movement in the area. There seemed to be dozens of scampering mouse tracks wherever I looked along the trail. I took notice of the bits of dead grass between many of their tiny footprints, which told me these little fellows were replenishing their food caches: the seeds were visible in the cut blades of grass. And what was more significant, these mice were in a feverish hurry to do so. This increased activity, in turn, brought the mink and weasel out. I hadn't seen many mink on the line, as yet, but I did catch the odd weasel. In fact they were the only fur-bearing animal I knew anything about, for I had been one school kid among hundreds in Western Canada who had trapped this little animal. Its pelt paid for part of our clothing, during the long months of winter.

But the squirrel activity was what mainly drew my eye. There were so many more than usual, scurrying over the snow hummocks, and through the trees, leaving their telltale, cone-seed trail everywhere through the large spruce. I often saw small piles of cones alongside holes in the snow. These holes likely led to dens under the roots of trees or to hollow logs buried deep beneath the heavy snow cover. What had caused this sudden increase in the squirrel population? In point of fact, there was no increase. Their normal numbers were simply out in full force, in plain sight, feverishly adding to their food supply. This, in turn, brought out the marten. On one particular afternoon, I caught an instant glimpse of a marten leaping over the snow. A dozen feet ahead, a squirrel crossed the trail and slithered up a spruce tree, followed by the marten. Other heavily branched trees cut off my view, so I didn't see the end of the chase. But I didn't need to; no squirrel can escape from a marten by seeking refuge in a tree. They are the masters in the treetops. This frenzied movement among these forest dwellers was a forecast, a warning that an impending snowstorm was brewing. I knew it was coming when I looked up and saw the dull grey halo encircling the hazy, orange-yellow sun. Back home, in the winter, this was always a sure sign.

The next morning when I was leaving my first night camp, I found it unusually warm—likely less than five below, if that. It reminded me of the February chinooks back home—and how welcome they always were. But this was not the beginning of a chinook. There was an entirely different feeling in the air—the unmistakable feeling that a real storm was on its way. Beyond the mountains to the west, a cloud cover was rapidly moving in. I wondered if this was going to be one of those "Yukon Blowouts" that Harry often talked about. Late in the fall of '35, he and Milt Campbell were crossing the mile-wide Liard River in a canoe, when a terrific Yukon storm hit them. They were forced back to the same shore they had just left and had to wait the storm out. Two feet of snow had fallen that night.

Well, more snow was something we didn't need. Harry had intentionally put the tomato wrappers fairly low on the tree trunks so that they would be more visible, but I could see that another foot of snow would cover them. I was thankful that he had put two tree blazes instead of the usual one, wherever a trap was set. After more snow, the marten sets would all need to be lifted and reset and new lynx pens built. "More snow, more work" was a truism of the trapline. The line, itself, was beginning to look like a miniature snow canyon.

At noontime, a strong breeze began drifting in from the northwest, straight downriver from the upper Nahanni country, bringing with it those familiar, star-shaped snowflakes—except that I had never seen any of this size before—or since. I'm sure they would have covered a twenty-five-cent piece. Nice and gentle they fell at first. Then big globs of the white stuff came floating down—increasing in volume until they were as thick as the leaves of a quaking aspen tree. Through this dense mantle of white, I could barely trace the outline of the olive-coloured conifers and it all took place in less than an hour.

By the time we reached the river, I couldn't see the opposite shore line. And now the wind began to blow! There was *power* and determination in that breeze, believe-you-me. Out here on the river, the gale had nothing to impede its force, so that the trail was almost filled when we reached the north bank. It was incredible!

Making the long climb up to the ridge of the small plateau wasn't going to be easy by any means, I could see, and I was beginning to wonder if I could reach the ravine (where I had found more dry timber on my previous trip) before daylight ran out. There wasn't a hell of a lot of daylight left out there now, as far as that mattered. They sky above was *black*. Most of the afternoon still remained, but I was finding it harder to pull the toboggan through the loose snow, as well as keeping myself over the hard-packed trail.

I was being reminded of the blizzards back home on the bald prairie, just north of Calgary. Some of them were dillies. I could still hear the announcer over the radio (CFCN) reporting: "Police close Calgary–Edmonton highway! Leave your cars and trucks at home! Use the streetcars!"

Well, there wasn't much I could leave at home where I was at. I was *here*! And it didn't matter a damn whether the road was clear or not. All I knew was that it wasn't closed. It's a free country up here in the Nahanni. But it was a road that I knew I had to go over—sooner or later. And there was no point in waiting for a streetcar.

The swirling snow gusts seemed to come in from any direction, making it difficult to maintain a uniform pace, a steady snowshoe stride, with the proper rhythm of movement that is essential in covering one's daily mileage.

Occasionally I would look back to make sure Liza was following. She was, but it was evident she had lost all enthusiasm for any further travel. As I mentioned earlier, Liza had a mind of her own, but when she didn't respond to my repeated warnings of "get with it, dammit, or else . . . ," it suddenly dawned on me that perhaps this dog was trying to tell me something: "stop, you fool—before you find yourself in trouble!"

Finally, common sense won out over futility. Was I trying to prove that I could beat old man weather at his own game? There was nothing to be gained by trying to force myself over the line: the traps would be buried again in less than an hour after they were reset. And trying to fight this storm over a further seven or eight miles was just plain stupid. I'd likely play myself out. No, I would go back to the river and make myself another lean-to camp. And if this blizzard continued for any length of time, I'd simply wait it out. Like the Indian had said on our plane flight: "Snow, she stop by an' by, mabbee." I sure hoped so.

An hour later, luck was with me. Through the blind of snow, I stumbled upon two big spruce trees. And they were both dry! They were standing side by side near a grove of smaller, green conifers.

Those two trees were as welcome as the sudden sight of a couple of yellow nuggets in a prospector's gold pan. The canopy of spruce would be of considerable benefit on this forthcoming night, also. As there had been no fire through this area in recent years, I assumed that these older spruce had likely been killed by insects of some kind. But I wasn't a biologist. And in any case, I was only interested in dry wood.

But I did have second thoughts as I noted the size of these trees. Both were more than twelve inches in diameter at snow level. I took my trail axe from Liza's pannier and examined the blade. It was what was known as a "two-pounder"—a boy's axe, actually. All trappers carried one on the trapline because it was light in weight and short-handled and could be carried conveniently in a dog pannier or on a packboard. What I needed for this job was Harry's big, double-bitted axe, which was at the home camp. Well, I'd put this puny little blade to work, and I'd bring the modest "giants" to the ground, supposing it took until hell froze over. Considering the frigid gale blowing from upriver, there was a possibility of that happening.

I didn't waste any more time thinking about it. I tramped the snow down around the base of the trees, removed the shoes, and went to work. The pile of chips grew higher and higher. Liza lay curled in the snow. Now and again when I stopped for a breather, she would raise her head and give me her usual, doleful look, her favourite expression in good or bad circumstances. She was also won-dering—I surmised—what was taking me so long with the fire. Fire time was mealtime to Liza.

Finally, after forever, both trees were down, almost buried in the snow. The very thought of digging out all that wood called for an intermission. Time to make tea. The fire was easy; I only had to toss a piece of birch bark on to the pile of chips, and light it. Liza came back to life when she saw the flames, and took up a closer position to the heat.

A tea break is not a tea break unless it's taken with a roll-your-own cigarette. The two go together out on the lonely trapline. They are as close as bacon and eggs or cream and sugar. When I sit by the night fire and watch the smoke curling upward from my cigarette, it gives me the feeling that I am not alone.

A man doesn't consume much tobacco out here on the trail. It's too damned cold to remove your mitts and build a smoke. It's too dangerous, as a matter of fact. I tried it one time. I managed to get the cigarette rolled, but by that time, my fingers were so cold and numb that I dropped the lighter into the snow. I was hunting for nearly an hour before I finally found it. You can't afford to lose an item such as a lighter when you are a million miles from anywhere. And so you reserve your smoking time until you have some heat on the subject.

My second cup of tea provided the pause I needed to think about the easiest way to make this wood supply moveable. Obviously I would be required to chop the trees into sections small enough to handle. Finally I decided to cut each tree into eight-foot lengths, then place the night fire in the centre of the two "butt" logs where they lay. This would eliminate the need to move the two heaviest logs at all. Thus only the other lengths would need to be maneuvered onto the fire. I was hoping I could do this by moving each end of the logs a few feet at a time. This wouldn't be any great feat if the snow weren't so damned deep.

The thing was to reduce the amount of axe work as much as possible. Let the fire do the cutting. Finally, in eight cuts, both trees were lying in five separate lengths. Harry's bucksaw would have done this job in a quarter of the time, but we had obvious reasons to leave both the saw and the double-bitted axe at the home camp.

This wood-surgery operation took up a large part of the afternoon, and I had to think about the night bed. And it had to be a better one than I had built up to now. A strong windbreak had to be built. And the only answer was a lean-to. I had previously constructed two of these shelters near the trail, and both of them had provided a certain amount of protection overhead, but neither had been of the proper size to be of the maximum benefit. It's the same in all endeavours; you learn as you go. Winter lean-tos require a considerable amount of effort to be worth their while, and I made up my mind that this night it would be done in a proper manner, with a reasonable amount of intelligence exercised. I was sick and tired of punishment.

The construction of a winter lean-to is a simple operation. But it must not be confused with its summer counterpart, which consists of a tarpaulin thrown up at an angle, between two trees. Every boy scout is acquainted with these.

Ever since the cave dwellers ventured beyond their diminutive territory, man has sheltered himself beneath some form of lean-to. And the material used was not always of wood and snow.

Expressed in simple terms, as applied to our Northern variety, a lean-to consists of a ridge pole (as in a tent) placed between two trees which are, preferably, about seven feet (two metres) apart. The pole is secured to each tree with strips of babiche or short lengths of rope. This *green* pole is placed no more than four feet (one metre) above the ground—the bare ground, that is. Slender poles, about two inches (five centimetres) in diameter, are now cut from green saplings, and evenly spaced about a foot (thirty centimetres) apart, against the ridgepole, at an angle of approximately forty-five degrees. Hence the name "lean-to." The slanting roof is then overlaid with spruce boughs, which must be amply covered with snow. The snow keeps the boughs in place and prevents them from catching fire. Usually the ends of the trees cut for the roof support can be used to frame the two ends of the windbreak. In turn, these ends are heaped with snow. Again, as with any night camp, the shelter must be put on bare ground, so as to be on the same level as the fire. The open side of this shelter is always adjacent to and parallel with the fire logs. This detailed description gives an idea of the amount of work involved.

The most important consideration to be taken in building a shelter of this kind, before a single axe cut is made, is the wind direction. The adjacent shelter and fire must coincide with the wind so that the smoke and flames will be blown *past* the open side of the lean-to. Otherwise—if a man happened to be dreaming of his girlfriend back home—he might be rudely awakened by finding his tarpaulin on fire.

It wasn't because I hadn't given the placement of the shelter sufficient thought. I had. It was just another matter that I would resolve later, after the wood supply was taken care of. My problem was I needed two ridgepole trees, and there was only one in proper alignment.

Well, this called for a liberal amount of cogitation aided by a roll of Turret tobacco. I stirred up the fire, which was still alive, and perched myself on one of the stumps. Liza turned her head in my direction, with a disgusted look on her face. She never could understand these smoke breaks; she considered them a waste of time. She reasoned that the night camp had to be built before she would be fed. And as yet, there was no sign of it even being started.

Well, I really wasn't trying to consume time. It was just that I happened to be a slow thinker. It always seemed to take me longer to analyse a difficult situation and come up with the logical solution than it should have.

Then suddenly I had the answer. And how simple it was: plant another tree in the required position for the one you don't have. It was as simple as that. It just hadn't occurred to me earlier, that I only needed to cut a four-inch post, six feet long, partially sharpen one end of it, then place the post upright in an indentation in the ground, which I could pound down with the head of my axe. After which the post could be pole-braced solidly from one of the stumps and another nearby tree.

Finally the job was finished. The lean-to had taken twice as long to build because of the terrific gale blowing in from the northwest. As the wind blasted through the spruce, it brought all of the previously accumulated snow off every tree in the grove, and deposited a fair amount of it down my back and through the work area. In every spare breath that I could muster, I cursed the snow, the wind, and each and every part of the Mackenzie Mountains. During the latter part of the afternoon, I created—and rapidly developed—an entirely original vocabulary which would have astonished Webster and his peers, but I doubt that any of the words would have been included in future editions.

It was nearing dusk when I lit the night fire. It was hard to believe that this logging, snowplowing, bedroom building operation had taken almost all afternoon. When the fire had firmly built itself into a bed in the butt logs, I put the tea billy on and reached for my tobacco pouch. Now I had a few moments to exercise some thoughts concerning things in general. Perhaps the life of a farm lad wasn't so bad after all. The food was first class. And the bedrooms were adequate, if not impressive (I really wasn't all that impressed by the one I had just finished) but they were always *warm*. And on those long, winter evenings there was always someone to talk to. And best of all was the music transmitted through miles of star-studded space to our old, battery-operated Marconi radio. From the deep south came the Cajun music—all the way from Shreveport, La., the old country songs from WSM Nashville, Tenn., and of course everybody tuned in the programs from KSL Salt Lake City on a Saturday night. I'm

hoping that tonight, in this little, snow-covered hovel of mine—
providing this damnable wind will die down a bit—I'll be able to tune
in, once again, to at least one of those stations—even if it's only in a
dream.

But there is always one form of entertainment here at these night
camps. And I am never totally alone. There is always that bird of the
forest: the whisky-jack. They flit from tree to tree, always keeping
their distance, as camp is being made. It is when the moose meat goes
into the billy on the fire, that the frenzied action begins. How those
dozens of birds know what's in that pot, is a mystery to me. So I eat
my welcome supper, listening to the delightful, discordant, cacophonous chatter until it's time to turn in. Did I use the word "delightful"?
Well, it is, if one doesn't have a radio.

But as the wind increased, a distracting bother was soon taking my
mind off country music: the gale began breaking the older, partially
dead branches off some of the nearby trees, and flinging them at random around the vicinity. It wouldn't take a very large tree to flatten
the lean-to, I reckoned.

I was up before dawn the next morning. How much before, I
didn't know, because my pocket watch had gone dead. Dead as a
doornail! Well, to hell with it; my stomach would tell me when it was
time to eat.

The water in the tea billy had barely thawed out when my fears
were realized. A splitting crash sounded out of the darkness somewhere between our camp and the river. A big tree had gone down for
sure. It wasn't close enough to make a man wet his pants, but it sure
brought Liza to her feet. She kept straining on her chain, trying to
seek protection inside the shelter. She felt it was a little too close for
comfort. As for me, I was beginning to wish it were daylight.

This must be one of those "tree-buster" storms that Harry had
talked about earlier back at the home camp, I thought. Apparently
Dead Men's Valley was a bad place for these blowdowns. Well, by the
time we reached that valley, come next June, we would be on the
water, and blowdowns would be the least of our worries.

I had learned something at this night camp: the two "butt" logs were
only partially burnt out and were still giving off heat when I arose to
make tea. It required only a few dry limbs to start the flames rising,

and I had risen only twice during the night. The size of the bottom logs was what had made the difference. At least two-thirds of the wood in the two trees was still left, which meant I could use this camp on two more trips. Of course this didn't mean that henceforth I would only fell big trees; one had to use whatever size was available.

The boiled meat was now finished and the last of the tea drunk, and still no dawn. I thought it would never come. I was eager to begin a new day. Yesterday had been a proper bitch, and one that I wanted to forget as soon as possible.

Daybreak brought a change in the weather. The wind was dying down, and the thing to do was hit the trail, if I could find it. I had to assume the storm had blown itself out. But down on the river, I could still hear the nor'wester howling down this waterway which never seemed to be without a certain amount of wind in the winter months, except during extreme cold. I sure as hell wouldn't have wanted to be out there on that river, travelling in the direction of its source on a night like the last.

But back here in the forest, or bush, as Northern trappers call it, suddenly it seemed as if I was in another land: it was so silent and still, now that the moan and shriek of the wind had almost disappeared. It was light enough now to detect the openings in the overcast where the star patches were twinkling through, another indication that the storm was over. Liza was standing and ready for action when I put the panniers over her shoulders. She was always anxious to be off after we were on the north side of the river, for then she knew we were heading for home. She probably knew more about this trail than I did. She was also as close to representing a certain segment of the "human" population as one would ever find: "I will do as much as I have to and no more." That was Liza's motto, always looking for the shortest way out. But—God bless her—she was company for me, and when supper time came around, she was always fed first.

By mid-afternoon we finally reached our second night camp. Roughly six hours (I guessed) to snowshoe eight hard-earned miles! And what about tomorrow? At this rate of travel it would likely take us eleven hours to reach home camp. Hell, we would run out of daylight. We could likely cover two or more miles yet, this afternoon, but that would find me building another siwash camp in the dark.

And that would be stupid. One slip of the axe, and I really would be in trouble. Better I stop here where I still had control over the situation. I would let tomorrow take care of itself. I could always spend the rest of the afternoon cutting wood. After all, I needed the exercise. . . .

A bitter, stinging chill bit into my face next morning when I crawled out of the lean-to. I noticed that Liza's face was buried in her body, tighter than usual. She never even looked up when I re-logged the fire. The temperature had returned to normal—and then some. It was cold. Damned cold. Twice during the night when I rose to tend the fire I had felt the chill penetrating through my parka trying to find its way through my heavy Mackinaw shirt. I could thank my dad for having the essential woollen underwear. Back in Edmonton, on an earlier trip to the city, he had said, "Here's some money. Throw that damned fleece-lined stuff away, and buy two suits of woollen Stanfields." That was in the late fall of 1936.

As stated before, my guests—the Canada jays—were always present. But on this morning, as I was boiling the meat, I saw only one or two. This seemed strange. I wondered where they had all gone, until I concluded these birds were likely back in the heavy spruce, trying to obtain a measure of protection from the searing cold.

Breakfast was short. Ahead of me lay twelve miles of snowbound trail. Although Liza's panniers were almost empty, except for the two-pound axe and the moose meat, she was having a tough time following in the open places where the trail was almost drifted in. Much of the way she was forced to flounder along in short, awkward jumps to stay in my shoe tracks. I was having problems also. There was more than a foot of new snow on the trail, and each time I put a shoe down, it sank through the new layer until it hit the old track. This meant, that for each horizontal step I took, I was expending more than an equal amount of energy in lifting the shoe out of the snow. In short, this form of perambulation was rapidly becoming the supreme shits—in more ways than one.

By mid-morning we had plowed our way across the rough country—through the ravines and over the ridges—until we came into the pine plateau. This was good fur country and where Harry had made a number of sets. The traps had produced two male marten, the first fur that this part of the line had yielded as yet on this trip. The reason was apparent: the animals as well as the birds had taken cover.

At midday I made my usual stop by the stand of silver birch trees, and lit a fire. There was always the odd dry tree to be found and in fifteen minutes the tea billy would be on its way to a boil. Slender birch limbs will provide instant heat in half the time of other wood.

Late in the afternoon, as we were coming off the plateau, I saw several plumes of vapour rising upward out of a heavy wooded area, about a half mile away. I was puzzled as to what this strange sight could be. Then I thought I heard the sound of animals moving about in crusted snow. It was a muffled sound, and yet there was something distinctive about it. It resembled that of cattle moving around in a far-off barnyard. And suddenly I realized what it was: a herd of moose were moving about back there in the timber. They had "yarded up," as moose do in periods of severe weather and deep snow. These animals are the largest of the deer family, and they must constantly forage for food no matter what the conditions. Aside from breaking through heavy snow more easily as a group, the added protection in numbers helps them to fend off the wolves.

Later, nearing dusk, I caught my first sight of a living thing (with the exception of Liza and a couple of whisky-jacks). I spotted a great-horned owl, perched up in a spruce tree alongside the trail. There wasn't the slightest flicker of an eyelid as we passed by. The bird might as well have been sculptured in stone. Queer birds, those owls.

I was running out of daylight, and I'd better think about it! There were at least three more miles of trail to break, and in the coming of the dusk, I wouldn't average more than a mile an hour. I had one alternative: I could stop where I was and sit up all night alongside a small fire, like the Indians often did out on their traplines, or I could push on and face the music. Well, I wasn't an Indian, and I didn't think I had their staying power, nor their degree of endurance. Those chaps were born into this kind of life; they were inured to it. And endurance it would take to crouch over a tiny fire until morning. And only God knew how long that would be! And what about Liza? I knew that she would never agree to that stupid idea of spending the night in the middle of nowhere.

So we pushed on. I was trying to remember the number of sets between where we were and the home camp. Perhaps a dozen or more. Well to hell with them. Let them *stay* buried; I wasn't about to spend more time poking around in the snow, trying to locate them. I was having enough trouble just trying to keep on the trail.

The colour of the snow was in my favour; it was white, which reflected some degree of light, as opposed to the dark outline of the spruce trees. Whenever I did step off the trail, I was quickly—and rudely—reminded of it: one or the other of my snowshoes would plunge into four feet of snow, and I would take a double-header into the raspberries. After a few sessions of this treatment, I smartened up; I cut a five-foot length of slender pole from the first green sapling I could locate. Thus by prodding the trail ahead of each step, I could tell when I was still on the original hard-packed trail. The drawback to this way of travel was that it took forever to get anywhere. An eternity had passed when we came to the spot where the line veered to the right, leading into the long stretch of spruce bordering the Nahanni. We were part way across the river when I saw the light of the candle illuminating the tent from within. As I write these lines, I still regard that sight as one of the greatest I have ever seen.

Harry had finished his supper and, when he heard Nigger bark, he immediately put two large moose steaks into the big fry pan, while I fed Liza and attended to her spruce bough bed. It was 8:30 by Harry's watch. After I had eaten, I almost fell asleep at the table. Harry didn't seem to be very perky, either. There were two tired men at the Rabbitkettle on this cold, starry evening.

Wolverine and Wolf

Harry and I had handled the storm in different ways. Having more experience than I, he had recognized that a blowdown was on its way and had dealt with it in a logical manner. On the following morning after reaching his first night camp, he knew that it would be a waste of time to make the full round of his line; the traps would be unworkable within an hour after reset. So he decided to head for the home tent by way of the river.

"This was a big mistake," Harry said. "I knew the snow would be hardened out on the river and I thought the going would be easier. But I couldn't face the wind. And neither could Nigger. So I was forced back to my second camp spot. Two days to get home, still facing into the wind. Six lousy miles a day. And no fur to show for my effort."

And I thought I had had it tough. When the brunt of the storm hit, I was *going* with the wind, until I decided to return to the river and build the new lean-to. Harry had made the mistake of challenging a storm that had free rein down an open river. It simply couldn't be done. Although I did have the two marten to show for my effort, our trip over the line, in this instance, was nothing more than a demonstration of sheer endurance for both of us.

The next day, after late breakfast was finally over, there wasn't much left of the forenoon. "This is going to be a short day in camp," I remarked. "Short and slightly frigid."

"I think we better stay in camp until this weather warms up, Friday, me lad."

I shot Harry a quick glance—just to make sure he meant what he said. Well, I certainly wasn't about to veto his suggestion. Too many things could happen out there to a man in this deadly temperature. As far as I was concerned, the traps would have to wait until we could reach them. And so we spent the afternoon playing rummy, stuffing the stove, and discussing whatever happened to come to mind. I mentioned hearing the moose moving about in the timber after the wind had died down.

"In heavy snow, they always yard up," Harry explained. "It's more for protection than anything else. Wolves like to single out an animal and put it on the run. But they have to think twice about attacking a yard full of moose, with no intention of running anywhere.

When it reaches forty below, according to Albert Faille, you can hear moose milling about in a yard-up more than two miles away. It's hard to believe how far sound carries when it's really cold. I remember hearing the Calgary–Edmonton passenger train going through Innisfail, one bone-chilling day a few years back."

"I do too," I agreed. "And our farm is nineteen miles west of Innisfail. You could hear the rumble of the drivers on the locomotive, and the long, mournful moan of the whistle as it blew at the crossing just before coming into the station."

The conversation returned to the fur-bearing animals of the region. I hadn't caught a single mink on my part of the line and had seen very few tracks. I wondered why. Harry had trapped only two here at the Rabbitkettle.

"This is primarily marten country, Friday. Mink follow streams that carry fish. This is poor fish country; high water takes the spawning grounds out. There may be more mink around the lakes. Dalziel seemed to be interested only in the marten and lynx. Perhaps the marten tend to drive the mink out. I don't know. I do know that a marten is much faster on its feet than a mink, especially in deep snow. A mink wouldn't stand a chance of escaping."

"What about the fisher?"

"I don't know a thing about that animal, only what I've heard,"

Harry stated. "I've never seen one to my knowledge. According to the trappers down on the Liard, they are few and far between. Apparently they are larger than marten but resemble them to a great extent. A trapper in Simpson told me that he once treed a fisher, and was about to shoot it, when suddenly it made a flying leap to the ground, and was running the instant it landed. He said he never even had time to pull the trigger. He claimed that the fisher was the fastest animal in the bush for its size.

"I do know this much: their pelts are worth more money than marten. So if you or I are lucky enough to trap one, we shall take the proceeds down to Andy Whittington's restaurant in Fort Simpson come spring, and buy the biggest meal of bacon and eggs ever served in the history of mankind. Forestood?"

"I agree, and I forestand," I said. This was my partner: a man who had the canny ability to add that touch of humour to any topic of conversation. I don't believe he ever had a negative thought.

I was becoming frustrated with these 500 rummy games. I had lost five in a row. The thought had entered my mind that in a reckless moment, I might burn that damnable deck of cards. The law of averages should have told me something at this late stage of the game but no, it was this cursed "luck" that I was having. It just *had* to change sooner or later.

Supper time was at hand. Nigger's tail always told one so; it was always arched high over his back at feeding time. Liza? Well, you could never be sure what was going through her mind. She showed little emotion about anything. Inwardly Liza was a pessimist; she spent most of each day dwelling on what a raw deal fate had dealt her. Life to her was to be endured.

After supper, out came the cards. But there is a limit to how much time two people can spend playing rummy, especially when only one is winning. So at ten o'clock we put the cards away. We had agreed to take turns stoking the fire during the night. "It's the only way you will get any sleep." Harry glanced at my "July and August" sleeping bag.

"That's a good idea," I said. "Somebody should keep watch over this bloody stove, or we will burn the tent down. It's either red hot, or as cold as an icebox." And I did not smile when I made the remark.

"You're right, Friday. We can either freeze or go to Hell. Personally, I'd rather freeze."

84

The driving cold kept us holed up in the tent for two more days, putting us into the third week of February. The trapline had now become totally unproductive. It had to be attended to. We knew that it would take four days instead of three to reopen the line and put it back in trapping condition again. So on the first indication that the weather might be moderating, we hit the trail.

And the extreme cold did recede, only to bring more snow. Each day on the line became another day of ordeal. Lift the shoes out of the snow, now put them down. Dig the traps out and reset. Come dusk, cut wood. Come night, burn it up. Come daylight, pick up the shoes. Now put them down. And it could go on forever.

A thought ran through my mind. What wouldn't I give to pass through this same area, view these same mountains at dawn in the early morning, stand on the highest hill and move my eyes up the Rabbitkettle Valley—*if* conditions were different! The word "if"— the longest word in the English language. But on this day, I only saw the same familiar scene: a canyon trail of snow.

As we reached the south bank of the river, I saw them—two wolves were lying down in the snow, near the north shore. I quickly brought down the Winchester and levered a cartridge into the chamber. I had some difficulty restraining myself from tossing a couple of rounds of lead their way, but it would have been a foolish gesture. Those wolves were too small a target at that distance.

When Liza saw the wolves, she suddenly perked up and gave her full attention to these four-footed animals across the river. Presently the wolves saw us, and immediately rose to their feet, but never made any move to leave the spot. Then two more of their clan came down out of the timber. Now there were four. Liza began whining and emitting low, guttural growls, urging me to do something about the situation.

I was waiting for them to bunch up and then I would chance a shot, hoping that I might pick off one of them, but this never happened. Two of the pack slowly began moving downriver, and after reaching a respectable distance, they crossed over to the south side, and stopped. Were these wolves waiting for me to cross the river? Well, I had to cross the river to go where I wanted to go. And I would oblige them. Liza followed as closely as she could, sometimes stepping on the toboggan. She didn't like the situation.

When we reached the centre of the river, I removed my pack-board, laid it on the toboggan, and sat down and waited. Finally one of the wolves near the north shore began moving upriver, and it too stopped behind me at a respectable distance. We now had wolves on *three* sides of us.

Well, if this was about to develop into some sort of an encir-clement, there sure as hell would be some serious complications in store for these four-footed fellows—whatever it was they had in mind. I had one cartridge in the barrel, five in the magazine, and five more in the inside pocket of my parka. And I had no intention of emptying eleven pieces of lead into thin air.

So I waited. And the wolves waited. And finally the wolves won out. I couldn't sit here in the middle of the Nahanni River forever. I tied Liza's chain to the packboard to counter ideas she might have about heading back to the home camp. Then I slowly made my way towards the nearest wolf, the one upriver.

Slowly now . . . one short step at a time . . . just another ten yards and I'll chance a shot. The wolf began to back off, and I just couldn't resist. I shouldered the rifle and fired. The bullet didn't find its mark, but it must have made an impression, because the wolf suddenly remembered it had an important engagement elsewhere as it loped off in long, struggling jumps through the deep snow towards the north shore. There it and its mate disappeared into the timber.

Meanwhile the other two headed for the centre of the river where the snow crust might support their weight, and in a very short length of time, they too were out of sight behind a bend in the river.

And so my little "brush" with the wolves hadn't amounted to much. But one such encounter certainly didn't justify any hasty con-clusions about these animals. I'd wait until the winter was over before I formulated any opinions regarding the wolf.

I did know that wolves hunted in packs and generally follow a planned strategy. And I had to admit I was uneasy about the situation. But I also knew that I had the superior weapon, the bullet.

What would have been my reaction had I not had my rifle? The answer is simple. I would not have left the spruce forest. I would have stayed on the south side of the river and built a fire immediately. All animals are afraid of fire. Of course the question is hypothetical because no trapper or prospector would leave his home camp without a rifle—unless he was forced to. When Harry's rifle blew up in January, he told me that he headed back to the tent in the shortest time possible.

The trail over the ravine and up into the plateau was easier to negotiate, having been partially packed down on my previous trip, and we were making good time. I half expected to find several traps robbed by the wolves, but there were none of their tracks along the line as yet. That meant they must still be on the river or on the other side.

This long day was nearly over, and the most welcome part of each excursion around our part of the trapline was the point where the trail abruptly turned to the right, leading down to the stretch of spruce bordering the river, for now Liza and I knew we were nearly home.

This particular trip hadn't been very productive. I had only one marten to show for my efforts. Harry had fared better: he brought back another well-furred lynx, which would be worth some money. During supper, I told him abut the wolf incident.

"You will see more of them on the river when the caribou begin to move," he said. "They always follow the caribou when migration begins."

"Do you suppose those four-legged friends had dinner on their minds, out there on the river?"

"Wolves always have dinner on their minds. And supper too," Harry said. "But that doesn't mean they might have attacked you. Not in daylight they wouldn't. There are too many caribou in this country; they don't need to take risks. You were likely the first two-legged animal those wolves ever saw, and you sure didn't have any resemblance to a caribou.

"But at night I wouldn't want to be surrounded by a pack of wolves without a campfire burning brightly, but who would be stupid enough to let that happen? It don't take long to build a fire.

"From what I've seen here in the Nahanni," he continued, "wolves carry out most hunts right on the river. They must force their prey into a run. Like Dalziel said, 'they relay hunt, and play their victim out.' Their ability is hampered in the bush, especially in deep snow. No doubt they do kill moose in deep forests, but these are generally animals far past their prime."

I knew that Harry had met most of the trappers on the Liard, plus a few around Fort Simpson, and so I put the question to him straight: "What is the general opinion down there about wolves? Will they or won't they attack a man under the right conditions?"

"Friday, me lad! When the wolf subject comes up among a group of trappers, you can ask ten questions and you get twenty answers. Nothing is ever resolved. It's always rather vague. Nothing is ever proven."

"How do you mean?"

"Well, everybody has a different wolf story to tell, but they all end up on the same note: 'You can bet I would have been attacked had this, that, or the other thing not occurred' or 'I thought I was a goner for sure—I was just lucky, I guess!' The actual attack never happens." I knew what Harry meant.

Near the end of February, I saw my first wolverine. It was caught by the front leg in a number three Victor double-spring trap. These large traps were always attached to a small log, the size of which would allow a certain degree of movement so as to prevent the animal from pulling itself out of the trap. The smaller, single-spring traps set for marten or mink were always fastened to a tree.

In this instance the wolverine had dragged the log into a dense stand of jackpine, where it had become entangled. There was a scene of destruction about the place that was hard to believe. This animal had chewed its way through an area that must have been thirty feet long and at least a couple of feet wide. These trees were about two inches in diameter and they were scattered in all directions. Some were bitten off at the snow line, others had been chewed off a foot or more below the surface. It was one weird looking sight.

As I approached, the wolverine crouched down in the snow and turned to face me. Then it began pushing its body deeper into the snow until there was only its head and shoulders showing. Those two beady, black eyes never left mine. I saw the awesome claws as it raised its front feet out of the snow, ready for action, and watched the saliva dripping from its open jaws, revealing a set of teeth that would make a full-grown bear shudder. A bullet put the animal out of its misery and rage. It was the only battle this carnivore had ever lost. But then, it didn't have a chance to use its weapons.

Had I not arrived on the scene when I did, I might never have seen the animal, for sooner or later, it would likely have chewed the toggle pin out of the log. How long it would have carried the trap through the timber, I did not know, nor did I care to contemplate.

Not many days later, I was to come upon another wolverine. But on this occasion the scene was of an entirely different nature. I was on the trail leading down to the line of spruce that ran parallel to the north side of the river, when I remembered that we needed some birch bark to replenish what we had at the tent. As I reached the small stand of silver birch overlooking the river, I saw a wolf feeding on a freshly-killed caribou down on the ice below, a few scant yards off shore. The bloodstains splattered over the area were still a bright red.

Then suddenly my eye caught another movement across the Nahanni on the south shore. In a slow, floundering manner, a small animal was making its way down the bank through deep snow. In short, clumsy half leaps, it began zigzagging across the river, and it wasn't until I saw the bushy tail wavering over its back, that I knew for sure what the animal was. Only the wolverine has that peculiar, side-loping mode of ambulation. It may have been an awkward sort of movement, but this animal knew where it was going—and how to get there. Veering from side to side, as if trying to find an easier way through the deep snow, it moved towards the kill. Part way across the river, it stopped, rose up on its short hind feet, as if the better to survey the situation and take time out to formulate a plan of action.

When the wolf saw the unwelcome visitor, it stopped feeding. The two animals kept their eyes on each other for a minute or two. The wolf made several attempts to resume feeding, but the wolverine just stood there—waiting—seemingly adopting the old Fabian strategy (delay of battle).

I was getting cold, standing there among the birches and was hoping that something would happen before I froze. Liza was back on the trail, tied to a tree. We were too near to the home camp to leave her loose.

Suddenly this small but formidable scavenger made its move: using the same short, floundering lopes, it bounded forward within twenty yards of the kill. The wolf was now fully disturbed, and began walking back and forth over the dead caribou, as if trying to contemplate a way of protecting its hard-earned property from this shaggy interloper.

Now the wolverine, seemingly taking all the time in the world, began making a complete circle around the area. Then another . . . and still another. And each circuit brought the shaggy scavenger closer to the kill.

It was plain there was going to be a dispute over the ownership of the dead caribou. It seemed to me there could be only one winner: the wolf must have weighed nearly three times as much as its adversary. But there were a few important differences between these two animals that I hadn't taken into consideration, as I was about to discover.

The wolverine now began to shuffle forward, a foot at a time, until there were only a few feet between it and the wolf. Strategy was being employed here: the wolf was being *forced* to attack. It was either that, or leave the kill. Meanwhile the wolverine had buried itself deeper into the snow, waiting for the impending assault.

Suddenly the wolf jumped. The impact bowled the smaller animal over on its back, deeper into the snow. All I saw was a white flurry and four claws flying under the wolf. It happened so fast I had trouble detecting exactly what did take place.

But I knew what I *did* see. I saw the wolf jerk back and break away. It was bleeding from its torn nose, and I saw a strip of skin trailing from its under-belly as it limped off down the river. I could have sworn this little scavenger *knew* it could win that battle. In the sense of the word, it didn't really amount to a battle; the affair couldn't have taken more than a half dozen seconds. The wolverine must have been desperately hungry, for it immediately began to feed off the caribou meat. It never even gave the retreating wolf a second glance.

But this amazing animal's victory was short-lived. I suddenly remembered the reason for me being here at this spot, in this particular country, in this particular vocation. And so I quickly raised my rifle. I had a partnership to uphold, and this so-called "glutton of the North," possessed a valuable coat of fur.

Liza, meanwhile, was barking her head off when she heard the rifle shot. Rifle fire meant food to Liza, and was the one and only thing that interested her to any degree. When I laid the animal down on the toboggan, she shied away. Whether she was afraid, or didn't like the permeated odour of the beast, I did not know.

In camp that evening, I related the unlikely drama to Harry. He listened with intense interest, then politely said, "Well now, Friday—if I may be permitted to say so—your story sounds a mite farfetched."

"In other words, you don't believe me?" There was more than a mite of irritation in my reply, and Harry was quick to detect it.

"No, no, Friday! I would never dream of suggesting such a thing. I happen to be a gentleman, you know."

"You certainly *did* suggest it!" I was becoming warmer under my collar.

"Well Friday must accept my most humble apology. It's just that my throat has been quite sore of late, and I have had considerable difficulty in swallowing at times."

That remark almost did it, and I had to exercise some control in my reply. "Now listen, Crusoe. Take a good look at that carcass (we had hung it under the ridgepole of the tent), does any one of those feet look like its been in a trap? Of course not. Did you not tell me earlier, that you could determine which leg an animal had been caught by, just by examining the broken blood vessels in the pelt?"

"I did, Friday, and I don't doubt your word, but some people might suggest that this wolverine had been in a tree, and that you shot it from the trail . . . now don't get all heated up; I know it didn't happen that way. I'm only saying it could have."

"Well, it damned well didn't!" I retorted. And then suddenly it occurred to me the obvious way to put this touchy matter to rest was to revisit the site of this episode. That would clear the matter up for good.

"Here's what we shall do, Crusoe: tomorrow is our day off. That caribou kill is not more than two miles upriver from this tent. In the morning we will go back up the trail and you can see for yourself. The evidence will all be there—tracks, blood, remains of the kill—everything. I don't think we will have any snow tonight; nothing will be covered. We might even get a wolf or two, who knows. We both need the exercise. Now how about it?

"Case dismissed, Friday. Case dismissed! I must give you three more apologies—one for each leg of this fellow. It will be a fine pelt. It's even bigger than the one you got the other day. You know, Friday, I think we should celebrate. What say we have a drink of Governor General?" This was a suggestion I wasn't about to refuse.

Over the years I have taken an avid interest in our Canadian wildlife, particularly the fur-bearing animals, a number of which are rapidly nearing extinction. The wolverine is one of them. Realizing there may be the odd member of the trapping fraternity who will strongly doubt the validity or truth of what I saw that cold February day in 1937, let us peruse a few pertinent facts about the two animals in question.

The wolf obviously has the weight advantage—one hundred pounds or more, against the wolverine's forty. But in contrast, the smaller animal has *five* distinct weapons: a formidable set of jaws, backed up by four powerful paws—each equipped with a set of claws that would (or should) make any adversary stop and take note. In the drama that I witnessed it is debatable whether the wolf's weight *was* an advantage. The wolverine had buried itself in the snow, so as to provide as small a target as possible, and when the wolf attacked, it faced a set of jaws built for close encounters. And when the smaller animal was knocked backwards, it simply positioned those awesome four feet into play. It must also be noted that the wolf's jaws are comparatively long and pointed, and much more vulnerable than the wolverine's wide, short-protruding ones, and therein lies the wolverine's distinct advantage—or at least one of them.

I once saw another example of this last point when our neighbour's bulldog in Victoria suddenly attacked a german shepherd that happened to come trotting down the street. The bulldog, being far smaller, and therefore faster, immediately put a death lock on the shepherd's throat. I ran to the scene and had to kick the bulldog loose from its fatal grip. The shepherd was later taken to the vet to have its nose repaired. The key to this short-lived battle was the impregnable shape of the bulldog's facial features—square-jawed and a non-protruding nose. Plus, of course, the unbelievable fighting ability of the smaller dog.

Another time I was vividly reminded of that cold day of 1937 when watching a TV wildlife film. The scene showed a grizzly—or brown bear—attempting to herd off a wolverine from the carcass of a dead animal. Each time the bear charged the smaller animal, it dodged the attack. Then circling from behind, it would take a sizable piece of fur out of the bear's rear. Again the bear whirled around to take a vicious swipe at its adversary, which was no longer there.

Finally, furious with rage, the bear tore a leg off the carcass and dragged it into the bush. The wolverine—without so much as another glance at the bear—began feeding on the carcass. This wolverine wasn't the least bit concerned about the bear. Why? Because it *knew* it could out-maneuver the much larger animal. (Size only counts in the boxing or wrestling ring.)

Consider this: In our Northern woods, I know of only two animals that are *slower* than a wolverine: the skunk and the porcupine. In the context of a particular animal being able to protect itself by outrunning another animal, would it not be reasonable to assume that the wolves and bears should have eliminated these three members of the animal kingdom hundreds of years ago? The fact remains that nature has endowed each animal with very effective weapons. Everyone is acquainted with the skunk. And the wolf or bear that receives a nose full of porcupine quills will not likely make the same mistake twice.

The wolverine is the true scavenger of the North. Being unfleet of foot, it must obtain food from the remains of animals that other predators have killed, and from those that have died a natural death. The wolverine may be a slow traveller, but it is not confined to a small area by any means. It can and will cover a large range, the size of which is governed by its degree of hunger. Trappers at least agree on this one characteristic. And what it lacks in speed, it makes up for in its relentless and tenacious search to appease its hunger.

Most trappers are only interested in the characteristics of the wolverine for practical reasons, either hating it for its greedy marauding of their traps or prizing it for the value of the pelt when it's caught. Thus I was later astonished to come across a book about furbearing animals in Finland that contained a photograph of a domesticated wolverine lying on a bed with a trapper's wife! The couple had raised a two-week old cub on a baby's bottle until it was old enough to eat its natural food. Later, when they moved to town, they would stroll the streets with their pet on a leash, much to the alarm of local citizens, who successfully petitioned their council to rid them of this potential menace.

During the month of March we caught very little fur. Most of the time the weather was against us—cold one day—warming the next. The third day would produce more snow. We spent most of the time resetting the traps, which were always freezing down in the snow. In some places the depth of snow would have covered the tomato wrappers, had I not tramped it down. I often wondered how damned deep the stuff could get. In the space of three weeks, we only spent two days at the home tent.

One bright wonderful morning a chinook wind blew in, out of the southwest. We stood by the tent and watched the arch grow larger and larger, and the exhilarating feeling that came over us is impossible to describe in so many words. By noontime it was above freezing, and in the afternoon it grew warmer. In the space of eight hours there must have been a rise in temperature of at least sixty degrees. It was hard to imagine. To me it felt as if I had been catapulted into another world. Only the deep snow reminded me of where I was.

The sudden change abruptly terminated our trapping activities. It was just as well, for from now on the fur would rapidly be losing its prime. But the weather was the main reason: when the snow begins to pack as the day warms, travel on snowshoes is an impossibility. The snow is no longer powdery and will not sift through the webbing of the shoe.

And so near the end of March we made our final trip around the line, collecting the traps as we went along. For me it was to be the end of a short trapping career. And on that last evening as I pulled the toboggan up the low bank, and hung it on a tree near the tent, I knew it was the happiest moment I ever spent on the trapline. There had to be better ways of earning a living, and sooner or later, I knew I would find them—Depression or no Depression. This matter of pride in proving to yourself that you can "take it," didn't get one very far that I could see. Common sense had vanity beaten by an exaggerated mile, in my books.

Beaver and Caribou

According to the notches I had cut on the outside pole of our table, today was April Fools day. And there was no fooling about it. The penetrating cold of winter was finally over. No more frigid siwash nights, wondering if the wood supply would last until dawn broke. No more days of fighting snowbound trails or digging out traps, wondering if the fading daylight would hold out until I reached my second night camp. And now there was the spring beaver hunt to look forward to, which would provide something of interest, no doubt, in days to come.

Ever since the turn of the century (and some years before that) men had been seeking the elusive gold that was supposed to be hidden somewhere up the Flat River or anywhere along the tributaries of the South Nahanni. (A glance at a map will give one a fair idea of the size of the "anywhere" country.) And when the long-time trappers (and numerous newcomers) failed to locate the yellow metal, they turned back to the old stand-by beaver hunt, when the "land fur" was in short supply.

There was no doubt about it; there were beavers on the Nahanni. On my part of the trapline near the river, I had seen several beaver houses. What I had failed to perceive was the fact that not all houses were necessarily occupied—any more than all wallets contain money.

In the fall of the year, the presence of beaver is easily detected by the fresh tree cuttings in the area, but not when there is a cover of three or four feet of snow on the ground.

During the latter part of the winter, Harry had never discussed the forthcoming beaver hunt to any great degree, except in a casual manner. Perhaps it was because he knew only what Dalziel had told him about the trapping of the animal under the ice. Dalziel, as Harry gathered, was primarily a marten trapper. Later, I realized that my partner hadn't wanted to raise hopes of a bountiful catch unduly.

Our first attempt at trapping under the ice took place about a mile below the home camp, on a large island in the centre of the river. The island had been built up through many years of spring floods. The remainder of the area was covered with heavy willow and a mixture of balsam and white poplar, the principal food of beaver colonies. At the western extremity there was a huge log jam, enlarged each succeeding year by the high water of the June floods.

Near the log jam was a large beaver house rising off the river to a height of nearly six feet. Here we set our first trap under the ice near where Harry thought the entrance might be. Did I say "we"? Hell, I didn't have a clue about any part of the operation. I merely provided the energy required to chop a large hole through the ice where the trap was to be set.

Upriver, above our camp, Harry knew of three other houses that he said showed evidence of being occupied, and we made ice sets at each one. These houses were all located in snyes along the river. A snye provides an ideal location for a beaver colony: there is usually very little current in the channel to hinder the building of the house and there is always a good food supply near at hand, both from the island and the mainland shore.

During the first ten days of April we managed to trap two beaver. An impressive number indeed! Thawing conditions often forced us to make new trails up and down the river from the home tent. And if we made our daily patrols right after dawn broke, we found that we could make use of our snowshoes as long as the crust remained on the snow. By midday the snow would begin to pack, rendering our shoes useless. Several times when this happened, it would take us upwards of an hour to travel a couple of miles. This limited the distance we could reach from the tent.

Now that we had most of the afternoon in camp, we had plenty of time to spend on several things that had been sorely neglected— mainly our clothing. We had long run out of soap, but I had heard back home that ashes from the stove, mixed in hot water, make a fair substitute. And we discovered this to be true to a certain degree. We spent more than one afternoon trying to wash underwear and shirts into some semblance of cleanliness. I'm sure most housewives would have shuddered on observing our ablutionary activities.

The single item that I missed above all, now that time was available, was reading material. All I had was my little dictionary, which by now was becoming dog-eared and soiled. Strangely enough, it had taken me all these years to discover the wealth of knowledge that a book of this size could bring. I actually was beginning to find a certain interest in looking up the meaning of words.

There was an added pleasure attached to my little dictionary. In the odd conversation with my partner, I found a tantalizing delight in using ten-dollar words where ten-cent ones would have been more appropriate. Harry, naturally, wasn't all that amused. An example readily comes to mind: we were changing our clothes that afternoon, after returning from a wet excursion after beaver, when a brilliant idea suddenly flitted across my mind.

"Crusoe!" I exclaimed in unrestrained excitement. "I have been engaged in profound cogitation."

"What the hell's that? You'd better hide that dictionary, Friday, I warn you, I'll use it to light the fire one of these mornings."

"Now, now Crusoe! You are just jealous. Is it my fault that my master cannot read? What I mean is that I have been thinking. In *deep* thought, I might add."

"Well congratulations, Friday, me lad! Is it the warm weather that has brought about this amazing change? Now what have you been thinking about?"

"Listen Crusoe, I have a proposal. Why can't we chop our way into these beaver houses? I admit there will be a certain amount of work involved, but think of the reward. Where could the beavers go? They can't swim forever under the ice. They must need air to breathe. Right?"

I studied Harry's reaction cautiously—lack of experience can be a serious handicap in the delicate art of thinking. But I could see he was mulling the suggestion over in his mind, a sure indication that there might be some merit in my idea.

"Friday!" Harry finally declared. "You just may have something! It might work. We shall try it."

At dawn the next morning we were at the beaver house downriver by the island. We had our rifles, axes, and tea billy. Generally on these short excursions, we left the dogs behind to guard the tent in case a wolverine should happen along. In my opinion this was a mistake. I couldn't see how a short-haired dog would stand a chance against a wolverine, especially when tied up—even the spunky Nigger. Liza, of course, would have been too frightened. It was also Harry's idea that the caribou would soon be on the move, and we could do with one or two. From that angle of thought, the dogs would be better left in camp in any case.

The trap we had set under the ice was empty, as usual, so we immediately set to work. I climbed up on the dome of the house and cleared the snow away. A search for the breather hole proved futile. I couldn't find anything among the tangled mass of debris that remotely resembled a breathing hole.

"Are you sure this house is occupied?" I called down to Harry. "No sense going to a lot of work if nobody lives here."

"Listen Friday!" Harry retorted. "There were fresh cuttings here last fall. I saw them. I firmly believe my helper is trying to get out of work. Now stop talkin' and start workin'. Forestood?"

"Yes, me Lord."

From the first swing of my axe, it was painfully apparent that these flat-tailed, furry engineers knew how to build an impregnable home. I had never encountered such a twisted conglomeration of willows, tree boughs, frozen clay mud, even roots, all entangled in a proportion that almost defied attack. We even encountered small logs four feet in length and as many inches in diameter, entrenched in the frozen muck.

There was only room at the top of the dome for one of us to work at a time, so we took turns spelling each other off. I was having a smoke down below when a most distressful thought crossed my mind. "Crusoe!" I called up to Harry. "Is this operation legal—breaking into a beaver house? There may be a law against it."

Harry paused for a moment, then laid down his axe. He stuck his thumbs under his suspenders and pushed his chest out another notch and said, "My dear Friday—you do not seem to understand the situation. I *am* the law! I am the monarch of all that I survey!" To emphasize the proclamation, he swung both outstretched arms in a wide arc. "And the reason this is so, is because there is no one in all this vast domain to dispute my claim. Forestood?

"Surely Friday would never think of disputing Rob Crusoe. However, if your conscience still bothers you, I shall make an official declaration which should serve to remove all your worries."

And in much the same manner of Mark Antony in his famous speech at the Forum in Rome upon Caesar's death, Harry raised both hands high above his head, beckoned out across the Nahanni River to an imaginary audience, then sounded forth with the proclamation: "Now hear ye! Hear ye, one and all! I hereby declare, by all the powers that be, that from this hour henceforth, it shall be legal to chop holes in beaver houses—providing that is, that all choppers are of noble birth." And then as if to seal the edict, he deliberately spit over the edge of the dome, took up his axe and resumed work. Now I wasn't too sure about my status of birth but I did feel more at ease when I exchanged places with Crusoe a few minutes later.

Luckily, as it turned out, my brilliant brain-child came to a sudden end: my axe made contact with a chunk of clay that made the sparks fly. The chunk of clay, however, was a rock about the size of a garden turnip. "Perhaps you'd better revoke that declaration, Crusoe," I said. "We are liable to ruin our axes."

Harry wasn't joking when he said, "It's a damned good thing it isn't thirty below today; you might have been minus part of an axe blade. I guess we better begin using our brains. That goes for the both of us."

Harry and I hadn't known at the time that beaver always have one or two escape routes under the ice to the shore where they tunnel upwards in the riverbank to a level above the water. These outlets are almost impossible to locate, except by a trapper with plenty of experience behind him.

The morning was still young by Harry's watch but there wasn't anything more to be done out here on the island. So we shouldered our packboards and began heading back to the tent. Just as we came to the point of the island by the log jam, we saw a cow caribou galloping downriver on our snowshoe trail. Now caribou do not normally gallop; they trot. This animal was running for its life.

I don't believe the cow ever saw us as she passed the point. She was so intent on escaping from the "death" following not far behind. I could see her bloodshot eyes, the dangling tongue, the spurts of steam shooting out from both nostrils, as she swerved off our trail at the point. With every lope, the cow's front hooves splayed out to either side of her body—the sure sign of a winded animal.

We both turned to look upriver. There, about a quarter of a mile back, we saw a black object swiftly moving down our trail.

"It's a wolf," Harry cautioned.

"Maybe it's Nigger! Nigger may have gotten loose," I said.

"No it's a wolf! Grab your rifle, Al, and nail him when he comes by!"

We dived behind the log jam to conceal ourselves as much as possible. I crouched down among a pile of stranded poplars, laid the Winchester across a big log, and waited. The wolf kept coming at a steady lope, directly in front of me. At less than thirty yards I fired. The shot was too high. The wolf skidded to a complete stop, then instantly veered to the right to pass the point. I took a standing aim and fired again. The wolf leaped high in the air, somersaulted and lay dead.

"Beautiful shot, Friday! Beautiful shot!" Like all trappers, Harry hated wolves.

But I was thinking about my first shot—which was a "rest" shot at no more than thirty yards. How could I have possibly missed at that range? It wasn't expert shooting on the second try, either; it was pure luck. It made me wonder about the accuracy of my Winchester.

It turned out that my victim was a female. I was always anxious to learn as much as possible about wolves, and so I opened her abdominal cavity. She was carrying six pups. I learned later that this number was an indication that the wolf population in this part of the Nahanni was on the increase because of an abundance of food supply, that is the caribou. It was thought that wolves had the natural ability to control their population in the years of food shortages, simply by having fewer young. But in this instance, of course, I had upset the balance of nature a little. Seven wolves had been taken to save the life of one caribou and possibly her unborn calf. Had we been really short of meat in camp, it would have been the other way round; I would have killed the caribou, and the wolf would likely have escaped.

As always, when we returned to camp, Nigger performed his usual series of calisthenics, capering and straining at his chain. He dreaded being left behind, always wanting to be part of the action. Liza's philosophy of life was entirely different. She was never overly interested in anything that required effort. Unless she could smell fresh meat when we arrived in camp, she seldom made any move to rise off her spruce bough bed.

Harry's mouse trap was still working effectively. When I went to make tea, there were four mice in the bottom of the water bucket. This necessitated a trip down to the river for fresh water. Neither Harry nor I liked our tea flavoured with mouse dung.

"There's a bit of extra work attached to this mouse trap affair, and no remuneration that I can see, Crusoe. Are you sure their pelts aren't worth anything?"

"They were only bringing three cents apiece down at Fort Liard, the last time I was there—that's providing the whiskers are not damaged," Harry replied.

"What about the tail?"

"The tail must be attached to the pelt, Friday. Surely you would know that. They won't take a bobtailed pelt. Now is the tea ready?"

How could anyone be low-spirited in the presence of this shaggy-haired companion? Although he knew our fur catch was not going to meet earlier expectations, he never once commented upon the fact, or showed the least trace of disappointment. Harry was not a man to be down on his luck for very long. To him, misfortune was something to be expected along the way. He seemed to possess that rare ability of turning adversity into jokes. When he lost a small fortune in the crash of 1929, at the age of twenty-two and was forced to sell his beautiful Peerless automobile, he said, "Oh hell! Come easy; go easy. They'll still be making cars before I'm ready to kick the bucket."

One evening, shortly after midnight, we were suddenly shaken out of our sleep by the dogs raising a terrible commotion outside. It sounded like they had gone stark raving mad. I leaped out of my eiderdown, grabbed my moccasin rubbers, and rushed outside to get my Winchester hanging from the tree. In the semi-darkness, the dogs seemed to be straining their chains towards the river. There had to be something down there somewhere. I stood for a moment, trying to listen, but the damned dogs wouldn't give me a chance. The candle light lit up the tent and Harry stepped outside.

"There seems to be something down by the river. Shut up, you bloody hounds—I can't hear myself think!" I said.

"By the sound of the dogs, it's probably a herd of caribou coming through. We could do with some fresh meat, Friday."

Slowly I picked my way down to the water hole, trying to give my eyes time to adjust to the outline of the trail. Somewhere out there in the grey gloom there were animals milling about on the river, and they had to be caribou. They seemed to be near the centre of the river; I could barely make out the grey outline of each one. Well, there was no point in shooting at something that I wasn't reasonably sure of bringing down. There was nothing for it; I had to get closer. Floundering through the snow towards the closest objects, it occurred to me that I should have put on my snowshoes and left my rubbers in the tent. When the range seemed close enough, I stopped, hoping that these "objects" would separate so that I could make an attempt to place my shot. My feet were okay but my hands were damned near frozen. I wondered how I would hold the rifle steady enough to hit anything.

Suddenly three of these greyish-dark objects appeared to be moving towards me. Now I knew they were caribou. This was crazy! I must be having some kind of a stupid dream. One of the three trotted up to within ten feet of me and snorted as it stopped. I just pointed the rifle at its head and pulled the trigger. It dropped in the snow. The other two turned and wheeled away towards the north shore, then on sudden impulse, they reversed direction and came striding back to where the first one had dropped. This was some kind of a caribou caper that I didn't understand. I fired twice in quick succession and both animals dropped.

Harry was already coming down the path, wearing his snowshoes, his Hornet slung over his shoulder. Harry never moved very far from the tent without his rifle. "How many did you get, Friday?"

"Three—and I think my hands are frozen. I'm cold! I haven't bled them."

"I'll take care of that," Harry said. "You go and get the stove going, and holler down when the tea is ready."

Nigger and Liza had now barked themselves hoarse. This was an old game to them and they knew one thing: the rifle shots meant meat. Harry was back in half an hour. He had had trouble keeping his hands warm too.

"This hunting in the dead of night is unreal, Crusoe. I still don't understand what happened out there. It's obvious I don't know much about caribou. Those crazy animals came within spitting distance. I simply pointed the gun barrel at them. It seems to me, a wolf could easily have hamstrung any one of them."

"Friday, me lad—if you had been a wolf, the animals would have been long gone. These Barren Lands caribou don't see many two-legged animals in their travels and they are very curious creatures anyway. Curious and stupid. Their actions don't make sense. Most of the trappers I've met, claim the same thing. But you can bet your last dollar a caribou knows a wolf when it sees one."

"Why didn't the herd take off when the dogs were barking?" This was another puzzle to me.

"Wolves don't bark; they howl," Harry explained. "And when they hunt, they hunt in silence. Wolves follow the migrating caribou and are often in plain sight of the herd. A healthy caribou can outrun a wolf and knows it. That's why wolves hunt in packs—when one tires out, another, stationed a mile or so away, takes up the chase. They play their quarry out. That's what took place with the one you shot."

Harry glanced at his watch. It was 1 a.m. "Let's finish the tea. We'd better get busy with the meat down there before the wolves find it."

It was going to be difficult butchering the animals down on the river, so we finally decided to build a fire near the cache and bring the three carcasses up on the toboggan. We needed both light and warmth to do this job properly.

Once the fire began throwing some light, it didn't take long to finish the work. One man can easily maneuver a Barren Lands caribou into position for dressing out without any help, and we made a simple job of it: we cut each carcass into four quarters. In a couple of hours we had the meat up on the cache and under cover.

As always, the jays were there by the dozens. All during the butchering, their incessant, discordant chatter never eased. I found it interesting to observe the persistent antics of these little birds as they took turns trying to reach the offal, which was lying too close to the fire for their comfort. But they didn't want for trying. I wondered how we would protect our meat on the cache if we hadn't had the big tarp. "Well Friday," Harry remarked, "You have heard that necessity is the mother of invention. Somehow we'd find a way—likely by covering the works with spruce boughs, perhaps."

Our first job was to take the offal and heads down on the river and, because of Gifford's toboggan, that task was made easy. We then set several traps around the remains. It was a safe bet there would be wolves out here, sooner or later.

Dawn was beginning to break when we got back to the tent. "What say we have an early breakfast? I'm hungry," I announced.

Harry paused for a moment, pretending to ponder my suggestion. Then spreading his arms out at maximum length, he called into the grove of poplars, "Now hear ye! Hear ye, one and all! It is the top sultan of the Rabbitkettle speaking: I do hereby proclaim a royal breakfast consisting of oatmeal sprinkled with dried prunes, fresh caribou heart, and tea. I caution my subjects not to rush in all at once!"

Hot porridge and prunes! What a treat—the second such since my arrival at the Rabbitkettle. Indeed, a breakfast to remember.

Although the dogs were usually fed at night rather than morning in order to keep them alert on the trapline, there was now no reason why they shouldn't join us in the morning feast of fresh meat. Since trapping was finished, their heavy work days were mostly over; once breakup came Harry and I would be concentrating on taking beaver in open water.

Waiting for Breakup

The warmer weather during the mid-afternoons had brought the snow level on the Nahanni down nearly two feet, causing an accumulation of water near the centre of the river. But the nights were still cold, and of course this water would freeze, only to begin melting again shortly after noon. This condition produced what we termed slush-ice—the more damnable stuff to travel through one couldn't possibly imagine. Over on the north side of the river, the sun's direct rays had melted all the snow off the high bank, which made that area look like summer until one ventured deeper into the spruce forest. And over on our side, the snow still seemed as deep as ever—unreasonably so, considering that it was mid-April.

We were sitting on the sawhorse one afternoon, soaking up the heat from a sultry breeze coming in from the Rabbitkettle Valley. It felt just like another Chinook wind, except that the arch was missing. We had been wondering whether the meat up on the cache might thaw out if this sort of weather continued. We finally decided we'd wait and see. If need be, we would dry the meat.

"But there is a job that must be done, and it's my guess there is no better time than the present, and I fully expect my man Friday to cooperate."

"It all depends upon what sort of a job Crusoe is talking about," I responded.

"We will have to move our camp to higher ground, Friday."

"Why so?" I could see that Harry was serious and I was puzzled as to the reason.

"Well, if we have a couple of weeks of this kind of weather, a million creeks will begin pouring water into the Nahanni, and if breakup comes in all at once, we can be flooded out of house and home."

"I can't see how that could happen," I said. "From where we are sitting, we must be at least ten feet above the river ice. I don't see how any river could rise that high."

"Well you'd better believe it can! The Nahanni is a mountain river. It starts in the mountains at the Divide (Yukon and N.W.T. boundary) and ends at the last mountain, Nahanni Butte, at the Liard River. From here to the Divide is about 140 miles, according to Dalziel. And only God knows how many mountains that distance represents. Just think of the tons of snow lying up there, waiting to come down in the form of water. Let's suppose you could flatten each one of those mountains out—like a piece of paper—just think of the total drainage area that would amount to. Millions of ravines containing snow twenty or thirty feet deep, or more. All it takes is a two-day rain and every one of those ravines will become a roaring creek. And the tributaries back there will all be in flood. I haven't seen a map of the Nahanni beyond the Rabbitkettle so I wouldn't know how many of them there are." Obviously Harry wanted to put me straight.

Not knowing the first thing about floods, and remembering that Harry had spent three springs in the Nahanni and Liard country, I deemed it prudent to listen to what he said, and not formulate opinions on something I knew nothing about.

As if he had suddenly thought of the perceptible evidence close at hand, Harry said, "If you want proof of what a flood can do to this valley, come with me. I'll show you."

I followed Harry back into the poplar grove where Dalziel's airplane pontoons were. "Now why do you suppose Dal bolted those pontoons around that poplar tree?" Harry answered his own question. "He wanted to make sure they didn't float away in high water. That's why."

"Now you shall see a sight that will really open your eyes!" Harry pointed up into the poplars." "See the dirt rings circling the trunks of those trees, the tufts of dried grass, notice the clumps of leaves and pieces of dead wood caught in the branches? How high would you say those rings are above ground?"

"I'd guess about eight feet. About room height," I said.

"Now look closely. You will notice those rings trace a straight line right through this grove of trees. Now that line, my friend, represents the high water mark of last spring's flood."

"That means the river level must have been about eighteen feet higher than it is now. That's incredible," I said.

"Incredible—but true," Harry observed. "I don't guarantee there will be a flood, but we sure as hell don't want to take any chances. Poole Field is an old-timer in this country. He's spent a lot of years prospecting and trapping in the Nahanni and knows the river as well as anyone. When I talked to him in the spring of '35, he told me that he had seen the Nahanni rise one foot in each hour for seven or eight hours straight. And more than once—when there was a heavy rain. Poole Field wasn't a man that would bullshit anybody."

Harry, of course, wasn't exaggerating. He just wanted to make sure that I realized what could happen in these Mackenzie Mountains.

We spent the remainder of the afternoon on the north side of the river, and almost directly across from the tent, we found a perfect camp site near the high bank. It only had one drawback: its access to the river. Each trip for water would mean descending the thirty-foot bank and making the climb up again at an angle which would be difficult to negotiate. But it certainly would solve the flood problem—if there was to be one.

Moving our camp across the river wouldn't entail that much work; it was the building of a cache that would involve a bit of energy and time. And as Harry said, "There's no time like the present! Let's have at it!"—another of his favourite expressions.

By late evening, the triangular notches were cut in the two trees, the two crosspieces were shaped, and most of the platform poles were ready. Tomorrow we would assemble the pieces.

This was the first real work we had done in ten days and we were hungry. In the fading light of what had been a long afternoon, we took turns frying caribou steaks and mostly just discussing the price of tea in China. At the rate we were consuming it, the price had better come down.

At noon the next day, the cache was ready for the meat and fur, except for the sheet metal. It would be transferred when we were ready to move camp. During the night the weather changed to our advantage: it had grown much colder, which meant there would be no meltwater on the river when we moved.

We were on the river at daybreak with the first load of meat. The little toboggan slid over the frozen snow and ice almost without effort, and shortly before noon the meat and fur were up on the new cache. Removing the sheet metal off the one in camp proved to be the toughest job of all. Luckily, Harry still had the pliers he had brought into the country in 1934. Finally, with the aid of our axes and a long thin wedge we had made from a sapling tree, we were able to remove both sheets so that we could reuse them around the trees of our new cache. A simple tool, such as a claw hammer would have been handy, but the nearest one was at the mouth of the Nahanni, about 200 miles (320 km) away. It was a bit of work that required the patience of Job because each and every nail had to be salvaged; we had no others.

And as surely as one day follows another, the whisky-jack battalion followed the meat to its new site. It was interesting—if not so amusing any longer—to watch our "ball-of-feathered" friends operate. We could be doing ordinary camp chores such as chopping wood or packing water, and nary a one would we see, but if we merely walked under the cache, there would suddenly be a dozen or more flitting from tree to tree.

Our new site on the higher elevation produced an excellent view of the Rabbitkettle River Valley, and also of the "Big Six," our name for the mountains that lay to the southeast of us on the right side of the river.

On one of the last toboggan trips, I brought our furniture across: the two, big blocks of wood that served as chairs, and the dismantled pole table. Now that the winter was over, we could dispense with the log framework around the lower part of the tent. We must have spent half an hour trying to put the table back together without the benefit of a few spikes. Had the ground not been still frozen, it would have been no problem.

"Listen Crusoe! I'm getting fed up frigging around with this damned table affair. Who needs one anyway? There are several more large blocks of wood over at our old camp. We could set them together right on the dirt floor. That would only take about five minutes, and we'd have our table."

Harry appeared to be immersed in deep meditation. "It would look kinda primitive, Friday. There's such a thing as pride you know."

"Are you expecting visitors, Crusoe? Mae West, for instance?"

"I agree it's not likely. You may bring the blocks and I shall arrange them in artistic formation."

"I figured that would be Friday's job," I remarked lamely.

During the following days we had little to do but wait for the breakup; on the Nahanni open water usually occurs in early May. Going any distance in the bush or on the river was next to impossible except in the early hours of the morning when the surface water was still frozen.

Being confined to our new home didn't bother either of us to any degree. Camp chores were now reduced to a minimum because there was no need for heat. Our new location had solved the mice problem (almost). Water was a bother, which we could have solved in a hurry with an ordinary pick or grubbing hoe by cutting steps up the hill. As soon as the ground thawed out, I resolved to try to make some steps in the hill with the butt end of my axe. That incline was a killer.

Harry never got tired of playing rummy. And why not—he always won. We also spent the hours away, reminiscing about the bygone days on the farms where we were raised in the area now known as Spruce View, in Alberta. We talked about the chicken suppers at the Bethel church, the box socials at the Spruce View school, the bridge parties, followed by the dances, where Danny M. fought Charles C. for the privilege of having the supper waltz with Sadie Perkins. Fist fights were something that Sadie was a genius in bringing about. As in all rural communities there are always special events and special individuals who stand out in one's mind and are not easily forgotten.

During supper one night I remarked about the number of squirrels there were at our new camp. They seemed to be everywhere, chattering away among the spruce. Over at the old camp, we only saw the odd one. Harry thought that Fritzie might have cleaned them out. We wondered about Fritzie. Would he cross the river to our high camp? We didn't know. We hadn't seen the marten for some time now. We had always left meat for him in the tent at our old site, and twice, at least, we knew he had taken his free meal.

The twilight hour is long in the North at this time of year, and the day seems to never end. Early rising didn't matter that much, now that we were in the "waiting period," as they called it, waiting for breakup. Judging from the past three springs, Harry guessed that the Nahanni might go out about the first week in May, depending upon the weather. The hours of sunshine were longer and warmer during these first days of May. A glance at our trail across the river served as a measure to calculate the number of inches each day the snow level was receding. The trail was beginning to resemble a manmade bridge of ice over to our winter camp.

Any day now, the meltwater accumulating in untold numbers of gullies and ravines would begin moving down the mountainsides from the timberline, sending billions of gallons of water cascading into any number of creeks—existing and newly formed—all dumping their tons of water into a common receiver—the South Nahanni River. This sudden volume of water, in turn, would cause the winter ice of the river to sag and groan under the tons of weight, and finally crack, splitting into an open channel of flowing water. And when this channel rose in depth, applying still more weight, the adjoining ice on either side would begin breaking off in ever larger chunks, finally to be pushed over to either shore, until at last, the river would be flowing free and unobstructed.

Early one morning—while there was still a crust on the surface of the remaining snow—we decided to snowshoe up to the mouth of the Rabbitkettle River, which was roughly two miles distant. Harry thought there was a possibility that Bill Eppler and Joe Mulholland had left a message somewhere in that area, which would provide a clue as to what may have happened to the two men who had disappeared more than a year ago.

And hour later, as we were following the left bank of the Rabbitkettle, I spotted a neatly folded green tarpaulin that had been placed between the trunk and one of the lower branches of a big spruce tree. We went over to investigate. It was a heavily-branched tree that one might select for protection during a heavy rain. We began poking around in the snow at the base of the tree and found an empty Turret tobacco tin and one front leg of a wolf. A further search revealed the remains of a campfire. But when it was built or at what time of year, we couldn't tell. There wasn't an axe mark in any of the few pieces of wood still remaining. We surmised that someone may have shot or trapped a wolf and skinned it out over a winter fire. But that didn't explain why the tarp was left behind. Trappers and prospectors are not in the habit of leaving tarps wherever they happen to stop along the way.

We searched both banks of the river until mid-morning, looking for a tree blaze, but found nothing. Harry picked up the tarp and put it in the pocket of his packboard. "We'll take it out to Nahanni Village when we go. There is a chance that Jack Mulholland may be able to identify the owner of this tarp—if it belonged to anyone at the mouth of Nahanni."

Later, back in camp, as we were busy changing our soaked footwear, Nigger and Liza began kicking up a real ruckus outside. "Sounds like something is after the dogs!" I shouted.

Harry grabbed my rifle and pushed open the tent flaps, then called back, "The caribou are coming through again! There's a big herd down on the river. Mostly cows and last year's calves."

We watched the herd go by in their ground-consuming trot, some in bunches, and others in single file. We could hear the rhythmic snap and click, snap and click of their hooves on the ice as the herd moved steadily downriver in their mile-eating strides.

Near dinner time I had brought a quarter of caribou down from the cache and was busy cutting it into steaks at the meat block. The jays were there as usual, and I impulsively tossed a piece of the meat on the ground. It was then that I saw something that aroused my curiosity: the odd bird would quickly pick at the meat, then fly away into a stand of tamarack trees near a small muskeg back of the tent. Meanwhile I saw several other jays flying back from the same area. I walked in among the larches, and a red speck caught my eye: it was a tiny piece of the meat, deftly tucked under a flaky scale of the bark of a tree. On another tree I found another particle of meat cached away in the same manner. So this was how the Canada jay stored its food supply for a rainy day. Apparently we two-legged animals weren't the first to use a tree cache.

Harry was standing by the cutting block when I returned. He pointed into the limbs of a nearby spruce tree. "Our little friend has found our camp, Friday!" And there sat Fritzie, watching every move we made. Harry laid a small slice of steak on the block, then we retreated inside the tent and watched.

Fritzie used a lot of caution before making his move. But the temptation was overwhelming. Suddenly, in a flash, the marten streaked down the tree, snatched the steak off the block, and retreated up to his perch.

"You have just witnessed a demonstration of speed by one of the fastest animals on four feet!" Harry exclaimed.

These first days of May were long, and very warm. Here on the north shore, the snow was almost gone. Water was collecting in deep pools over much of the river, confining us to camp during most of each day. But there was always something to be done—clothes to wash and mend, and most important, time to spend discussing plans for the spring beaver hunt, come open water. All trappers look forward to this hunt, but for us it was also our last chance to improve our dismal winter catch of fur. The adult beaver might bring from twenty to twenty-five dollars at Fort Simpson.

I had an armful of questions that needed answering about taking beaver in open water, and one afternoon Harry explained the more intricate parts of this operation in some detail.

"Soon after the river is clear of ice, the 'tramp' beaver will begin swimming upstream and back down again, looking to find a new home. These are the ones we'll be going after," Harry explained.

"What do you mean by tramp beaver?" I asked. "And how do we go after them? Neither of us can swim."

"One question at a time, Friday. Just listen! When the young are born, usually in April, they remain in the house with their parents until they are two years old, along with the previous year's kits. Then they leave their home to start or find a new colony. These are called tramp beaver. I've been told it's nature's way of preventing inbreeding.

"Beaver are most active at dawn and in the late evening. During these stages you position yourself on the edge of a low bank of the river, with your rifle by your side and your pike pole within reach. The pike pole is a slender sapling about twelve feet long with a hook shaped out of a piece of heavy wire attached to its smaller end. Mr. Beaver swims up to the bank and begins nibbling the fresh green grass sprouting above the water line. You aim for the beaver's head—bingo—you are twenty dollars richer—providing, of course, you hit the beaver on the head; otherwise it will dive at once, and you won't have time to hook it with the pole. Sometimes you can nail them as they swim by, if they are within reach. You have to know the length of your pole."

"Sounds like a tricky sort of business to me," I remarked.

"It is," Harry admitted. "Ole Lindberg, down on the Liard, was the trapper who told me about this method when one doesn't have a boat. I've never hunted beaver in this way. When Milt Campbell and I came into the country in '34 we had our canoe and outboard motor and were able to pick off the odd one from the boat, but primarily we were on our way into the Flat River area to hunt for gold, not beaver. It was illegal anyway, as we had no license to trap any kind of fur. The same thing applied to '35 and '36, unless we could join someone who did have a licensed trapline. That's why I hooked up with Dalziel.

"But you and I don't have the luxury of a canoe and outboard motor. From here on, we're confined to shore."

"That reminds me, Crusoe, I must look the word 'luxury' up in my dictionary. There was a time when I thought I knew what it meant."

But if we did lack certain material things, there were others that mere money couldn't buy: we were now enjoying to the fullest, the grandest days one could imagine. Warm and balmy they were, and each succeeding one seemed so much longer than the one before. One of these days we would have to gaze above timberline on our mountains, to be reminded of what snow looked like. Now that would be something to look forward to.

On May 10th we were sitting in the tent, mending our moccasins when we heard the first loud report. It sounded similar to an underground dynamite blast from upriver (a comparison I learned later while working at the Con mine at Yellowknife). The dogs immediately began barking. They thought someone was firing a rifle. Then two more reports came in rapid succession.

"The ice is breaking up!" Harry exclaimed. We put our moccasins back on and went outside to the high bank. A few hundred yards upriver we could see blocks of ice being pushed aside, as though by some giant hand. We could hear the grating, crunching movement and the rumble of slabs of ice sliding over other ice near the centre of the river.

Fifteen minutes later, we saw a wall of water coming down the Nahanni that was awesome to behold.

"Something must have been blocking up the meltwater upriver," Harry said. "The Rabbitkettle probably has gone out, and the ice has been accumulating at the mouth."

The dogs were straining at their chains. Harry went over and untied them. Liza was uncertain. She decided to stay where she was. Nigger rushed along the river bank a few yards, then suddenly returned. Whatever was going on out there, he didn't want any part of.

The ever-increasing weight of the oncoming water was slowly breaking down the river ice, and by evening an open channel had been bulldozed down the centre of the Nahanni.

Throughout the next day, huge slabs of ice were breaking off on either side of the midstream rush of water, and by late afternoon of May 12th, there were only a few yards of ice remaining on either shore line.

"All we would need now is a two-day rainfall, and you would see a flood that Noah wouldn't believe," Harry observed.

But the rain never came. The following mornings dawned bright and clear and somewhat colder, thus reducing further snow melt. We could just as well have stayed in our old camp, but who was to know? Drifting ice did come down from the upper reaches during this time, but Harry, having witnessed four breakups on the Nahanni, considered this one to be as normal as any of the others.

Bears and Berries

While waiting for the ice to clear we made a discovery: the remainder of the caribou meat up on the cache was tainted. The past nights hadn't been cold enough to keep the meat from thawing out. There wasn't a great amount of meat spoilt; two hungry dogs and two hungry men can make short work of a caribou carcass. While neither of us liked to see food wasted, during breakup Harry had mentioned that from now on, we wouldn't need to worry about meat. "We can always get a moose in the Big Muskeg," He had said. "Dal and I shot two there last fall."

Since Harry's back had been bothering him of late, it was decided that I would go upriver to the big muskeg and hunt for a moose. I knew about this muskeg: my part of the trapline had circled its south end and when I reached this area of stunted, black spruce, I always knew I wasn't much more than a mile from the home tent. I was also aware of the predominance of red willow and the young larch trees growing around the fringe of the lowland. It was prime moose habitat.

"From here on in, Friday, me boy, it's a dried meat diet for us. I can't say I'm looking forward to it."

I had never eaten dried meat so I wasn't able to offer an opinion.

As the dogs had been tied up for a number of days now, Harry

115

suggested I take them with me. They needed some exercise. There was always the chance they might spook an animal and spoil a shot, but we couldn't keep them chained up forever.

When I slipped on their panniers, even Liza was ready to hit the trail. The panniers always meant action. Just as we were leaving, the high sultan issued an order: "Don't come back empty-handed! And please do not shoot an old, ancient bull—like the one you got last February. Pick out a nice, young, fat one. Forestood?"

"I shall do your bidding, Crusoe. I'm sure that muskeg will be swarming with moose of all ages," I retorted. As we approached the fringe area, I hadn't the same degree of optimism about the moose population here as he had. But as usual, Harry wasn't far wrong. When we came out of the willows, I counted eleven bull moose in an area of less than twenty acres.

I quickly turned back into the heavy spruce and tied the dogs to a tree. If Nigger spotted one of the animals, the hunt wouldn't even have a beginning.

I gathered a handful of spruce needles and tossed them into the air. They floated away in the soft breeze, indicating a cross-wind that wasn't entirely in my favour. I decided to circle the muskeg area until the wind was right. Then I saw two bulls ambulating slowly in my direction, stopping momentarily to browse as moose generally do when they are not headed for any particular destination. I decided to wait.

Suddenly I heard the branch of a tree breaking in among the spruce off to my right. I turned to see another bull moose emerging from the heavy timber. He stopped and swung broadside to me, as though he had detected something he didn't like. I raised my rifle and fired. The moose moved forward then stopped again. Then the dogs let loose with a barrage of barking that could be heard at the mouth of the Nahanni (if the wind was right). The moose still stood there. "Why hell," I thought, "the animal must be stone deaf."

I couldn't believe it! At fifty yards, broadside, how could I miss? Was there something wrong with the ammunition? Now that *was* a bad thought. I held the rifle up and watched the lever action put another cartridge into the chamber. Just as I was about to fire again, the animal's body began to waver, then slowly sink into the moss cover.

It had been a lung shot. The big bull was glassy-eyed and breathing his last when I came into the hollow where he fell.

Such is the luck at times when one is hunting. Had the dogs seen the moose first, he would have turned back into the spruce, and I wouldn't have seen him. The dogs, of course, should have been left in camp, but it's not always the best thing to do: a dog can be a source of protection when there are bears around, as will be seen later.

So that Harry would know that I made a kill, I gave our pre-arranged signal: two shots in rapid succession. And as I was gutting out the moose half an hour later, I heard a loud "halloo" behind me. He had come as soon as he heard the rifle shots.

The mid-morning sun reminded us there was work to be done—and plenty of it. It was going to be a warm day and the sooner this meat was up on our cache, the better it would be.

We didn't waste any time. At 6 p.m. most of the moose was in camp and covered with the big tarp. There were still about eighty pounds left at the kill and after a smoke and three cups of tea, I volunteered to take Nigger and make the fifth trip. I was concerned about Harry's back, but he never complained about the loads he carried on his packboard, which were heavier than mine, although I carried the only rifle. Harry was not one to shirk hard work by using excuses.

Nigger and I were back at eight with the final load. Into the big fry pan went most of the heart and kidneys. It's hard to believe the amount of meat that two men can consume at one sitting.

After the feast, we finished building the meat rack that Harry had started early that morning. It consisted of seven slender poles placed about six inches (fifteen centimetres) apart upon two heavier cross poles that were secured between four trees. This "platform" formed a rectangle in shape, which measured about 3 1/2 feet (1 m) wide and 7 feet (2 m) long. It stood a little over 5 feet (1.5 m) off the ground, which we later discovered was about the right height.

We were up at 5 a.m. the next morning to begin cutting up as much meat as possible before the heat of the day began bringing the flies out. The procedure, Harry explained, was to cut the meat into narrow strips or thin slabs that were then draped over the poles. The idea was to provide enough heat from the fire underneath the platform, to produce a thin crust over the surface of each strip, sufficient to keep the meat from spoiling. During the drying process, a small amount of moss is placed on the fire to control the heat and keep the flies away. "This was the way Milt and I had seen the Indians do it, when we were prospecting on the Flat River," Harry said.

Initially, Harry was left with the main job of cutting the meat, while I folded the strips over the poles and tended to the wood gathering. We would put off lighting the fire as long as possible.

Early in the forenoon, while I was up on the cache after another hindquarter, I saw two, fat bluebottle flies buzz out from beneath the tarp.

"The bloody flies have been at the meat, Crusoe! Some of this stuff will be flyblown."

"Don't let it bother you, my boy! We'll scorch the eggs dead with heat. They'll never get a chance to hatch," Harry said.

I thought of several comments I could have made, but lack of experience in the meat drying business, reminded me to keep my silence. I did notice, however, that Harry lost no time in lighting the fire under the rack.

At 5 p.m. the job was finally finished. The cool of the evening would soon be settling in and that would help to keep the damnable flies down. Despite the heat and smoke, the devils were still trying to get at the rack.

The tiring work was now over. All that remained was the tending of the fire. This would be an all-night session extending into sometime tomorrow, depending upon Harry's opinion about the condition of the meat. I found a piece of birch bark and pencilled "heads" on one side and "tails" on the other. We would flip to see who took the first shift looking after the rack. I won the toss. I had swallowed a lot of smoke during the afternoon and I was tired. After a bite to eat, I felt as though I could go to sleep floating down the Nahanni River.

It seemed as if I had just gone to bed when Harry woke me at 3 a.m. to take the next watch. I didn't know the first thing about this meat-drying process. I simply went through the act of turning the strips over on the poles, so that hopefully, each side received an equal amount of exposure to the heat. As to the amount of heat required, I didn't have a clue. I didn't have a meat-drying manual. I merely followed Crusoe's vague instructions.

At noon that day, Harry spelled me off. I snoozed during most of the afternoon and then joined Harry at the rack. He removed several strips from the poles and began examining them closely. "Well, what do you think of it, Crusoe?" I asked.

"Looks about right, Friday. We may have used a mite too much heat, but that's better than not enough. At least I'm sure we've killed the flyblows. I think we've done an excellent job. There's a good crust on the meat. Keeps the damned fly eggs from penetrating."

I was watching the high sultan closely as he gave his verdict. I wasn't entirely convinced that we had made an "excellent" job of this operation. I found myself wishing that we could have an Indian's opinion. All I saw were seven, shredded, black rows of the most repulsive-looking stuff that anyone could possibly imagine in the way of food. It was really a distasteful looking sight. It was difficult for me to imagine myself eating this stuff. But I had a problem that I wasn't aware of: I hadn't been in the North long enough to know what it meant to be hungry. Dalziel had left four gunny sacks with Harry. We filled three with the strips of dried meat, then stored them up on the cache, making sure the tarp was tucked tightly under and over them.

"What will we do with these moose ribs, Crusoe?" I asked. "There is quite a bit of meat on them."

"We will separate some of the ribs from each rib cage and give them to the dogs. Then we shall hang the two cages over the fire with a couple of green forked sticks. Crusoe, the expert, will show Friday how it's done. Then we shall have the largest rib roast ever held in North America," Harry declared. And with that pronouncement, we did just that. By shaping the forked sticks properly and using a short length of babiche, either rib cage could be twirled around with the slighted touch.

We feasted on roasted moose ribs for nearly two hours before the evening dusk finally faded into the dark of nightfall. The dogs were still chewing on their share of the bones when we crawled into bed.

May 14th—if my notches were correct. I had been cutting them into the ridgepole of the tent, now that we didn't have the pole table. This was to be the first day of our beaver hunt. In the early dawn we took up positions along the north bank of the river. Harry chose to patrol the shore near the beaver house on the island where I had shot the wolf. I stationed myself near a snye, upriver from our camp.

119

There was this much to be said about lying on your belly in the prone position, with your head hanging over the edge of a river bank: at least you weren't wearing out your footwear, nor were you exerting yourself to any degree. But if one merely wants to rest, I can recommend better positions. And after a couple of hours waiting, watching nothing but the cold, clear water gliding by, I was beginning to find this new adventure rather boring. If the tramp beaver were supposed to be using this side of the river as their highway, there sure as hell wasn't much traffic. By using sheer willpower, I managed to endure another hour's eternity before I finally terminated the morning's vigil, leaving the river to the beaver.

Rather than follow the game trail back to camp, I decided to cut into the big timber and pay a visit to the muskeg. I was curious to learn if the moose had returned there to feed.

Making my way through a deep carpet of undergrowth, I came upon a large windfall. How long ago the fire had swept through this area, only a dendrologist could hazard a guess. Many of the criss-crossed trees were almost hidden under a heavy carpet of moss. A new growth of pine forest had sprung up here years back. Many of the tall trees were six or eight inches in diameter. There was something about this place that I had never experienced before. I felt a certain sense of well-being and exhilaration as I slowly picked my way over the mounds of moss-bound trees. I had the feeling of entering a great cathedral of the kind that only nature could create—truly a sanctuary of peace and solitude.

But as I ambled deeper into the secluded area, I soon discovered something of greater interest than its scenic wonders: I found that I was on the outskirts of a huge cranberry patch. There were still a few spots of snow lying in the hollows, but on the log mounds, the red, heavy-clustered berries could be seen hanging from the low bushes carpeted over the moss. There seemed to be an unlimited quantity everywhere I looked. To me, it was like discovering a pot of gold.

I must have eaten a gallon of berries before I made another discovery: I found a half-buried log from which the berry bushes had been ripped clean. Claw marks in the ancient bark were clearly visible. And then I saw the bear dung, and bear tracks in one of the snow hollows. My cranberry feast came to a sudden end. A short investigation of the area proved that I was in a bear's banquet room. At this moment, he or she could by lying asleep in one of these hollows. I decided to vamoose, promptly.

Harry was back in camp when I returned. He hadn't seen any beaver either. His eyes lit up when I told him about the cranberry patch. "You have made a discovery that will make our lives more bearable. Did you know, Friday, that if you have never eaten dried moose meat smothered in cranberry sauce, you have never lived?"

"Are you sure you're not being carried away, Crusoe?"

"You just wait and see, after you discover it yourself. I think you will agree."

"There may be a slight disagreement over the ownership of that berry patch, Crusoe. The bears have been in there and they have seniority rights."

Back in Edmonton, Dalziel had mentioned that the Rabbitkettle area had its share of bears. "They come out of hibernation as the snow is leaving the ground. You will see them along the river and in the berry patches. Be on the look-out. Best give them a wide berth." Harry and I had discussed the possibility of meeting up with grizzlies. The danger lay in an unexpected meeting. We were far from home, and the last thing we needed was a confrontation with bears. Constant precaution would be required—both in and out of camp.

"Not to worry, me boy! Not to worry," said Crusoe cheerfully. "Once it becomes known to them that *I* am the supreme monarch over all that I survey, I feel certain that an agreement can be reached whereby each party shares the patch at different times. Everybody shall have a turn; I am not an unreasonable man."

"That sounds like a logical solution to me, Crusoe. I'm more than willing to let you do the negotiating."

Harry suggested that we should celebrate the cranberry find with another royal banquet—the usual oatmeal and prunes affair. I was in total agreement. Our banquet dinners were few and far between, and each succeeding one was something to look forward to. We often talked about our daily breakfasts back on the farm. Oatmeal was always on the menu—every day of the year. It was a prairie tradition—and for more reasons than one. Here at the Rabbitkettle, one didn't take a feed of rolled oats for granted.

We snoozed for a couple of hours after the feast, then Harry proposed that we pay a visit to the cranberry patch, after which we could still take up a watch for beaver at the snye. Harry had been living on a meat diet longer than I, and he knew the importance of having a fruit supplement. I was just as eager to go, but I still had those bears in mind.

"We had better take the dogs along," Harry said. "They will warn us if there are bears present."

Sometime later, after we had reached the windfall, I spotted a tall pine tree near where I had found the berries. The tree was heavily limbed and one that would be easy to climb. "We're getting close to the patch, Crusoe. I'm going to shinny up that tree and have a look around. If the bears are here, I would suggest we wait our turn."

I found a perch among the branches and carefully scanned the area. Three grizzlies were feeding on a log-mound near where I had found the berries that morning—a sow and her two, two-year-old cubs. Suddenly out of a group of pines, I saw an older bear saunter into the area.

I signalled Harry to come up and join me. He then tied the dogs to another near-by tree.

Meanwhile, the big bear stood up on his hind paws to better survey the situation, thrusting his nose in the air as though he had scented something unfamiliar to him, which might mean danger. Finally the grizzly lumbered over to the log-mound and began raking off the berry bushes with a forepaw, stuffing the vines, leaves and berries into his mouth, then using his teeth as a sieve to separate the fruit from the unwanted material.

Harry had now taken up a position just beneath my perch, and when he saw the big bear, he exclaimed in a voice barely above a whisper, "That's old Scarface! I'd recognize him anywhere. Dal and I saw him last fall when we were setting up the tent. We watched him through Dal's field glasses."

I could understand how Harry had identified this bear so readily: one of his ears was missing and the other was partially chewed out of shape. His coat appeared matted and scarred in several places and from where we were, it was plain this old fellow had been in a battle royal with one of his kind sometime in the past. And it would have been something to watch! This one-time monarch "of all that he surveyed" had seen a few seasons come and go, and some of them hadn't been all that easy. This much was evident.

At one point, as we watched, the old bear decided he wanted to get at the berries lying partially hidden underneath the mound. He reached out with one paw and sank his claws into the half-submerged log and reared back. The end of the rotten log broke off and Scarface tumbled backward. This seemed to infuriate him to a degree, and with an angry snuffle, he ambled over to another mound near where the sow and her two cubs were. This was a mistake. In an instant the she-bear rushed him. The skirmish didn't last long; Scarface was no match for this mother. He took off at a lengthy lope into the far side of the patch—presumably in search of a friendlier place to finish his meal. The cubs, meanwhile, had retreated to a safe distance behind a large tree root.

After observing this performance, I didn't have any desire to pick cranberries. It was obvious old Scarface was not the friendly type, and the mother bear didn't seem to be in the negotiating mood.

"I have a solution to this situation," Harry said. "How about you take your Winchester and go down and drive old mother bear out? She's had her turn; now it's ours. Meanwhile, I'll stand guard up here in the tree, with my .22 Hornet."

"I have a better idea, Crusoe," I retorted. "I'll lend you my Winchester and you can go down and chase mamma and her cubs out of the patch. I'll stay perched up here with your pea-shooter."

We both grinned, knowing that neither rifle had the potency to deal with messy bear situations. Even had we had two elephant guns, we certainly would not have used them. We didn't come to a cranberry patch to kill bears.

We sat there among the branches for a couple of minutes, waiting for the she-bear to discover that other visitors had come to dinner; we thought she would have heard us talking by this time. Harry casually rolled a cigarette and lit it. "She'll smell the smoke and then vamoose," he predicted. But for some reason she didn't.

Suddenly Harry sounded forth with a shrill "Halloo-o-o-ah." It sounded like the wild Indian war-whoop, signalling the attack on Custer's men at the battle of the Little Bighorn. In a split second the mother bear whirled around in an attempt to discover where the sound came from. Then she saw us.

Then the dogs began to bark. They had finally caught her scent. With lightning speed, she turned to face the spot where the dogs were tied, but she wasn't able to see them. The sow hissed and grunted, calling to her two cubs who rushed out of a hollow behind a tree stump, taking refuge directly behind her. She was a mad bear looking for trouble.

I climbed a little higher up the tree. She kept turning from side to side, expelling spurts of air from her nostrils, reminding me of an old sow with her litter of pigs that we had on our farm when I was a six-year-old boy. How could I possibly forget! An automobile salesman happened to be standing at the board fence and rescued me from the sow's attack. I had been playing with her young.

Sooner or later something had to give. Finally we both let forth in unison, shouting and yelling in a chorus of calls that would have wakened Rip Van Winkle. This time she circled slowly around and again called to her cubs. Then in one, swift motion, she set out through the windfall, turning back to make sure her young were following.

I still believe to this day, that had we encountered her at close quarters, she would have charged us. But in this instance she had an alternative and she took it.

We did, however, want the cranberries, and there were one or two safety measures available. We could light a fire in a snow hollow where we would be picking. That would be sure protection. But this was a poor place to start a fire, unless we were certain we could stamp it out. Fires had been known to smoulder throughout an entire winter in the type of moss-covered terrain that we were in. We decided against it. We would take turns filling the water bucket while the other stood guard with the Winchester.

On the way home, we spent an hour by the snye during dusk, watching for beaver but none swam by—at least we hadn't spotted any. But we did have our berries, and when we reached the tent, we soon had them on to boil. A lengthy discussion followed about whether or not we should use a cupful of sugar to sweeten them. I reminded Crusoe that there was less than a quarter of the sack of sugar remaining and that perhaps we should leave it for the tea. Harry agreed.

While we were waiting for the fruit to boil, we talked about the Sunday berry-picking excursions we often took each fall out west to the Clearwater River near the foothills, during the Twenties. Many families counted on those trips for the winter's fruit supply.

Cranberries and low-bush blueberries. Family picnics they were, and fun for everyone, as well as work.

"We didn't need to worry about bears in the patches in those days," I remarked.

"No, any grizzly that showed up on the Clearwater was a dead bear," Harry agreed. "Bears and cattle don't mix—and the bears have to go."

It was a late supper we had that night. And Harry was right: the cranberries *did* make a world of difference to the *flavour* of our dried meat (and that took some doing). We would look forward to more of the same when the opportunity presented itself.

Two caribou on the river just before spring breakup, May 1937.

Rabbitkettle Valley taken from the spring camp, 1937.

*Stan McMillan and mechanic fixing a strut on the Norseman
at Fort Simpson, February 1937.*

*Harry, Nigger, and Liza taken the morning the four
Dall's sheep were killed.*

Four sheep heads. It could and should have been a different picture, May 1937.

The author not so proud after a second thought.

Harry holding one of the rams on the summit of the mountain where the four sheep were killed.

Three caribou looking down river, mid-April 1937.

Virginia Falls, June 1937.

Harry holding the blown-up 280 Ross rifle.

The author with Nigger and Liza, 1937.

Dall's Sheep and Other Encounters

May 21. The weather in the Nahanni Mountains can change from summer to winter overnight during this month. There were two inches of snow on the ground when I lit the morning fire to make tea. We thought it better to postpone watching for beaver and spend the day in camp tending to the odd chore.

I was out by the sawhorse chopping firewood when I happened to look up on the south slope of the mountain that rose to the north of our camp. Suddenly my eye caught the movement of a greyish white object in a ravine near the summit. Or was it my imagination? The object was probably a small patch of snow. Then the white dot slowly began moving up the ravine where it disappeared into a forested area near the summit. It was a Dall's sheep—the first I had ever seen.

Our plans for the day were now changed. "It's going to be a cold day," Harry observed. "This might be a chance to get some fresh meat and keep it from spoiling for a few days, unless the weather changes. It should be an easy climb to the top of that mountain; it's forested all the way to the summit on the east slope. Let's have a go!"

After our dried meat diet of several days, I didn't need much coaxing to go on a sheep hunt. We ate a hurried breakfast, shouldered our packboards, and with the dogs following behind, we headed out across the slough back of the tent. When we reached the foot of the mountain, we made better progress on the firmer ground, even though we were beginning the ascent. Tramping through foot-deep moss for any distance can be a tiring ordeal even on level ground. Negotiating the famous Nahanni moss is not recommended for the weak.

Two hours of steady climbing brought us just below the summit. Harry had hunted Dall's sheep on occasion during his time on the Flat River creeks, and he advised that in approaching these animals, the secret was to climb *above* them whenever possible.

As we were now about as high as we would be going, we stopped, rested on a dead log, and had a smoke. Tired hunters don't usually hold their rifles very steady.

"That sheep you saw was likely a ram. And where there's one, there will be others," Harry explained. "At this time of year the rams herd together in groups. The ewes keep in secluded places to have their lambs, usually in rocky areas where bears and wolves are not so apt to be. We'll look the gullies and ravines over carefully after we get to the summit. That's where your ram will be unless he's left the country."

As we continued up the slope, I was in the lead when I saw them: four, white rams resting side by side in a small grove of spruce. I reached back and touched Harry's arm. He had also spotted them. Harry whispered, "Take the two on the right." The four sheep turned their heads in perfect unison when they heard our sound. Four shots rang out! Four heads slumped to the ground, resting sideways and silent in the duff! They never knew what hit them. Only for an instant did they know they were in any danger. It was finished before I had had time to think. Each ram had been shot in the head from a distance of about twenty-five yards.

"They never made any attempt to get up," I said. "That's not the way our bighorn sheep act back in Alberta."

"We're not in Alberta, now, Friday. It's a pretty safe bet we were the first two-legged animals those rams had ever seen. Curiosity stilled their instinct to react. One day in the summer of '35, I was up Bennett Creek, off the Flat River, panning for that yellow stuff. I looked up to see *seven* sheep watching me. They just stood there like seven statues. I'll bet I could have killed three of them before the others took off."

133

Such was Harry's comment—expressed through experience in a part of the Territories that at that time had seen few hunters. And it was all true what Dalziel had said that evening in the Leland Hotel in Edmonton when I inquired about the game situation at the Rabbitkettle. "If you and Harry can hit the broad side of a barn at fifty yards, you fellows won't have any trouble keeping meat on the table. You will find plenty to shoot at."

We quartered the sheep out in a snow-covered nook just below the summit, then built a small fire and had tea. "That wasn't much of a hunt, was it," I remarked.

"I've had longer ones," Harry replied. "It isn't always this easy, believe-you-me!"

I had brought my folding camera along, and we took several pictures at the site. Then fully loaded with meat, we headed down the slope, using the same route taken on the ascent. I didn't think it possible that so much could happen in so short a time. It seemed so unreal.

Back at the camp I was wondering how long we could keep the fresh meat from spoiling up on the cache. "I suppose it all depends on the weather," I said. "Tomorrow it could turn warm again."

"You worry too much, Friday," Harry replied. "How do you suppose I became the high sultan-supreme ruler over all I survey? Was it because of my good looks? Of course not. It was because of my fantastic ability to improvise in time of need."

"Improvise what, may I ask?"

Harry repeated his "thumbs through suspenders" performance once again and replied, "I propose to build the first refrigerator ever constructed on the South Nahanni River. Henceforth, me lad, you may cast all further worry aside."

After dinner I suggested I go back to the summit and bring home the remainder of the meat that we had left hanging in a tree. I knew that Harry's back was still bothering him, and I was more than a little concerned. As far as I could see, the less back-packing he did, the better it would be for both of us. Meanwhile, he could stay in camp and begin constructing his icebox.

It was a scene to remember as I reached the summit and ran my eyes westward over the mountains. There rose our favourite landmark, Pyramid Mountain, our name for Mount Macbrian, directly upriver from our camp. It stood in sempiternal splendour, the snow-capped sentinel of white outlined against the clear blue sky of the late afternoon.

I walked over to the spruce grove and lowered the meat to the ground. It would mean a heavy load for both dogs and me, but it was a downhill pack all the way, which would compensate for the added weight. Just before leaving, I turned to take a last look at the four sheep heads lying neatly in a row where we had placed them just a few hours before. An uncomfortable feeling of distress suddenly came over me. Why had we shot *four* sheep? Wouldn't one have been sufficient? The longer I thought about it, the more it bothered me. It wasn't as if there was a shortage of food in camp; there were three large sacks of dried meat up on our cache. I certainly didn't care much for the stuff, but I knew that everyone in the North ate dried meat in the summer months.

No, this kill had been nothing more than a short-sighted exercise in extermination—an impulsive action containing no forethought. In this instance—as in far too many, no doubt—the bullet had proven to be faster than the thought of preservation. I walked over and laid my hand on the head of the largest ram—one of the two that I had shot. It had been the oldest ram of the group, with a set of beautiful horns. Would it have made the Boone and Crockett Club? I had no idea and couldn't have cared less. I had read of Daniel Boone and Davy Crockett, but I knew nothing about the club—and if I had, I can assure the reader that my thoughts at the moment were far removed from the "trophy head" line of thought.

The snapshot I had taken of the four heads was mainly on my mind. I was thinking of the picture I *could* have taken had I pressed the camera button instead of the trigger when I first spotted the rams. That was at the moment when they turned their heads in unison, as if posing for the camera. Then I would have had a picture I could have been proud of for the rest of my life.

At the summit I paused for a moment, and regretfully gazed into the little glade beneath the grove of spruce where the four rams had been having their last siesta. Then I called to the dogs and we made off down the slope. I just wanted to be away from that place.

Harry had supper waiting when we finally got back to camp with the last of the meat. It had been a long day and I was tired and hungry. My first meal of wild mutton was a welcome change from the diet of dried moose, I must admit, and would have tasted even better had it been obtained under different circumstances.

Early the next morning, we set to work building the refrigerator. In spite of his back problem, Harry had cut the logs the evening before. He was not a man "to let trivial things bother," as he put it, when I reprimanded him for not taking it easier until he felt better.

Our "fridge" was constructed of four-inch (ten-centimetre) logs and consisted of one frame placed inside another larger one. Nahanni moss was then stuffed between the two frames to act as insulation. The outside frame was about three feet (about one metre) square and stood almost four feet (1.2 m) in height. The structure resembled a miniature log cabin, minus the roof.

The slough, back of our tent, provided a perfect site for our storehouse. We simply removed the moss from the underlying ice that served as a floor for the log structure. The hardest part of the job was chopping the amount of ice required for packing around the meat after we had cleared the moss away from the slough. Placing the quarters of sheep in position, interlaid with the chunks of ice inside the inner frame, was the easiest part of the job. Now all that remained was to put a "roof" of moss over the topmost layer of ice.

The only witnesses to our day's work were the whisky-jacks; they knew where the meat was but they couldn't get to it. Their frenzied efforts were emphasized by their incessant cacophonous chatter, which was beginning to get on our nerves. Still, one had to give these birds credit for their untiring determination.

That evening we talked about our return to Nahanni Village. We decided to continue hunting beaver until the end of the month. "Then we will build the log raft and kiss the Rabbitkettle goodbye," Harry stated. "What dost thou, Friday, think of that?"

"Friday is in total agreement," I said.

During the latter part of May my daily vigils at the snye produced only one solitary beaver. And my boredom of late had now become a feeling of extreme frustration. A person can stare at running water just so long—if he wants to keep his sanity.

During one evening's watch at the snye, my patience finally snapped. "To hell with lying in this prone position, nursing a sore belly button morning and night!" I muttered to myself. And so I spent the rest of the watch sitting in an upright position with my feet dangling over the edge of the bank, and enjoying a Turret roll-your-own. If the beaver didn't like the smoke, they could bloody well stay on the other side of the river.

On this particular evening, I had left Liza in camp. She had been limping about with a sore foot, although we couldn't find anything wrong with it. It was important to have a dog with us on these beaver watches. One never knew when a bear might come ambling down one of these game trails that invariably followed the river banks.

At dusk, I left the snye, and was returning home on the main trail. Part way across a small marsh, overgrown with tall, dry slough grass, I spotted a small, reddish object lying under the dense grass cover. I stopped and stood there for a moment, wondering what this strange thing could be, lying there off the trail about thirty feet away. Finally I laid my rifle down on a hummock and picked my way through the grass to where the object lay. It was a moose calf, only a couple of days old. The little fellow never gave the slightest indication that it saw me. It laid there, still as a statue, not an ear wiggled, not an eyelash blinked—a perfect example of the self-protective instinct endowed by nature in the young of many cloven-hoofed animals. I was fascinated. Except for the enlarged ears and protruding upper lip, it bore a striking resemblance to the new-born Hereford calves raised on the farms of Alberta.

I reached for my tobacco pouch, and in that instant I heard a tree limb crack. And then I saw something that made my blood run cold; a cow moose was striding into the marsh, hell-bent-for-leather. I headed for the nearest tree on the opposite side of the marsh. And believe-you-me, I was moving! I went up that tree in nothing flat. I shot up that spruce and didn't stop until I had reached the topmost branch. And when I looked down, the cow was at the base of the tree. She was one mad mother! To this day, I can still see those two big bloodshot eyes, and the white foam dripping off that brown-black muzzle.

She kept circling the tree, tearing up the duff-covered ground with those two front cloven-hooves, making the dirt fly in all directions. Then suddenly she stopped, wheeled around, and ran back to her calf. Then back to the tree she came, her two ears stretched straight backwards in an unmistakable warlike position. She repeated this maneuver once again before she finally gave up, then calling to her calf, she slowly trotted into the tall timber.

I debated what to do; the cow and calf were between me and the camp, and the camp was a mile away, and I didn't have much daylight left. I couldn't park in this tree too much longer. And a tree is a poor place to spend the night.

What I needed was a smoke. I reached into my back pocket, but the pouch wasn't there. "Now what in hell did I do with my pouch?" I must have dropped it somewhere when I ran for the tree. I slid down to the ground and made a beeline to the rifle. If I was forced to use a bullet, so be it—God forbid. I found the pouch where the calf had been lying.

I didn't ponder the situation any longer. The key to my predicament was daylight; I needed every bit that was left. I levered a cartridge into the chamber of the Winchester and proceeded down the game trail towards camp. I was cautious. I didn't pass a single tree without wondering if it could be climbed. And then I remembered that I had another weapon; it wasn't as potent as a rifle bullet, but surely one that would cause any *sound*-thinking mother moose to head for far pastures.

I broke into song at the top of my voice, choosing the fourth verse of a song I had memorized back in 1925 called "The Wreck of the Old '97." I chose to repeat the fourth verse because I was able to give a much louder rendition of it than the others for some reason. And repeat it I did! By the time I reached the tent, I must have driven most of the wildlife out of the area, including the squirrels. Harry was cooking supper when I came in. He wanted to know if I was intending to become an opera singer.

"I believe you have a reasonable chance of succeeding, Friday, but you must learn more than one verse. There are only so many times an engineer can be scalded to death when his locomotive leaves the track."

I was still shaken, and Harry immediately sensed that something had happened. I told him about my skirmish with the cow moose. He seemed quite perturbed about the incident. "You likely made the right move, Al. If you had gone for the rifle, it would have meant a head shot or you would have been dead. Everything probably depended on that tree. For my part, I think I'd just as soon mess around with a bear. You should have had the dog along; the cow would have gone after the dog."

"I should have gotten the hell out of there when I first saw the calf!" I said.

I had no desire to waste any more time at the snye, and so I suggested that I make a three-day trip upriver in the hopes of finding fresh beaver sign. Harry agreed. In the meantime he would patrol the area east of the island. Liza and I left camp early the next morning. We were travelling light: she carried the axe, tea billy and fry pan; I had my rifle, tarp, and a couple of oilcloth bags (in case I shot a beaver) on my packboard, along with some meat.

On several occasions as we moved along the river bank, I saw flocks of ducks swimming near the water's edge. As we drew near they would quickly rise to find a safer place either up or down the river. These flocks were every bit as skittish as the ones that were to be found on the sloughs in Alberta. In any event, they had nothing to fear from us. I had no desire to waste ammunition on ducks.

I saw species of ducks that day, I never knew existed. The variety most prevalent seemed to be the Red-breasted Mergenser; there were dozens. The fan-shaped crest on the heads of these ducks easily identified them. Groups of Canvasbacks alternately rose and landed on the river as we passed by. Green-winged Teals flew low over the water, fast as fighter planes, as they wheeled and dodged the trees onshore. The King Eider were also present but in no real numbers. There was another species that seemed to keep to themselves on the far side of the river; they weren't inclined to associate with other ducks. (I learned later they were the Northern Pintails.) The common Mallards seemed to be in the greatest numbers, next to the Mergensers. There must have been a reason why so many species were gathering in this particular location. There appeared to be an extensive area of low-lying terrain between the river and the mountains to the south. Perhaps there was a marshland, a prominent nesting ground for migrating waterfowl in this region.

Early in the evening we came to a backwater of the Nahanni. At first I thought it was a snye, until I noticed there was no prevailing current, no sight of flowing water. Around a wooded bend in this stretch of still water, I saw a beaver dam that extended across this narrow inlet not far from its upper end. And back of the dam was just what I was looking for—a beaver house. Both sides of the inlet were covered by a dense growth of aspen poplar. It was a perfect location for a beaver colony. And what was of more importance, I spotted cuttings. They were fresh. Beaver had definitely been working in the area since breakup. Suddenly I heard an unmistakable slap on the water—the beaver's danger signal.

That settled it. Today's journey was over. Keeping well distant from the dam, I found a grassy knoll near a grove of pine—a perfect camp spot. Fifteen minutes later the water was boiling in the tea billy. I tossed Liza a few pieces of dried meat. She looked at the meat, then looked up at me in that woebegone manner she often displayed when she thought she was being ill-treated. It was an evening of utmost contentment for me, as I lay stretched out beside the campfire, drinking tea and watching the pine tinders exploding, one by one, above the flame. No siwash camp needed this night. No wood to cut—just a small fire of dead branches gathered close at hand. And no snow to shovel. Just spread the tarp out on nature's bed, pull the parka over your head, and fall asleep, dreaming that you are now in heaven—which in fact you are.

The morning dawn had given way to the sun's first rays, streaking in brilliant lines of light over the summit of the mountain skyline to the east. Curse me for sleeping in! This was a little late in the morning for beaver watching. I should have been out there two hours ago. I rolled out of bed in a hurry. No breakfast for me this morning. Ten minutes later I was lying out prone by the edge of the inlet about fifty yards from the house. I had tied Liza well back among the trees where she couldn't be seen from the water. Beaver are not slow in detecting movement along a shoreline. Near where I lay on watch, I saw an aspen hung up in the branches of a big balsam poplar—which proved that beaver don't always fell a tree towards the water.

I chided myself for not being on the watch earlier. Beaver are nocturnal workers; these occupants were probably all back in their lodge, having breakfast—or would it be their supper? I waited—and watched. And waited! How many minutes were there in an hour? If there were only sixty, they were the longest ones I ever endured. All I could do was stare at the murky brown water below, and wonder what my ex-girlfriend was doing right now (the one with the blonde hair who had been charmed by a stump rancher with a 1922 coupe). Then my eye caught a movement. I saw a bubble on the surface of the water. It was moving! A bubble moving in still water? How can that be? The bubble became a brown spot no larger than a twenty-five-cent piece, as it glided past. I aimed the rifle just below the brown blob and pulled the trigger. In the same instant a dark-grey paddle hit the water. "Slap!" The instinctive reaction was lightning fast—even in death. I grabbed the pike pole with its wire hook and pulled the dead beaver to the water's edge. The morning's hunt was now ended. There would be no more beaver coming by this spot for a few hours.

Back at our night camp, I began the operation of skinning my first beaver. I had carefully watched Harry perform the act on the other one I had killed. Beaver are difficult to pelt. Since the hunting knife must be razor sharp, it requires a certain degree of dexterity if one is not to end up with a punctured pelt. By heedfully following Harry's instructions, I finally finished the job, overseen by the watchful eye of Liza, who obviously was more interested in the meat than the fur.

A hot fire was soon burning in last night's bed of burnt-out coals, and fresh beaver meat filled the cast-iron fry pan. I tossed Liza several pieces, which she devoured in mid-air. I then put the remainder of the carcass in one of the oilcloth bags and hung it up in a pine tree some distance from the night camp, in case a bear smelt the meat. The pelt also went up in the tree in another bag. It wasn't long before the Canada jays found the camp. That meant I had to use my tarp to wrap securely both the carcass and pelt from the numerous intruders present, as well as the four-footed ones that might amble along later.

A full stomach, fur in the bag, and still well before noontime. What to do while waiting for the late evening watch? Just back of our camp, I had noticed a long, rocky ravine extending upwards almost to tree line on the south slope of the mountain. At that point there appeared to be a levelling off of the slope into a large plateau. I decided to hike up to the area; it appeared to be an easy climb, and would certainly give an excellent view of the upper stretch of the river.

I wasn't long on the incline before I realized that this wasn't going to be an easy stroll. Rock boulders waist high, and windfalls strewn across the narrow ravine were beginning to slow us down. I debated whether to continue. One careless step and I could by lying among these damnable boulders with a broken leg. And Harry wouldn't have a clue as to where I was. A rifle signal would finally lead him to me, but how would he get me back to camp? And what then?

Perhaps I should have listened to Liza. She was following behind, but not without protest. Liza was a smart dog; whenever we came to a really bad spot, she would simply stop. Period! And I would have to lift her over the windfall or boulders. Of course if one stayed in bed every day of one's life, one might live to a ripe old age, but it wouldn't be of much interest. So whether Liza liked it or not she was going to come with me up to the plateau.

Two hours of heavy slogging finally brought us to tree limit. Here the ravine widened out into a broad stretch of tableland covered with snow at a higher level, and finally rose into a series of rock gullies. We stopped for a few minutes at the head of the ravine, and when I looked down the incline, I realized that we had just ascended a dry creek bed. In a few more weeks it would be anything but. For those gullies (or small canyons) must have towered a thousand feet or more up the slope of the mountain, and when the warm July weather hit, there would be tons upon tons of meltwater flowing across this small plateau, into the ravine. When that happened one wouldn't know it was the same place.

At this time of year in the mountains, the higher one climbs, the colder it gets, and I was feeling chilly. Well, a fifteen minute hike up to the foot of those gullies would take care of that, and at that altitude above the tree line, I should have a view that would cover a sizable stretch of country. There was a heavy crust on about eight inches of snow still lying on the plateau, obviously wind-blown since the last snowfall; it was almost like walking on an asphalt highway.

Near the upper part of the plateau I found a number of sheep tracks crisscrossing one another. Sheep had been foraging here, as was evidenced by the many places where they had dug holes through the shallow snow cover to reach the dead grass below. We were making our way up the ridge of the nearest canyon when I saw three Dall's rams climbing out of a second canyon or rock gully. I grabbed Liza's collar and pulled her down below me as I crouched underneath the edge of the rim. The trio were soon joined by four other rams climbing in single file out of the same gully. This made a total of seven animals standing on the slope just below the rim. Here they engaged in several rounds of "horseplay," squaring off at each other in a series of comical, mock fights, staring at one another with horns arched high and feigning battle in their peculiar, stiff-legged maneuvers.

Suddenly one of the larger rams stood up on his hind feet and executed a perfect pirouette, then bounded down the slope. Part way down he seemed to lose footing; I saw him fall on his side and lower his horns into the ground, sending pieces of snow crust flying in every direction. Then seeming to use his lower horn as a brake, he came to a complete stop, then rose to his feet and turned back up the slope, proceeding in that same show-off, stiff-legged manner. Holding a respectable set of horns high in a haughty, superior manner as he rejoined the group, he seemed to say, "Now match *that* caper if you can!" I wondered: had that ram actually lost his footing— or was the display deliberate?

While I was busy watching the sheep, I had forgotten about Liza. I suppose she was wondering why I was kneeling there so long in one place, staring over the edge of the rim. So she decided to have a look-see. At sight of the sheep she began barking. Seven rams shot across that slope faster than I could blink my eyes. One of the larger rams was leading the herd as they galloped eastward into another gully. That was the last we saw of them.

I was wishing that I had the camera with me, but there were only three frames left on the roll of film, and I wanted to save them for the Virginia Falls on our way out to the mouth of Nahanni.

Up on the ridge I let my eyes wander over a sweeping, panoramic view which displayed an Alpine wonder that I would not soon forget. Down below, the river resembled a grey-green ribbon meandering out of the mountains in the west. My eyes, after much searching, finally picked out part of the backwater where our night camp lay.

Just as I was about to head back to the river, my attention was drawn to what appeared to be a cave, or a cavern in the east wall of the canyon. I decided to go down and investigate. After a fair amount of effort I was able to slide to the floor of the gorge, followed by an unwilling Liza. Near the entrance to the cavern I found the bleached head of a Dall's ram, frozen in the ice-covered ground. When I peered into the murky-looking cave I counted eight sheep heads—six rams and two ewes. The horn curls of the rams revealed they were of different ages when they died. All heads were bleached, and I had the impression these animals had been here a very long time. A few body bones were scattered about but the greater part of the skeletons appeared to be missing. Perhaps the odd, roaming bear had found this cavern.

Liza and I were back at our night camp by the river at the usual time for the evening meal. I missed not having my watch during these long days. It was harder to judge the time accurately. Just before dusk, I took up watch for beaver at the inlet near their house but saw no sign.

We were back at the Rabbitkettle the next day in time for an early meal. Harry had been watching at two separate beaver houses down-river from the tent, and had three pelts to show for his efforts. We now had fresh meat for awhile. We needed it, for Harry had discovered that the sheep meat had spoilt in the icebox. The Rabbitkettle refrigerator had been a complete failure. And so that sheep hunting affair of ours had been a *total* disaster that should never have happened.

I told Harry about finding the cavern in the gorge. It was his opinion that these sheep had come there to die of old age or because of sickness. "These caves are more numerous than you may think. They also serve as a place of refuge in bad weather for these animals." His explanation was reasonable.

Goodbye to Rabbitkettle

Our days at the Rabbitkettle were coming to an end. I remembered Harry saying that we should leave for Nahanni Village by the beginning of June or soon after. At breakfast that morning, I suggested we think about building our raft, unless we intended to swim out to the Liard.

"What's the date, Friday?" Harry asked.

Just to make sure, I reached up to the ridgepole and counted the notches. "It's the last day of May," I said.

"How can you be so sure of that? Friday could have made a mistake, you know."

"Friday almost never makes a mistake. I've counted the notches twice—all thirty-one of them," I retorted.

"Are you sure there are thirty-one days in May? I always thought there were thirty."

"Listen Crusoe! I can prove it!" I reached into my dunnage bag and drew out the dictionary.

"Why should I take Webster's word for it?" the high sultan asked.

"For the same reason that I always understood you went to public school. Tell me, Crusoe: what grade were you in before you were expelled?"

"Be careful, Friday! You are treading on dangerous ground, my fickle servant!"

145

"Listen Crusoe: Thirty days hath September, April, June and November. All the rest have . . ."

"Hold it! Hold it right there!" the sultan interrupted. "I now officially declare that we begin construction of the raft immediately—if not sooner. That's final."

Harry had wiggled neatly out of that one—as usual.

I had a number of pertinent questions I wanted to ask Harry about rafting the Nahanni River. I'd heard a thing or two about this tributary of the Liard, and naturally I harboured a few misgivings. I was aware of the fact that Harry had made a total of four trips up and down the Nahanni as far as the Flat River, but what about the area between the Virginia Falls and the Flat? I'd heard a few stories about that part of the river. One also had to remember that Harry and his partner, Milt Campbell, had made their trips in a canoe powered by a five-horsepower outboard motor. Harry and I would be negotiating over 200 miles (over 300 km) of *June* water on a log raft.

Considering my total lack of experience with *any* form of watercraft, and the fact that my idea of a raft was a wooden article that would float, a contraption that consisted of a few boards nailed across a couple of poplar poles, which had served to carry us school kids across the odd slough back on the farm, it is understandable that I might have some cause for concern. But after considerable thought, I deemed it prudent to conceal my ignorance for as long as possible. In any event I knew I'd learn soon enough.

After breakfast Harry outlined the plan of procedure. "We'll build the raft on a level spot, right here near the bank. Then when we've finished, we can just push it over the edge and slide it into the drink. It will be as simple as falling off a log," a favourite expression of Harry's.

Our main job was to locate five fire-killed, standing trees, from which we would cut the logs necessary for the raft. Had we been across the river we could have found the material close at hand, but on our side of the water, we had to search for nearly a quarter of a mile before we found suitable timber. "These logs must be straight and sound, and free of any sign of rot," Harry explained. After careful selection, we cut the trees into five logs, each measuring approximately fifteen feet long and not less than eight inches in diameter at the small end. Packing the logs into camp took longer than expected.

146

I prepared dinner while Harry assembled the logs into a compact unit, ready for marking the position of the crosspieces.

During the meal, a question came to mind. "Crusoe, how do we attach the crosspieces to the logs? Do we use babiche?"

The high sultan looked at me in feigned surprise, which also suggested a degree of disdain for my obvious lack of intelligence. "Friday, me boy! You must have been a Boy Scout at one time. I've heard they use ropes. . . . Babiche! I do declare! The raft would fall apart!" Harry raised his hand and pointed to our cache. "We shall use the triangular notch—the same cut that we used on those trees where the two crossbars are driven through. I should have thought Friday would have guessed."

Harry was right, of course. It should have been evident after helping build the cache. And I was aware that babiche stretches when wet. By using it, we would have had a raft of loose logs after a day in the water. On the second day we would likely have drowned.

"How did you know about the triangular notch, Crusoe, did you invent it? That's hard to believe."

"I never lie, Friday. A trapper by the name of Ole Lindberg showed me how to make that cut. He and his wife live down on the Liard. There would be more than a few men alive today, had they known about that notch. We will likely be seeing Ole and his family when we go down the Liard to Fort Simpson."

I think Harry could sense that I had a few apprehensions about rafting the Nahanni, and he knew it was important that any forebodings be dispelled at the onset.

"Friday, me lad, when we finish putting this vessel together, it will be strong enough to sail the Atlantic Ocean. Neither hell nor high water will tear it apart. I promise you. Rest assured that when you put your life in the chief sultan's hands, you will be as safe as a baby in its mother's arms."

After this piece of eloquent enunciation, it may have occurred to me that I really didn't have anything more to worry about.

A raft is built in much the same manner as a cache, described in chapter 2. Obviously there is more work involved in building a raft, even after the logs are procured. But this is partially offset by the advantage of working at ground level as opposed to exerting one's efforts twelve feet above the ground. Of course a higher degree of exactitude is required in the alignment of the notches (fifteen in all) in the raft construction.

The actual procedure was as follows: a "pilot" log was selected on which the first three notches were cut—one for the centre crosspiece, and one for either end. We made sure all five logs were tightly placed side by side on level ground. The alignment for the other notches was the key part of the entire operation. We carefully marked them off with the bucksaw, by using a length of my brass snare wire as a straight-edge. While Harry was busy with the notches, I went back in the muskeg swamp and selected three green tamarack trees from which the crosspieces would be cut. The shaping of these to fit snugly through the notches proved to be the most difficult part of the job—and one that would try the patience of Job. The grain of the wood of this larch tree is whorled, as opposed to being straight in other tree species, hence the fitting problem. Finally, after much trimming, we were able to drive each crosspiece into position.

The key factor in using the triangular notch is easily understood: when the raft is put in the water for a couple of days, the dry logs swell and the wood is expanded around the green crosspieces "tighter than a bull's ass in fly time," as the high sultan put it.

The following morning, June 1, we added a "superstructure" to our vessel. It consisted of six, two-inch poles laid lengthwise across three shorter poles (the width of the raft) which were firmly secured to the crosspieces with—of all things—babiche, no less. Harry didn't like using these moosehide strips, but they were all we had. We didn't want to cut my three-eighths rope into small pieces. That rope had been used for a number of things. Baling wire would have been the ideal requisite, as would a few pounds of nails.

This pole platform was a necessity. Something had to be added to keep our possessions out of the water, especially the fur.

At noon, the raft was ready to launch, and we did have spectators: a platoon of whisky-jacks occupied the choicest seats in the tree stadium—on hand to witness the Rabbitkettle's Event of the Year.

"We must christen this vessel, Friday. Have you any suggestions?"

"How about calling it the *Rabbitkettle Clipper*?"

"Excellent, Friday. It's so original. The *Clipper* it shall be."

"We could use our bottle of rum for the launch," I suggested. "I'll break it over the bow, as you begin heaving the raft over the bank."

The high sultan paused a moment, apparently in deep meditation as he casually stroked a grimy hand through his long beard. "That is a logical suggestion, Friday, but we should explore all alternatives. . . . Ah yes—I have it! We shall fill the tea billy with water and you can splash that over the *Clipper*. We have more water than rum." Harry waved an arm out over the Nahanni.

One final but important part of the entire operation before launching was to attach the three-quarter-inch mooring rope to the bow of the raft. Harry carefully tied one end of the forty-foot rope around the centre log, just back of the forward crosspiece. Then using short poles, we pried the raft over the bank and followed it down to the water. Five minutes later the *Clipper* lay in shallow water, moored to a tree on a lower part of the high bank, a few yards below the tent.

The most tedious job of all was the shaping of the paddles that we hewed from a green spruce tree. The big, double-bitted axe and the bucksaw speeded up the work somewhat, but it still took all afternoon to shape anything that remotely assembled a paddle.

As I was standing on the bank, gazing down on this "modern day" watercraft, a puzzling thought entered my mind: what position does one assume while paddling a raft. Do you sit, kneel or stand? Well hell, one would only stand if he were poling the raft *against* the current, near the shoreline (as with a canoe). I couldn't see any place to sit; the pole platform was only about six inches *above* the logs. (In marine terminology, I suppose they would have said "above the hull.") And if a guy had to kneel all the way from the Rabbitkettle to the Liard River, he sure as hell would need a pair of cast-iron knees. The more I mulled the situation over, the more perplexed I became. Well, no one wants to demonstrate total ignorance about something that should be obvious, so I decided to keep my silence and wait to see what position the high sultan took. Who knows—perhaps the proper position was to lie *flat* on one's stomach.

After supper we took the *Clipper* out on its trial run—I in the bow and Harry riding the stern, in the sitting position with his feet stretched out in front of him. Naturally, I followed suit, but I wasn't comfortable. I could see where this was going to take some getting used to.

We made several runs across the river to our old camp and back, and although the heavy raft didn't maneuver like a canoe, Harry felt certain that we could pilot our craft across a strong current when the occasion demanded. I soon learned that the bowman's job was much the same as being in a canoe—that of handling the mooring rope when tying up on the shoreline or wherever. But there is a difference: one needs a higher degree of agility, and damned good sense of balance on a raft. Just try it sometime on an angry river—but make sure you're sober when you do.

Later that evening, I asked Harry when he thought we would reach the Liard.

"If we leave tomorrow, we will be feasting on bacon and beans, fresh bread, strawberry jam, and chocolate bars not later than June 10. That's providing Jack Mulholland's trading post is well stocked with those items. That would leave us two days to build another raft at the Falls," the high sultan stated.

I crawled into my eiderdown, our last night at the Rabbitkettle, in a happy state of mind—yet with just a tinge of regret. How different it all would have been under other circumstances. Perhaps it was just a coincidence, I do not know, but during the night I dreamt I saw a three-ton truck coming down a gravelled road. It was loaded with hundreds of tins of Malkin's Best strawberry jam. I waved to the driver to stop as he drove past, but he just kept on going. It's strange how little feeling some people have for others.

Harry was still asleep when I made the fire the next morning. It was 5 a.m. by his watch—time for two river-runners to be up and about. As usual, the water pail was empty. Well, one more trip down the bank wouldn't be all that much exertion; from this day on, water was going to be mighty handy to reach. And plenty of it.

Just then I heard Nigger growl. Then there was the sound of heavy footfalls near the tent. I reached for the Winchester and opened the tent flaps. A big grizzly was settling down on his haunches, trying to lick the dried blood off the meat-cutting block. Finding this a futile effort, the bear rose to his feet and lumbered over to the drying rack. He sniffed the structure over for a few seconds, then casually reached up, and with a single swipe, the grizzly brought the rack to the ground. Then both dogs began barking. I fired a shot in the bear's direction, then sounded forth with a blood-curdling yell that must have shaken the boulders loose on Pyramid

Mountain. The bear made one mighty jump, scattering rack poles in all directions, as he loped off across the slough, then into the tall timber.

Harry came out of the tent in a hurry, holding the *.22 Hornet* at the ready. "What the hell happened, Al?"

"A bear in camp! He must not have liked the way you built the meat rack. It's a good thing I heard Nigger growling. In another half minute I would have been down the bank after water, with no rifle."

"It's a damned good thing it wasn't a sow with a pair of cubs!" Harry exclaimed. "I guess we should have pitched the tent farther away from the game trail."

"What difference would it have made, Harry?" I said. "There are meat smells all over the place. Anywhere you want to go. To be safe we'd have to be away from the river a quarter of a mile—and perhaps not then."

Harry agreed, but he was partially right—putting the tent smack on a game trail *was* asking for trouble. As for myself, I was glad we were leaving this place today. I had a feeling that bear might be back, because this camp fairly reeked with the smell of meat. And a hungry bear is a hungry bear!

Harry and I knew that this incident could have ended on a more serious note. Had the dogs been chained on the "river" side of the tent, they might have both been dead. It would have depended on the bear's reaction. These bears were not long out of hibernation and they were hungry. But men in bear country can only take so many precautions. The worst place a man can be is asleep in his tent when bears pay a visit. Reaction time is the key!

We ate our last breakfast at the Rabbitkettle under a note of surveillance, and while we were loading our gear on the raft, our rifles were always within reach.

Considerable thought was given to the manner in which all items were stored on the raft. The fur was packed in our dunnage bags, which we made as waterproof as possible. Vulnerable items such as tea and matches—and what little sugar we had—were put in empty tobacco tins, the lids of which were sealed with melted spruce gum. My camera, wrapped in one of the oilcloth bags, was put in my packboard knapsack, along with part of our tobacco and my ammunition. The axes and rifles were tied to the pole platform with short lengths of babiche. The bucksaw was placed underneath the platform. These were "survival items" and were secured where they could easily be reached. Harry and I also each carried twenty rounds of ammunition on our person, as a safety measure. The last item to go aboard was Mrs. Mulholland's packsack. The big tarp, off the cache, was now tied tightly over all, using the three-eighths rope.

"We will leave the tent standing with the flaps turned back. It belongs to Dalziel. He will be back sooner or later."

While Harry was chaining the dogs onto the raft, I pencilled a note on a piece of birch bark. It read:

June 3, 1937
We leave on log raft for mouth of Nahanni.
We have rifles, ammunition and two dogs.
Al Lewis. Harry Vandaele.

I then put the note in an empty tobacco tin and placed it up on the cache. It was time to go.

We pushed the *Clipper* out from shore and headed the bow towards the centre of the river. I turned to look back for the last time. There, upon the bank, standing boldly out in white, against the olive-green background, stood the lonely tent, rapidly receding out of sight as the raft hit the current. And through the tall spruce I caught a fleeting glimpse of the Pyramid Mountain in the west. Somewhere back there off the river, lay the remains of several siwash camps, and for a brief moment I felt the sting of those long, cold nights and the bite of the wind, howling through the trees. It was something to remember.

Nigger and Liza weren't too enthused about riding on the *Clipper*. Several times when the current brought us near to shore, both dogs would cry and whine, begging us to unsnap their chains so they could swim to shore. They just didn't want any part of this mode of navigation. It was much better (and safer) in the bush, having all four feet on terra firma as far as they were concerned.

I could understand their feelings. The only river craft I'd ever been in were canoes. Here we were *on* a log raft, which is about as foreign as one can get, positioned about ten inches above the water, with our legs stretched out forward on the pole superstructure.

Superstructure! Webster defined it as being a structure above another. Well, that was a logical definition as far as our craft was concerned. The word "super" was defined as a prefix meaning "above." And again, Webster was correct. I had thought that it meant "superior"— and that really had me confused. Well, it was true: we *were* sitting above the water—but not to any noticeable extent. And comparing canoes to rafts, I soon discovered the difference between the meaning of the prepositions "in" and "on."

By noontime I found myself actually enjoying this ride. It's an accepted fact that man quickly adapts to almost any situation, especially when there is no alternative. On a raft you either stand, or sit or kneel. Here we were, cruising down the river at seven miles per hour (Harry's estimate) seldom having to lift our paddles, just reclining on our buttocks, watching the trees on shore drift by. And nary a worry in the world.

"This is the life, eh Friday!" Harry called from the stern. "I wonder what the peasants are doing back home on this bright and beautiful day?"

"Likely busy cleaning the barn out," I offered. I thought of what my Indian friend had said about our plane ride to Fort Simpson on that stormy afternoon. And it was true: perhaps the *Clipper* wasn't as fast as the plane, but it sure beat backpacking on the shore.

Early in the afternoon we beached the raft on a sandbar at the head of a small island near the south shore of the river. Here we made tea and let the dogs have a good run. The afternoon was hot, more noticeable, perhaps, because of the much cooler temperature out on the water.

Several times I noticed Harry looking up into the mountains to the north. I knew what he was thinking: a few days like this one, will bring a lot of that snow-melt down in a hurry.

At 7 p.m. that evening, we put the raft into a snye near the right shore, and tied up on the low bank of a large island. It was a much better mooring place than the one we had at tea time, where we had to pry the *Clipper* off the sandbar. Here the raft was floating in dead water and quite manageable.

As in most of the snyes, there were many flocks of ducks landing then taking off when they discovered our presence on the island. It was a sparsely treed area consisting of low, marshy terrain covered with many grassy hummocks—a perfect nesting place for waterfowl.

Leaving Harry to make supper, I took the dogs for a run. I had the .22 Hornet with me, thinking I might be able to bag a duck, but of course the dogs would have precluded any chance of that.

Near a small pond, I suddenly heard the skirr of wings. Directly in front of me, a Mallard duck flew out of a hummock. And there it was in the tall grass: a nest containing five eggs. I gently placed each egg in my beret and slowly picked my way back to the campfire. One handles a find such as this with caution.

The high sultan took one look and reached for the fry pan. "By all the fickle fingers of fate! Friday has made a discovery more precious than gold! There shall be three for his highness and two for his devoted servant!"

"The hell you say!" I countered. "Don't be carried away just because we happen to be on an island. We will split that fifth egg. Forestood?"

"Whatever you say, Friday. Whatever you think is fair. I am not an unreasonable man."

"Perhaps we should have these eggs for breakfast," I suggested. "That's when people usually eat them."

"No, no, Friday, me boy! That would be taking too big a chance: they might spoil before morning."

Even in my teens I was always an early riser. There was something about the stillness of early morning that seemed to give me a feeling of exuberance, eager to discover what the new day might bring. And this morning was no exception. Out on the snye the utter calm and stillness was only broken by the swish of webbed feet as the odd duck landed on the water, or the occasional whirring of wings when they hop-skipped back and forth across the narrow snye.

When I stepped on the raft to fetch the breakfast water I realized how quickly this river could rise. Last night the water in the snye was almost languid, and now a visible current had tightened the mooring rope, pushing the *Clipper* parallel to the island shoreline. But the most noticeable difference was in the height of the raft; it must have been nearly two feet closer to the top of the bank.

At breakfast, when I drew Harry's attention to this, he said, "A rise of two feet during the night is nothing, Al. You will see the Nahanni climb one helluva lot faster than that when conditions are right."

"When are conditions right?" I asked.

"A combination of hot days and rainy nights. We've got high water on the way, Friday, me boy! I can feel it in my bones. Let's get the dogs on the raft and be on our way."

This was the first time that Harry had outwardly expressed his concern about the river.

As we passed the eastern end of the island, we gradually nosed the raft into the main channel. Once into the current, the rate at which the objects along the shoreline were drifting by, was a good indication of how fast we were moving. One would have thought the *Clipper* had shifted into a higher gear and pulled its throttle back.

"If we hold this pace we should reach the Falls early this evening," Harry called out from the stern. This was music to my ears. The sooner I could sample that fresh-baked bread, the better it would taste.

By mid-afternoon the valley widened, leaving the mountains in retreat, which slowed the current down to some extent because the volume of water could now spread over a larger area. But we were still drifting along at a mile-eating rate.

Two hours later, Harry called out, "Let's pull the raft over to the south shore. I have a feeling we're not far from the Falls. According to Faille there is a long straight stretch of river above the cataract. We'll pick a good place and tie up."

I had barely gotten the mooring rope around a tree trunk when I felt a trembling under my feet—something akin to a mild shudder. Then downriver we could faintly hear a rumble—like thunder in the far-off distance. It was a surge of sound that seemed to rise and fall in unison with the reverberation underfoot.

"Are you *sure* the portage trail is on the right side of the river, Crusoe?"

"Well it better be, Friday, or we will have some backtracking to do. That's where Dalziel said it was."

While Harry brewed a billy of tea, I took the dogs for a short run along the shore. And a short run it was. We ran into a mess of fallen timber and bog moss that would put an army obstacle course to shame. I didn't waste much time going nowhere.

After having tea, I climbed a tall spruce tree to try to determine how far we were from the Falls.

"There seems to be a bend in the river, about a mile from here," I called down. "I can see a grey cloud rising from somewhere back of the bend."

"That must be the spray from the drop that Faille was talking about down at Simpson," Harry said. "We'll keep the raft in close to the bank and work our way down to that bend. The old portage trail is near the bend, according to Faille—just above what he called the first chute."

"What's a chute?" I asked.

"Search me, Friday. The only chutes I know anything about are the ones they have at the Calgary Exhibition and Stampede, where the cowboys saddle the broncs in preparation for the bucking horse event."

"Well, I sure know that kind," I added. "I can still hear the announcer: 'Now folks, keep yore eyes riveted on chute number 3. Pete Knight will be coming out on Cyclone, the horse that nobody's ever rode.' Or was it Dynamite? I forget the name of the horse."

As usual, the dogs used every ruse they could think of to avoid boarding the raft, so we let them follow along the shore. As we were nearing the curve, the muffled rumble had increased to a steady, rhythmic thunder. And the louder the thunder, the closer we hugged the right bank. A hundred yards ahead, we saw tree-blazes that apparently marked the portage trail.

The dogs were waiting for us as we brought the raft up to the low shoreline at the bend. Liza had accepted this unusual, booming sound coming from back of the canyon somewhere, but Nigger showed his obvious excitement by staring in the direction the pounding thunder seemed to be coming from, and warning us with a series of low, guttural growls.

We stood there for a few minutes, watching the big, standing waves rolling across the narrowing canyon, pounding down to the north wall, then suddenly being forced into a sharp, ninety-degree turn. Here our vision was cut off by the right-hand canyon wall. Now it was easy to understand why Faille had used the phrase, "the first chute," for that was precisely what it was. The wide expanse of water at the bend could be compared to a Stampede "corral" which abruptly narrowed into the canyon or "chute," as it were.

Somewhere in that gorge, out of our vision, there was a lot of water taking a big drop! That was for sure. But the Falls could wait for later; at the moment there was work to be done. After our provisions were safely on shore, I helped Harry remove the superstructure. Retrieving the lengths of babiche proved to be a time-consuming job, requiring more than a little patience. When you have only a limited amount of anything in the Nahanni Country, you try to conserve what you have. We would need these strips of moose-hide when we built our second raft below the Falls.

We fed the dogs, then cooked our supper over a small fire at the water's edge at the bend. Later, we said goodbye to the *Clipper*. "It's a shame to see her scuttled," Harry remarked. "She was well built." Then he went to the bow and removed the mooring rope. We pushed the vessel away from shore and watched the current swing it sideways into the first wave. The big roller flipped the heavy raft over as easily as one would turn the page of a book. We saw the *Clipper* hit the north wall, then roll sharply to the right, out of sight.

After breakfast the next morning, we loaded our packboards, and with the dogs following behind with heavy panniers, we set off over a footpath visible only by the deep depressions made in the moss-covered terrain. We were likely following the least used pathway on the North American continent. A half mile of heavy-foot-slogging over mossy marshland brought us to the summit of a narrow ravine. It looked like it may have been an old creek bed at one time. Here we stopped and rested. It was plain to see that this steep decline wasn't going to be easy to negotiate with heavy packs.

There were old tree stumps on both sides of the steep ravine, among many cuttings that were made in recent years. These trees had been cut into short logs about three feet in length, and were evenly spaced across the bottom of the ravine. Many of the larger logs had been split in half and placed with their flat side down to prevent rolling.

I asked Harry how long ago he thought this skidway had been used. Some of the cuttings looked very old to me.

"Well we know for sure that some of the Klondikers laid those logs here in 1897," Harry said. "They brought their boats up this ravine. It's generally thought that only a few parties used this route from Edmonton."

"Did they reach Dawson City?"

"There's a lot of speculation about that. At Fort Liard, I was told that most of them died long before they ever reached the Yukon border. The odd one may have made it.

"As far as some of these cuttings are concerned, they could have been made before 1897. That's only forty years ago. There are stumps here a lot older than that, I would think. You have to remember there were men hunting for gold in the Yukon long before anyone had ever heard of Dawson City. And the Indians have surely used this route around the Falls from time to time."

"Would the Indians have used skin boats?"

"No doubt about it," Harry said. "The Hudson's Bay men vouch for that. But we white men like to believe we were here first. We don't even have any idea when the Indians built their first skin boats. You can bet it was long before we brought the canoe. We don't like skin boats because we don't know how to build them."

We soon discovered how steep this portage trail was. Part way down we had to lighten our packs. "Stumbling over these logs [they were crisscrossed all over the place] with an overload on one's shoulders, can lead to a broken back—or worse," Harry remarked. And I agreed.

By the time we reached the river, we realized the work that must have been involved when those Klondikers pulled their boats *up* this narrow incline. We rested awhile among the big boulders, gazing up at this huge waterfall and the cloud of spray that enveloped the big rock pinnacle in its midst.

We likely would have sat there much longer, had we not suddenly realized that we were wet—wet from the rain of mist rising and falling from the churning pool at the bottom of the drop. We shouldered our loads and began picking our way through an obstacle course of heavy rocks to drier ground downriver.

We hadn't gone more than fifty yards when I saw something that made my eyes blink. I wondered if I was seeing things: there was a green canoe sitting up on a ledge about five or six feet above the rocky shoreline.

"That looks like Faille's boat!" Harry exclaimed. "Let's go see." Except for a neatly folded tarp lying in the bow, the canoe was empty. On the flat surface of the bench there were dog footprints plainly visible. Close examination indicated that Faille had three dogs—the number that he always used on his excursions into the Nahanni.

"Where do you suppose he is now?"

"That's hard to say," Harry said. "He must have had a small canoe above the Falls, otherwise his paddles would be here. He's most likely exploring some creek upriver. Albert is a roamer; he could be anywhere."

So we were not alone in this Nahanni land, after all. I was disappointed in not meeting this man, since the opportunity had been so close. Harry had talked so much about him, and his exceptional ability as a river man.

After making a third trip over the portage trail, we finally had all our provisions stored above the beach on a moss-covered slope. We weren't taking any chances; we hoisted the dunnage bags containing the fur, and the two sacks of dried meat (we had consumed the third one) high in the branches of a nearby spruce.

Never before or since, have I traversed a rougher piece of real estate than that hundred and fifty yards of boulder-strewn beach between the bottom of the portage trail and our camp on the slope. It was torture. Harry nicknamed it the Rock Pasture.

Most of the rose-coloured hues had vanished on the mountain overlooking the Falls (now known as Sunblood Mountain) and the dusk of late evening had begun to obscure the rise of fog cloud above the Big Drop. Through the dim haze of mist, the outline of the pinnacle was still visible against the dark background of the mountain.

Time for tea. And then to bed in a mossy hollow—minus the spruce boughs, listening to the rumble and pounding thunder of Virginia Falls.

"Crusoe, are you still awake?"

"Of course I'm still awake; I just got into bed. Why do you ask?"

"I've been thinking—and wondering. How long do you suppose the Nahanni has been rolling over that drop?"

"Ever since water began running down hill," was the high sultan's answer. Way before Noah built the ark. You *think* too much, Friday. It's time we were asleep."

And indeed it was. The nights are short on the South Nahanni River in June.

As always, of course, I was the first one up next morning, and when I went to fetch the tea water, I noticed something strange about the beach: it didn't look near as wide as it had been last night. And of course, the river seemed a lot wider.

Harry was standing by the tiny fire I had made on a slab of rock, as I put the billy on the coals to boil. He was steadily eyeing the river, I took notice. "Looks like we have high water on the way, Al. We'd better get the raft built and high-tail it to hell out of here as soon as possible." It was plain that Harry was concerned about the situation. We didn't tarry long over breakfast.

Back on the slope, above the river, we finally located five suitable trees. They weren't fire-killed, but they were dry and sound, which was all that mattered. However, they were lying over a large area and were a considerable distance from the river. I suggested that I cut and skid the logs down to the water, using the mooring rope, while Harry shaped the three crosspieces. Harry agreed.

At six that evening—eleven hours after we had made the first axe cut—our second raft lay floating in the water, moored to a boulder on a rock shelf. Tomorrow we would attach the pole platform.

I was about to put the usual dried meat on to boil when Harry said, "I have a better idea." Thereupon, he climbed up on the rock shelf and began rendering another of his famous, Roman proclamations. It was comical to watch him act out these little dramas: "Now hear ye! Hear ye all! I now propose a feasting in lieu of tomorrow's maiden voyage of the *Nahanni Queen*. On this fair evening we shall partake of the largest bannock ever constructed at Virginia Falls. All in favour, raise your right hand."

I raised *both* my hands. "Carried!" the high sultan declared.

The baking of a bannock takes time, and as only one cook is required, I decided I'd take the .22 Hornet and try to locate a covey of ruffed grouse I had seen earlier in the day. Beyond the crest of the slope, I headed towards a grove of evergreens where these birds are usually found in the evening. Just beyond the grove, I came to a grassy knoll fringed with wild rose bushes that were now in their advanced stages of spring growth. Suddenly there was a fluttering of wings in front of me, and three grouse flew off and landed in the

160

grove of trees. Apparently, these birds had been feeding on last year's rosebuds.

Ruffed grouse are stupid birds; they almost invite themselves to be shot. (I, as a young boy, used to snare them by the neck with a length of copper wire tied to a pole.) In less than five minutes I spotted the birds, all three conveniently perched in the same tree. I picked off two with head shots, but I was low on the third; the bird was badly torn with a breast shot. It was always a mystery to me why spruce grouse (as we mistakenly called them back on the farm) didn't fly immediately when approached from below. Apparently they considered they were safe when they were up in a tree or high willow brush.

On the far side of the grove, as I headed back to camp I came upon a number of old stumps, the trees of which had been felled a long time before. These stumps were three feet or more in height, indicating that this had been a winter campsite. It was in a small, meadow-like area overgrown with dead grass and willow bush, and when poking about in the clearing I found nine logs placed side by side on the ground—some of them partially buried in the ground. They were all of equal length—about twelve feet—and had been cut with a two-man cross-cut saw. The intention had been to erect a cabin, there was no doubt about that. But if there had been two men here, which was likely, something had made them change their minds.

I spent another fifteen minutes probing around in the ground cover and found four rusted tin cans. That was all. I found myself wishing that I could determine the age of saw or axe cuts to any degree of accuracy. But such knowledge is only gained through long experience and close observation. The age of cuttings (I was to learn much later) depends upon a number of factors—mainly in what part of the country they are found and from what tree species. The degree of protection from the elements can be another factor. There are many others.

Back in camp, the dogs suddenly came to life when I approached with the grouse. Harry wanted to know if I had had to go all the way to the Rabbitkettle to get the birds. I told him what I had found. "Could that camp have belonged to one of the Klondike parties?" I asked.

"It's possible," Harry said. "It doesn't sound like an Indian camp. It's known that Klondike parties did winter in the Nahanni, but as I said before, there must have been other white men pass through this country. However, any assumption as to who cut those logs you found, would be pure guesswork—and we have enough of that in circulation." I knew what Harry meant.

I skinned out the three grouse, and divided the breast-shot one between the two dogs. Their portions disappeared in four seconds. Bones and all. The other two went into the fry pan. The bannock, turned to a golden brown, was a beautiful sight to behold. I made sure I witnessed the operation as Harry carefully cut this delectable creation into two equal parts.

"Hell's bells, Friday! We may as well splurge! Let's each have a tin of the butter to go with the bannock."

I was astonished! Was Crusoe out of his mind? One huge *pound* of butter to each! Unthinkable! But I had a thought that deserved a certain amount of contemplation: I knew I could polish off a can of butter at one sitting, easily enough. God! When was the last time I had had a taste of butter?

After we had finished the meal of a lifetime, Harry said, "It was a banquet for the rich! Our last evening at Virginia Falls is one that neither of us will soon forget."

For breakfast, we boiled the last of the rolled oats. I think we both realized that our paltry bit of "white grub" was about to be generously diluted with Nahanni River water before long, anyway. If there was any doubts about that, we only had to glance at the river across from our camp to figure that one out. Or listen to the thunder of the Falls which seemed to grow louder by the hour. The flat rock where Harry had baked last night's bannock was now completely submerged.

"I think we should check Faille's boat," Harry said. As an afterthought, he added, "We have plenty of tobacco; let's leave a can for Albert. I know he will appreciate it."

The water was only a foot below the stern of the boat when we got to the portage trail. We pulled the big canoe farther up on the ledge and tied both stern and bow securely to the willows, out of reach of any possible rise of water. We then put the can of Turret under his tarp. Harry seemed surprised that Faille had left his boat so near the water.

Now that we were back this far, we decided to climb up the cliff overlooking the main drop. From this vantage point, we had an unobstructed view of the "chutes" as Faille had called them. There were two, or possibly three smaller drops in a series of steps towards the main fall, as near as we could judge. I would have liked to have spent another day here, but we knew we had to be on our way.

"These chutes are different than the ones at the Calgary Stampede, Friday," Harry remarked. "Here, the gates are always open and the action never stops. And there is no admission fee; it's all free—each day and every day. That's what I like about the Nahanni; everything is free."

I wasn't sure that I agreed with this last statement, but I didn't comment. I didn't want to break this indescribable feeling that came over me as I gazed for just a few more times at the surging volume of water boiling over the Big Drop.

"Let's go, Friday," Harry called out, as he led the way back to the portage trail and over to our camp. There was much work to be done before we could leave.

Trouble on the River

When we finally had the superstructure in place, most of the morning was spent. The excursion up to Faille's boat, and the time taken to view the Falls from the high cliff had consumed at least an hour or more, but as Harry said, "I don't think it makes much difference at this stage. We will be caught in high water anyway! We will not beat the meltwater down. It's already on its way."

I had only to glance at the river to realize what he meant. Worried thoughts were running through my mind as I stood there, watching the surge of water rolling downstream. I didn't like the looks of that current. There was a lot of power out there. I was trying to remember the name of the author who wrote: "There is a tide in the affairs of men which taken at the flood, leads on to fortune. . . ." Well, we sure as hell were taking the right tide; where it might lead to was what bothered me.

There was another matter which gave me cause for concern: we had no life preservers and neither of us could swim. Harry soon put me straight about that.

"You needn't worry about life jackets, Al. Just stop and think about it for a second. If we lose contact with the raft, it's curtains with a capital 'C.' What good would it do to reach shore? All our essentials would be gone. You can't walk out of this country—not from where we are. No, we go where the raft goes—or we don't go at all!"

Harry was only stating the obvious—a fact. He just wanted me to understand what the situation was. He was simply "laying it on the line," as they say.

I made tea while Harry began loading the raft. Keeping the fur dry was going to be our main concern. We had no proper way of sealing our dunnage bags. But we did take extra precautions: we tied each bag and pack separately onto the pole platform, including the axes and rifles. Then, as before, we covered the lot with the big tarp. Nigger was chained aft of the supplies, while Liza's position was just behind me at the bow.

At 1 p.m. we were ready to go. One last look at the great cataract, then we pushed away from the rocky shore, into the rolling water. Down we swept, around the first bend, then into the narrow canyon (now known as Fourth or Five Mile Canyon). The only scenery I recall seeing through the entire five-mile stretch, was the vivid colours of the low, ninety degree canyon walls and the huge standing waves. I was no longer sitting on my fanny, gazing at the scenery; I was suddenly up on my knees, waiting for something to happen.

Riding on this stage of water was a different sensation. There was no sense of "drifting" down the river as before; all objects on either shore seemed to be moving at an unbelievable rate *towards* us. It was an eerie feeling. Like the dogs, I would rather have been on shore.

"There's rough water ahead!" Harry shouted. "Keep the bow heading straight into those waves!"

I didn't need to be told. They were coming, sure enough—big five-foot rollers!

When the first one hit, the *Queen* shuddered a bit, then shot straight through it, and the wall of water knocked me back against Liza, sending both of us against the mound of gear behind. Then two more waves hit.

"There's a big one coming up!" I heard Harry shout. It was more like a yell. "Keep the bow straight into it or we'll roll, sure as hell!"

Well what did he think I was trying to do? Hit it broadside?

It was instinct rather than thought, and at the moment before we hit, I suddenly turned on my belly and flattened myself out on the platform, holding the paddle in one hand and grasping Liza's chain with the other. I could feel the bow rise up on the crest of the wave, then plunge down in the trough below. When the raft surfaced I raised my head and opened my eyes. Harry had made the same move. He too, was stretched out, facing me. Nigger was already on his feet. He seemed to be able to react instantly to any situation. Liza had jammed her head between my legs. If the dog was seeking protection from me, she was sure making a mistake. I was too busy trying to take care of myself.

Well, we got through that one; now to get back into position so I could do something with the paddle—before the next one hit.

It couldn't have taken us more than half an hour to go through that canyon, but to me it seemed like a lifetime in which I had died at least once.

Out in the open valley, we went to work with the paddles. We had to; we were freezing. God, that meltwater was cold! All four of us were drenched to the skin.

During the next hour we really drifted. An onlooker would have thought we were in some sort of a river rafting race with a lot of money riding on the outcome, judging by the way we bore down on those paddles. But it was the only way we could keep warm.

We had been moving through open country since leaving the canyon, and except for the one time when we were passing a large creek that was pouring a lot of water in from the left shore, we were having no difficulty controlling the raft. But the clear sailing didn't last very long.

We were on a straight stretch of water when I saw a right-hand bend coming up about a half mile downstream. "I believe Hell's Gate is just around that bend," Harry called out. "There's supposed to be a portage trail on the right. Let's pull over to the shore and tie up where we can. We may have to portage."

"Portage," I called back. "How do we do that? Two men can't pack this raft anywhere."

"I know," Harry replied. "We will just have to build another one below the Gate."

Well, that was good news—nothing like learning how to use an axe. Cripes! We had just finished building the *Queen*. I was beginning to wonder how many we'd have to make before we reached the Liard.

Hell's Gate! That sounded like a nice name—very intriguing to the reader, perhaps, but a trifle formidable to me. Yes, I'd heard and read about that place. And here it was—presumably, just around that turn.

We weren't taking any chances. We hugged the right shoreline around the bend and steered the raft into a rocky shoal on the north end of the eddy. This brought us to a stop in a hurry, which was just what we wanted.

The clearly defined trail led us up to a high cliff overlooking the river's jackknife turn into a narrow gorge. From this lookout we had an aerial view of the course of the water after it hit the canyon wall directly below us. On the far side of the gorge, just below the turn, was a wicked-looking whirlpool—a surging piece of water, formidable to see.

Harry and I had never discussed Hell's Gate to any degree, mainly because all he knew about this place was what Faille and Poole Field, another veteran of the Nahanni, had told him down on the Liard. These men had put flat-bottomed boats under power through this gorge in low water. But this was flood time, and the only power we possessed was in the pull of our paddles.

Back at the eddy, Harry was of the opinion that we could run Hell's Gate, and he carefully outlined the plan of procedure: "We will track the raft back upstream as far as possible, so as to give us more time to cross over to the left side. The current will put us into the crest of the main rush of water. We have to keep on the crest until we reach that left point of the Gate. When we reach that low wall [he pointed to the north wall of the gorge] I want you to pull the bow into the gap."

"Won't that put us into that whirlpool beyond?"

"We will go into it, regardless," Harry explained. "We have to make sure we're not carried into that south wall. Sure as hell we will roll if we do, and then we could wind up in the eddy on this side. That would put us right back where we started—upside down."

Harry's plan sounded logical enough, and besides, I wasn't keen on building another raft.

Putting the raft into the centre of the current didn't present any difficulty and we made the right turn perfectly. I remember Harry shouting, "More to our left! More to our left! Pull her over!"

Well, I was on my knees pulling water as fast as I was able, wasn't I? I remember looking up to see a huge wave breaking against the south wall, then rolling backwards into the one following. This put a new fear into me—one that I never knew I had. I dug my paddle into the water with a reborn vengeance, but the *Queen* didn't seem to be moving over. Suddenly I saw daylight on my left. This meant we had reached the entrance to the gorge. I didn't wait for Harry's order.

"Pull the bow into the gap!" he yelled.

Well what the hell did he think I was . . . suddenly a curl of water rolled back off the wall and hit the bow at a right angle. It spun the *Queen* around as easily as one might brush a fly off the dinner table, forcing the raft off the crest towards the whirlpool below. This back-wash off the south wall was what "saved our bacon," as Harry admitted later.

I remember the bow dipping down in the water as I grabbed the mooring rope to keep it from sliding off the platform. It was always kept in a coil in front of me at the bow. Seconds later we were caught up in the merry-go-round, but the pool actually seemed smooth, as I remember. After half dozen circles, we finally managed to coax the *Queen* onto the outside of the boil, where the surging outflow carried us downstream.

Now that we were out in smooth water again (after a century) Crusoe called out, "By God, we made it Friday! Nothing to it eh, boy! You did a fine job—bringing the bow around. You couldn't have timed it better."

Nothing to it, my fanny! Just par for the course. If I had had a rock handy, I think I would have hurled it at his head. He knew damned well that I had nothing to do with the timing of anything. It was the backwash off the wall that did the timing. I was merely a pas-senger along for a *free* ride.

There was one virtuous thing to be said about Hell's Gate: it was aptly named. And my "living" death was brief, for we did come through in short order. And the ride did dispel any doubts in my mind about the talk of "life in the hereafter." Now I knew there was.

It was a relief to be riding in smooth water once again, until we reached another creek boiling down in the Nahanni off the north shore. We became turned around in the confluence. Here again we were lucky. We should have been over near the right bank of the river. And I should have been keeping my mind on the duties of a bowman, instead of gazing around. It's hard to imagine how I could have enjoyed the scenery, being soaked to the skin and cold. It was a nasty piece of water that should have been avoided.

By this time, Nigger and Liza had assumed the only position on the *Queen* that seemed to give them a feeling of safety: they lay with their bodies stretched flat out, and their heads resting between the poles of the platform—in a posture of resignation.

Apparently, Harry's Big Ben pocket watch had survived the Hell's Gate trip, for I heard him announce: "We have made good time, Friday. It's not gone five o'clock yet. We are nearing the mouth of the Flat River which comes in from the south just past that island downriver. We'd better cross over to the north shore and keep to the left of the island. There will be a lot of water pouring out of the Flat, and we don't want to be caught in the cross current. It might prove to be exciting."

That's just what we needed, I thought. More excitement. It had been such a boring afternoon.

Always, now, when circumventing a potential place of danger, we took the precaution of hugging the shoreline, so as to take advantage of the slower water. This practice however, contained an element of risk: around sharp bends, we could easily encounter a "sleeper" and have no time to avoid it. (A sleeper or "sweeper" is a tree undermined by floodwaters now lying out over the river with its roots still attached to shore.)

As yet, we hadn't had any trouble keeping clear of these overhanging trees, mainly because for the most part we had been drifting well out from shore. And here on the north side of the island, we had full view downriver, which gave me a chance to relax and observe the wide flow of water coming from the Nahanni's largest tributary. It was a light brown in colour, forming a distinct dividing line against the green water of the Nahanni. Obviously the Flat was in full flood—there was a lot of driftwood bobbing back and forth, rolling into the main current of the Nahanni.

"We have company!" I called out, as two big balsam poplars came floating by.

"We'd best stay near the left shoreline," Harry answered. "Keep your eyes peeled and the pike pole handy. We don't want to tangle with those buggers. We don't need their company."

This was beginning to resemble an army obstacle course under enemy sniper fire as I watched the two trees roll by, each trailing a massive set of roots. So a new danger began to take shape along with those we already had.

Well, at least we were in "Crusoe country" now. Since Harry had spent two summers up the Flat River, he must have seen his share of driftwood and overhanging trees. And the fact that he knew the Nahanni every stroke of the way from here to its mouth at the Liard helped to overcome much of my concern.

As for myself, I was beginning to learn a few things about a mountain river. I no longer wondered how driftwood islands were formed, nor what the force was that tore them apart.

And there was one thing certain: whatever the high sultan gave in the way of commands from here on in, Friday would obey them in haste, and without protest—until "death do us part." Primarily for the simple reason that Friday had no other choice.

Over the next hour more driftwood followed us downstream (we made sure we stayed ahead of it) but we had smoother water now and more room to maneuver.

"We'll camp for the night at Mary's River," I heard from the stern. "There's a good spot there with plenty of wood handy. We can tackle the Second Canyon in the morning."

There was that word canyon cropping up again.

We tied up on the right-hand shore near the confluence and prepared to make camp. The dogs went wild when we unsnapped their chains. They had had their fill of the *Queen* for one day, and so had we.

Harry began unloading the raft at once; I knew he was worried about the fur. I set to work building a fire which was designed to raise the temperature of the Nahanni country by several degrees. Thank God for birch bark, dry spruce, and the Kaschie lighter. One would have thought I was constructing my night fire on the Rabbitkettle trapline. We had been soaked ever since leaving the Falls and we were cold—even the dogs were crowding around the fire.

Harry came over when I had the tea ready. "Friday, me boy! I bring you good news. The fur is still dry! It's hot rums tonight, me lad. Which pack is the Governor General in?"

I suddenly came to life. "The bottle is in Mrs. Mulholland's packsack. It's wrapped up in that pair of woollen bloomers. How could I forget?" The dogs began cavorting around the fire and I resisted a strong impulse to join them.

We four were a happy lot that evening as we crowded around the fire. We didn't mind that supper would be the "usual." We had conquered Hell's Gate hadn't we? The worst was over and done with. Nothing more to be excited about. All we needed now was another shot of rum.

Harry squatted down by the fire and removed his water-logged moccasins. "What did I tell you, Friday? You can't *sink* or *swamp* a log raft! It's impossible. We've proved it today. We never had to bail a single drop of water out of the *Queen*; it sheds water like a duck's back. I'll tell you something, boy: the *Queen* is going to make history; our trip will revolutionize all further white water travel. You will see."

I had my doubts about Crusoe's prophecy—mainly because I was afraid I wouldn't live that long to "see" much of the future, considering what I'd *seen* this day. But I didn't wish to spoil such a persuasive speech that was intended to keep Friday's spirits up. I would most likely have used the same recourse had the situation been reversed.

And what Harry said was true: you cannot sink or swamp a log raft. But the main fault I found with our present mode of transportation was the same as I had from the very beginning: how *do* you ride a log raft? One would have thought I should have discovered the secret by this time. The high sultan seemed to favour the buttock position. But he was occupying the stern. How does one use the pike pole, sitting on his fanny, with his legs stretched out towards the bow? It's the same with the paddle; one is too far away from his work. The prone position, of course, is the safest; we both made that discovery five minutes after leaving the Falls. But it is not a popular paddling posture.

After supper I walked up Mary's River a short way, just to take the kinks out of my legs and bring my knees into proper working order again. It was a small waterway compared to the Flat, but in full flood now, it was carrying a sizable amount of water into the Nahanni.

There was a story about this river that I had vague recollections of hearing, and back at the fire, I asked Harry if he knew how this tributary got its name.

"It was named after Poole Field's wife, Mary Lafferty," Harry said. "The Laffertys are an old and well-known Metis family of Fort

Simpson. Some of the members were at Simpson before the turn of the century, I've been told. Poole is one of the old-timers also, and lives down at the mouth of Nahanni when he is not in the mountains somewhere, searching for gold and trapping in the winter. He was in the Klondike in the early days after the gold rush, and spent some time across the Divide on the Pelly and Ross rivers in the Yukon. He and Mary travelled with the Slavey Indians most of the time, and they often camped here at the mouth of the river.

"There's a sad story connected with this place, Al," Harry continued. On one of these occasions—I believe it was the spring of 1921—Poole and Mary, and a party of Indian hunters had just returned from a winter's trapping back in the mountains. They were waiting here for the Nahanni River to lower.

"According to Poole, the young girl in the party—a cousin of Mary's, whose name was May, had not been well for some time. Very often she appeared to be quite depressed and wanted to be back with her folks at Fort Simpson. One day she disappeared and was never seen again. Poole and several Indians in the party set out to search for her. These Indians knew a thing or two about tracking and soon picked up Mary's trail. They followed it for more than a week until they lost all sign. They finally had to give up the search and return to their camp. Milt and I met one of the trackers in 1935. His name was Diamond See. We may meet him down on the Liard this summer."

This was Harry's story and a sad one indeed. It had happened in mid-June of that year, and one could imagine the torture that girl must have gone through, fending off hordes of mosquitoes, as she struggled through dense bush, over the creeks and high cliffs. Sometime later one of the creeks was named after her, as shown on the maps of today.

It would have been a terrible end for any human being to endure, to say nothing of what it must have been for this poor girl, steadily losing her strength *and* her mind.

There were dark clouds rising over the mountains in the west, abruptly reducing the usual long hours of daylight on this June evening. There wasn't enough breeze to rustle the leaves on a quaking aspen tree. And now, as the rain threatened, the mosquitoes began invading our camp.

Mary's River—at its mouth, at least—possessed the main ingredients required to produce a mosquito haven: moisture and moss, nurtured along by the right amount of June heat. The moss in our camp must have been a foot deep, which soaked up water like blotting paper, resulting in a perfect breeding ground for these hungry pests.

Another look at the sky brought instant action. We quickly spread the big tarp between two trees, making a hurried shelter lean-to where the fur and packsacks could be kept dry. There was plenty of firewood lying about and we soon had enough of that under the canvas to last the evening out. They were a determined lot, these mosquitoes. I believe they thought they were going to have a banquet at our expense, but a big fire—and what was turning into a steady rain—soon put an end to their persistent efforts. As Harry so aptly remarked: "There's nothing like fire or rain to stop the little bastards."

We had much to talk about, here at Mary's River. For only a dozen miles away, to the west, lay the valley of the Flat River where Harry and Milt Campbell had prospected during the summers of '34 and '35. Harry had mentioned very little about these two seasons, and even less about last summer's excursion on the Liard, where he and Milt had brought in an expensive pumping outfit to wash for gold on the Liard, or one of its tributaries. I never did get the exact location. Harry was a man who found it extremely difficult to admit defeat—in any endeavour he undertook to take. Failure was a foreign word to him, and he didn't talk much about his hunt for gold.

And as we sat there in the moss under the fly-cover, keeping the fire stoked, and watching the steady drizzle, there were so many questions that came to mind about his sojourn in the Flat River country— this part of the Nahanni country of which I had heard (and read) so much about. There were questions that I knew Harry would answer in a straightforward manner, sans all the current mystery and sensationalism that had been bandied about for so long.

"I know you mentioned it during a poker game we had at our farm during the winter of '35, but I have forgotten. Just where were you and Milt prospecting on the Flat?"

"We were about seventy miles up the river. Most of our sluicing was done on Borden and Bennett creeks," Harry said. The two streams are about two miles apart."

"Did you have any trouble getting up the river?"

"No problems that I remember. Milt and I had the eighteen-foot canoe and two five-horsepower, outboard motors—the same outfit we started out with from Fort Nelson in '34. We did have trouble with one of the kickers; we should have thrown the damned thing in the drink."

"I've been told there was a gold rush up the Flat in 1934. Was that just newspaper talk?"

"Well, you couldn't call it a stampede. Milt and I staked some claims on Bennett Creek, and there were several two and three-man parties working in the area—mostly trappers from the Liard. In '35 there were men prospecting on both Ervine Creek and the Caribou. I think everybody and his brother staked on McLeod Creek. It's just downriver from Bennett a short distance."

"Is that the creek where the McLeod brothers were supposed to have found gold?"

"That's the one. That's where all the B.S. began."

It wasn't hard to detect the note of cynicism in Harry's answer. It was a statement well taken and I knew he meant it. Harry and Milt—like dozens of others—had bought those tall stories of the early Thirties, stories that grew taller by the telling.

"Yes," Harry continued, "there have been men looking for gold on McLeod Creek ever since the Klondike days, and the boys are still hunting for it back there. Gus Kraus and Albert Faille were sluicing for gold on Bennett Creek just last summer. Faille has been up nearly every creek that empties into the Flat River. He knows that river by heart. He has several cabins up there. Milt and I stayed in one of them at Ervine Creek for two days in 1935."

"Do you think there is any gold in that country?"

"I have no idea and I don't much care. I think Milt and I found about two ounces during the two summers. Hell, we could have washed gold on the North Saskatchewan River west of Edmonton and made a couple of dollars a day. There were guys doing it."

There was an unmistakable bitterness in Harry's words, and I found myself wishing I hadn't mentioned the gold at all. I already knew their search had been futile. I should have chosen my questions with a little more tact. No one takes pleasure in reminiscing about his three lost years of hard labour.

Then suddenly—to dispel despondent thoughts of the past, I suspect, and to put himself in a better frame of mind, the high sultan issued an order. Actually, it was a request, rather than an order: "Friday, me boy! Would you determine the amount of Governor General rum there is left in that bottle, then kindly report back to his highness at your earliest convenience." I made a quick dive for Mrs. Mulholland's packsack. "It's more than half full," I announced.

"I want the truth, Friday!"

"Well, you be the judge, then." I held the bottle up for his inspection.

"Your judgement is extremely accurate, Friday. I'm sorry. I should have known you would never lie to the sultan. Kindle the fire. We shall have a hot one—or perhaps two. It looks like we're in for a wet night."

It was easy to read Harry's thoughts: if this rain lasted for a couple of days, and was covering a wide area upriver, we were going to be caught in water that we may not be able to handle.

Ever since prospectors or trappers have gathered together around their campfires, these men have rehashed the ongoing stories of the day. And on this dismal evening, Harry and I were no exception.

Being, at the moment, in the area where other depressing stories had originated, it was inevitable that the name of Martin Jorgensen should come to mind. Mainly, perhaps, because his death also involved Poole Field.

Jorgensen and Field had been partners on the Ross River on the Yukon side of the Divide prior to the First World War. Rumours of the gold strike by the McLeod brothers (presumably) had drifted into the Yukon, and in about 1912 or so Jorgensen went up the Ross and over the Divide to the headwaters of the South Nahanni, his destination being the Flat River country. Sometime later, Field received a letter, brought by an Indian from Jorgensen, saying that he had found gold and wanted Field to join him. Poole set out in 1915, following Jorgensen's route over the Divide, and located his burnt-out cabin near the mouth of the Flat River. His bleached bones—or what was left of them (according to Field) were scattered about the area. His rifle and axe were found nearby. Apparently Jorgensen had sent a map along with the letter, showing the location of his cabin. This was the story that I had heard from Harry's brother Joe.

Harry reached for his tin cup and took a hefty swig of rum, then offered a few pertinent remarks. "There are numerous versions of the Jorgensen story, Al. I haven't had the opportunity to discuss the case with Poole. But others have, and from what they've told me, Poole would have had to have given a different story to each. Poole is not the sort of man to make up stories out of thin air. The different accounts I've heard simply don't add up."

"Your brother Joe believes that Jorgensen may have met with foul play," I said.

"Listen, Al! Every death in this country has been put down to foul play by somebody or other—or implied as much. As I said before, Joe wouldn't go out of his way to spread rumours, but he's inclined to believe anything he hears about these cases.

"We know that Martin Jorgensen died near the mouth of the Flat River. And that's all. Poole found his skeleton, but Jorgensen obviously died months before that. Any possible clues as to the real cause of his death would have long vanished. Within a week after Jorgensen died, the bears—or wolves—would have changed any evidence considerably."

"Tiny Gifford mentioned something about a man named Angus Hall who died up here on the Flat. What do you know about him?"

"Hall disappeared eight years ago—almost to the day," Harry explained. "He and two other men came in from Fort Nelson in the spring of 1929. They were headed for McLeod Creek. Where else? Everybody, before or since, has made that creek their destination. Anyway, Hall's party ran into high water on the Nahanni. So they left their boat at the mouth of a creek somewhere downriver from here, and decided to walk overland to the Flat. As the story goes, Hall was dissatisfied with the progress the three were making after a couple of days, so he struck out on his own through the bush, leaving the other two to follow."

"It was a number of days before Hall's partners reached McLeod Creek, and when they did, there was no sign of Angus Hall. It's a cinch nobody will ever know how he died—or where, for that matter. This is a big country. Milt and I were never able to determine for certain the creek where the three men left their boat—not that it matters."

Harry uncorked the bottle of rum and poured himself what I

thought was a stiff drink; I was a keen observer in those days. He handed me the bottle and I poured out what I *knew* was a stiff drink. The rain was beginning to come down with some authority now, and our fire, which was only protected on one side, began to sputter and smoke. But we were warm *inside*, thanks to Dalziel.

As the evening wore on, I remembered another life that the Flat River country had taken. I had heard the details from Harry himself, when he and Milt had returned to the farm in Alberta in mid-November of 1934.

In the fall of 1931, Phil Powers, a veteran Northerner from the Liard, had gone into the Flat River country to trap. When he hadn't returned to Nahanni Village by late fall of 1932, a search party consisting of two RCMP constables, Poole Field, and Albert Faille went up the Flat River to investigate. They found his skeleton lying in the ruins of his burnt-out cabin at the mouth of Ervine Creek, which is about fifty-five miles (eighty-eight kilometres) up the Flat.

"There was also a lot of speculation about how Phil Powers died," Harry remarked. "I heard conflicting stories about his death at Fort Simpson. There is always these mysteries attached to the deaths in the Nahanni."

"I don't understand why there should have been any confab about Powers," I remarked. "Four men reported what they found. If he died in his cabin when it caught fire, what was the mystery?"

"I agree," Harry said. "Cabins *do* catch fire. Powers could have come in off his trapline one evening, cold and dead tired, put on a big fire, and fallen asleep on his bed. A rusty stove pipe could have caused the fire. Or a dozen other reasons. He could have been sick, or hurt, and not able physically or mentally to look after the stove properly. It's as simple as that. There are plenty of reasons why cabins burn."

As for my own thoughts, I deemed it more than likely that Jorgensen's death stemmed from the cabin fire. And the same could be said of Mulholland and Eppler.

I recalled what Tiny Gifford said that evening in his cabin at Fort Simpson: "And be careful of fire; it's your worst enemy in that country." How true. I also remembered Harry mentioning something about being careful about using a candle in the tent at the Rabbitkettle. "There was an old trapper at Fort Resolution that lost his only shelter that way, in the middle of the winter." Yes, it was also true: even experienced men can be careless in the bush.

It was still raining the next morning when we crawled out from beneath the tarp. Our breakfast was later than usual, due to the extra time it took to hunt up dry wood. I finally cut down a dead, standing spruce and sawed it into firewood chunks underneath the tarp. I had learned that trick (if it could be called a trick) on different sojourns in the foothills back home.

I had had a restless night under the lean-to, trying to keep dry. And I also had some unpleasant thoughts.

"Crusoe! I had a bad dream last night!"

"You did? And what was the dream about? Don't tell me—I already know: your girlfriend ran off with some character from Caroline, and now she's pregnant."

That brought a measure of amusement on this wet morning. "No, nothing of that nature," I said. "I dreamt we both fell asleep on the raft and lost our paddles."

The high sultan mulled that over for several seconds, then said, "Yes, I must admit there is a definite possibility of that happening."

"Well, we don't have any spares. What do we do when we wake up?"

Neither of us could answer that question, and so we spent a wet day carving out two extra paddles. It was something that should have been done before we left the Falls. Aside from the dream, I suspect it was the ride through Hell's Gate that motivated the decision to make the spares.

As we were making ready to leave the following morning, it looked as if the *Queen* had found a new mooring place during the night. The river must have risen at least three feet during the past eight hours. The Nahanni was on a roll—that was plain to see.

When we drifted out from shore, the dogs were still on their feet, eyeing last night's camp. Had we unsnapped their chains, they would have immediately swum to the bank.

There was plenty to think about as we swept into the western entrance of the Second Canyon. (On modern maps this section is now called Third Canyon; the canyons are numbered one to four as one travels *upstream*.) The rain had eased to a drizzle but the heavy over-cast threatened more to come. I wanted to look up at the sloping canyon walls and try to remember a few of the sights that were here to be seen, but always there was driftwood following close behind us, and always a lonely tree trailing the *Queen*, looking for companionship on its way down to the Liard—if it didn't get hung up on some island.

And then there were the sleepers. If we ever ran into one of them, it would be "goodbye Charlie." We were trying to keep that from happening by keeping the raft out from shoreline, staying away from the outer perimeter of the wooded bends where the main current was undermining the banks, and bringing trees into the water. But this was easier said than done. The *Queen* wasn't responding to the pull of the paddle as before, and it was plain that we didn't have full control over the raft. We simply didn't have enough power to overcome that of the current. And we sure as hell tried! There were times when I felt my arms growing numb from pulling the full blade of the paddle against the force of the current when trying to bring the bow around. The man in the stern wasn't shirking either; I could feel the *Queen* quiver with every stroke that Harry made with his paddle. The high sultan was a strong man!

Two hundred yards downstream, I saw a canyon wall looming up out of the overcast. We were approaching a sharp bend in the river and were heading straight for the wall. I shoved my paddle between my legs and reached for the pike pole—just barely in time to push the raft back from the wall. The backlash of a big wave hit the bow and swung it into the surging current, as gently as you please. It was as if we and the river had rehearsed that maneuver a dozen times, earlier.

"Nice going, Friday! You timed it just right," Harry called from the stern.

"Nice going, my arse! I thought, as I put the pole back in its slot and grabbed the paddle. What really annoyed me was when I turned to look back, and there sat his highness, hardly touched by a single drop of water, except from the sky drizzle—and here was I, in a desperate crouching position at the bow, soaked to the skin. Now I knew why novices were always installed in the bow of a boat. They could be compared to the people in the passenger seat of an automobile in a head-on collision; they usually came out second best.

During the next hour, the Nahanni decided to give us a break; we enjoyed clear sailing—but not for much longer. Harry suddenly called out: "We are coming to The Gate! Better have your pole ready. There's another bend to the right!"

The Gate? I thought we'd already been through The Gate. Then suddenly I saw a torrent of water rolling into the Nahanni on our left. Another creek in flood, boring a path through boulders and loose gravel—a perfect example of the power of water pouring out of the mountains. But this one was a godsend: the heavy, incoming flow brought the bow of the raft around the ninety degree bend, into The Gate, almost in mid-stream.

I heard Harry mention something about Sentinel Rock (now known as Pulpit Rock) being on our left, as we rounded the bend. But I don't recall seeing it. As a matter of fact I don't remember seeing much of anything while going through this part of the Second Canyon. I was too busy watching the water ahead. I wasn't interested in the scenery. Harry told me later that he and Milt camped near the Rock several times on their way to and from the Flat River.

There was a breeze blowing through parts of the canyon, which produced a strong degree of undulation on the water, and on the straight stretches of the river the *Queen* rose and fell in perfect unison with the motion of the current. It was a gentle, soothing motion—if that can be believed—which tended to take one's mind off what may lay ahead. Which was just as well.

"We're really drifting now, Friday. At this rate we should be in Dead Men's Valley by the middle of the afternoon. It's about fifteen miles away, I reckon."

Well that was good news. I was wet and cold and just wanted to see the end of this canyon. Like the dogs, I felt much happier with my feet firmly planted on mother earth.

Sure enough, another bend was coming into view. The river seemed to be wider here, and we weren't anticipating any trouble making the right-hand turn. But we did err in judging the force of the current. We tended to equate the power of the current by its speed, rather than its volume. It's a common fallacy attributed to the inexperienced raft runners, as I was about to learn.

To start with, we were much too close to the left side of the river when we tried to make the turn. The raft did not respond to our paddles, and the bow refused to come around. I put the pike pole into action and managed to push the *Queen* back from the wall, but we were now at right angles to the flow of water, and we hit the first wave broadside. The raft rolled upside-down without the slightest bit of hesitation.

I remember grabbing the high log of the raft as it rolled. When I looked around, I saw that Harry must have made the same move, for we were both on the top side—and we each had our paddle. We couldn't have pulled that feat off again in a hundred years. The dogs were still in the water, pawing frantically, trying to pull themselves back on the raft. Thank God their chains were ten feet long; both dogs would have drowned had they been short-tethered.

In that one, short moment, I'm sure we both acted by a common instinct to survive by reaching for the highest part of the raft above the water at the right instant. As Harry had said on the morning we left the Rabbitkettle: "Come hell or high water, we go with the raft or we don't go at all." The fact that neither of us could swim, had no bearing on the situation whatever. Not in the least.

I remember being bewildered (if that is the proper word) by realizing that I had nothing to hang onto except Liza's collar, and my paddle. It finally dawned on me that the end of the chain I really needed was "down under"—somewhere in Australia.

The *Queen* was barren! No superstructure! No nothing! Everything was underwater except two dogs, two men, and two paddles. I felt like a naked person kneeling on five moving logs. It was so unreal it could not have happened.

There was no panic, no shouting out there as we floated down the centre of the canyon.

There was the fear of being swept off the raft during the first few seconds, but there was no time to dwell on that: I had to get that mooring rope. That meant letting go of Liza's collar. Holding my paddle underneath me with one hand, I crawled to the bow with the other and reached beneath the centre log until I found the forward crosspiece where the rope was tied. Now it was pull, pull, hand over hand—forty feet of it. Then I felt Harry's hand grab my belt from behind. Now there were two of us yanking on that rope. It was a precarious situation for both of us, lying flat out on the logs, until we could bring the rope back to the stern where Harry secured it to one of the logs. We now had something to hang on to, leaving about twenty feet of rope left for mooring this outfit to we knew not what.

181

I thought about the big tarp. We had taken pains to tie it down securely to the superstructure. If it held there was still a chance for us, for even though each bag was tied down individually, in our situation any sort of cover was bound to help.

This raft had to be stopped one way or another. And soon. But it was easy to act on impulse. Whatever move we made had to succeed.

Then Harry called out, "We'll ram the raft up on a gravel bar. The first one we come to. It looks like our only chance."

A few minutes later, I heard him say, "It won't work out! Forget the gravel bar! We might tear the superstructure off—going at this rate. Then we could lose everything. We have to keep the raft afloat and try for either shore."

"There's an island ahead of us," I shouted. "If we put the raft into that snye we'd at least be in slower water."

"Let's try it, Al. Let's keep to the right-hand shore."

But I was wrong: it wasn't an island that lay ahead, and we were not in a snye. We were in a backwater. A backwater! Luck was with us when we really needed it. Now the *Queen* had suddenly slowed down, and as we approached a grove of trees, we were only moving at about two or three miles an hour. Our relief was unbelievable!

Unknowingly, we were reaching what was to be the best "beach" (in our circumstances) that we could ever have hoped to find. Now we could stop this outfit among the trees and still be totally afloat. If we had opted for a gravel bar, and even been partially grounded, we would have run into all kinds of problems.

Harry was crouching at the stern, now, as we glided into the poplar trees, and had already loosened the mooring rope at his end, to give me slack at the bow. The *Queen* hit one of the trees with a thud and I put a loop around it in short order. This brought the stern around against another tree and Harry lost no time in securing it. It was so incredibly easy—pure and simple luck. Luck spelled with a capital "L."

We stood there for a moment, leaning against our respective trees, with the raft jostling about under our feet. Then, with obvious relief in his tone of voice, Harry said, "Turn the dogs loose, Al, then get the axes and the rifles. I'll hold the raft steady. I think we're in about three feet of water."

I shoved my paddle into the water. "I make it closer to four," I said. Nigger and Liza lost no time in swimming to higher ground—anywhere away from water. And that's where I wanted to be as soon as we had this mess under control.

I thought I knew where every item was tied, but the raft was upside-down now, and I had to adjust my thinking. I found my .30-.30 rifle first and cut it loose with my hunting knife. Now where the hell was my axe? I remembered putting the big axe aboard and quickly retrieved it. Finally, after God knows how long, I had the three axes and rifle on top side. The tree at the stern prevented me from reaching the .22 Hornet, and we had to move the *Queen* backwards a foot or more, which also took up time. The dogs had found the best spot available. It was a small knoll, just above the poplar grove. Now to get the key items on dry land above the overflow.

We were working in the water above our navels and it took us more than an hour to put our supplies up on the knoll. Harry had the tricky job: once the big trap was opened, and the babiche line was cut, he had to feel for each bag, separately, making sure that none were lost. During all this time, he had to put up with the raft jostling about: the overflow was still coming in.

As for me, I must have made about ten trips through that water jungle, tripping over submerged trees, through hollows which brought the water up to my breast in places before all bags were on dry land.

As I write these words, fifty-eight or more years later, I recall my advanced training in the Canadian Army in 1944. The Army thought it had an obstacle course second to none. A few of our high-ranking officers should have witnessed our eighty yard, water jaunt through that submerged poplar grove in 1937.

God, that water was cold! Flood water from high elevations always is. But standing there on the knoll, staring at our worldly possessions—and Nigger and Liza watching every move we made—was more than worth the effort.

What I needed now was a smoke. I reached for my leather pouch, but the papers and tobacco were wet. "Damn the luck, anyhow!" I exclaimed. Harry saved the rest of my day: he handed me his multi-folded rubber pouch. Three summers in a canoe on Nahanni and

Liard waters, had taught him a thing or two about keeping tobacco dry.

Then Harry gave me the bad news: the fur was soaked! It came as no surprise. How could it be otherwise? The entire outfit had been underwater for so long—at least two hours or more? I couldn't remember. It was more like an eternity since we had rolled that raft over.

Now there was work to be done. A fire had to be built—right pronto—and plenty of wood gathered from somewhere. Harry wasn't sure whether the fur could be dried out or not, but we were determined to try. And there was the dried meat to think about. It had been stored in two gunny sacks, which would shed water about as efficiently as a wide-meshed sieve. Consequently, the meat was a soggy mess.

Well, it was one job at a time, so we covered the fur and meat with the big tarp to provide a certain measure of protection from the flies, then we both went to rustle wood. We finally found a few dry spruce back of the knoll, and here I began gathering fuel while Harry built a makeshift drying rack.

The sun had broken through the overcast and the afternoon heat began beating down on the knoll. The sudden warmth was beginning to dry out our clothes, saving us the trouble and time of removing them. But the sun was a mixed blessing: it brought those blue bottle flies to the meat and fur in a hurry—as steel is drawn to a magnet.

How do you dry out wet fur above an open fire? We tried every way we could think of. The fire had to be dampened with moss to prevent the flames from singeing the pelts. This resulted in less heat—and intense heat was what we needed. Actually, all we had was a big smoke smudge, but it did serve to keep the damned flies at bay. The "cased" hides gave the most trouble. The "fur" side acted as an insulation, preventing the heat from reaching the "skin" side to any degree.

Something now had to be done with the meat. The flies had found their way under the tarp. Leaving Harry to the fur, I hit upon an idea: I'd build another fire, and I would roast those goddamn flyblows in a hurry. That I would!

No sooner said than done. I filled the large cast-iron skillet, along with our two smaller ones, with as many pieces of meat as each would hold, and placed all three directly over the flames. Turning the meat piece by piece in each pan was time-consuming, but it worked. The only change to the meat was its colour; instead of the usual, brown murky shade, the strips were now a dirty black—just as unpalatable as ever, but still food to a hungry man. The dogs provided a reliable indication of the condition of the meat. When they smelled the stuff "cooking" over the fire, they came over to investigate. I tossed a piece to each. It must have taken them all of ten minutes to muster up enough courage to tackle the filthy looking strips. Hunger will overcome any degree of revulsion—be it in man or beast. By late afternoon, I finally had the meat dried and the sacks hanging in a tree.

All the work seemed to come at once. There were the rifles to be cleaned with the Neatsfoot oil—as soon as I could locate the bottle. The only items that hadn't gotten wet were the tobacco, matches, and tea (all stored in unopened and empty tins) and my camera and dictionary, which were wrapped in two oilcloth bags. Our four Kaschie bullet lighters, which we always carried on our persons, all lit at the first turn of the flint wheel—which proved the wilderness-worthiness of these lighters.

There were our packsacks containing what few clothes we possessed, which had to be hung out to dry, item by item. Mrs. Mulholland's pack took considerably longer. There were some valuable pieces of clothing there, and I took some pains with its contents. I thanked my lucky stars that I had purchased the coil of three-eights rope in Edmonton. We had found so many uses for it. And now it served its worth as a clothesline.

After Mrs. Mulholland's clothes were spread out, the place resembled a women's outdoor camp. A few minutes later, Harry came over where I was working on the rifles. He glanced at the clothesline. At any other time, the scene would have drawn a witty comment from his highness, but he was in no mood for humour. In a quiet, casual manner suggesting total resignation, he said, "Al, what say we polish off the rest of that rum? I think now would be as good a time as any."

I didn't need to be told; I knew he had given up on saving the fur.

"I'll fetch it out," I said. "It's in Mrs. Mulholland's pack. I was intending to make billy of tea, but we are into our last package."

"By all means—it's better to save the tea and drink the whisky," he said. There wasn't the slightest trace of humour in his comment.

I found the cups, poured two stiff drinks, and handed one to Harry. Then we walked over to the drying rack. I put my hand inside one of the "cased" lynx pelts: the skin was still slick with moisture. As I opened it at the "tail" end, two bluebottle flies buzzed out. The marten pelts weren't in much better shape. Only two could be kept. It was a grim situation. But Harry did manage to save three beaver pelts out of the nine we had. Because beaver are stretched in the "open," rounded form, he had been able to hold the flesh side of each pelt directly to the heat, thus drying them out in a matter of minutes.

We stood there for awhile, looking up at our hard-earned fur draped across the rack. As for me, all I saw were those cold siwash nights and snow-bound trails.

Harry downed a long jolt of rum, then reached up on the rack and began tossing the pelts that couldn't be saved—one by one—into the fire. The stench of burning hide floated through the air. Nigger and Liza had been lying on the knoll, and they now came down to investigate this strange, putrid smell. I walked back to my fire and heated some water. The overproof rum was too potent for me to take straight.

Long June evenings and hot rums are great motivators—which prompted me to suggest that we go back to the water jungle and try to put the *Queen* right side up. Harry agreed. "It will give us an earlier start in the morning. The sooner I'm out of this place, the better I'll like it."

My own sentiments couldn't have been more clearly expressed.

The job proved to be a lot easier than it looked. We were able to reposition the raft against two trees which were in a more favourable distance apart. We then went to opposite ends of the *Queen* and tipped it down vertically against the trees, to its side in the water. The weight of the raft in a vertical position, sank it. We then took hold of the superstructure as low as we were able to reach in the water and pulled the bottom side out. The buoyancy of the water pushed it to the surface, leaving the *Queen* right side up. One couldn't imagine a simpler operation.

We wanted to pull, or paddle the raft to a better mooring location, but there were none that we could see, so we tied it where it was, and waded back to the knoll. Soaked again.

Off with the clothes again! Wring pants, shirt, socks, underwear out—the works. Squeeze the water out of your moccasins. Damn the mosquitoes! Get your clothes back on! I need a smoke. Where in hell did I leave my tobacco pouch? You left it lying on your packboard, stupid. There didn't seem to be any end to the torment of this place. I was beginning to become short-tempered.

"I promise you, Crusoe! If I ever get out of this country in one piece, I shall *never* take another bath. I may hang my clothes once in awhile, but you will never get me into a bathtub."

"I know how you feel, Friday. Throw some more wood on the fire and we'll finish Dal's bottle."

In the dusk of the evening, we set our mosquito bars up on the highest part of the knoll, to take advantage of the cool night breeze that was drifting in off the flood water.

I was beginning to feel better—now that we had resumed using our "designated" names, once again.

Dead Men's Valley

"The river must have risen again, during the night," Harry observed as we reached the raft, after our first trip through the water jungle, the next morning. He pointed to a knife mark that he had made on one of the trees the night before. The water was now over the mark by about four inches.

Our camp departure on this morning must have been the longest ever taken in the history of the North. More than an hour floundering through that overflow, wrestling with the bags, trying to tie them down properly on a vessel that wouldn't settle down. At least it was easier than getting them out from under. The worst part of the loading was getting the dogs aboard. We had to make them swim back to the raft.

After an awkward siege of poling and paddling, we managed to leave the backwater behind, and were swiftly moving towards the river proper. It was a blessing to be riding right side up once again, although I hadn't noticed any change in the seating or kneeling arrangement.

According to Harry's estimation we were about twenty miles (thirty-two kilometres) from Dead Men's Valley (represented on modern maps as Deadmen Valley). At the rate we were moving we would be in the valley by noontime—or sooner, if we paddled.

And paddle we did. Aboard the raft, we could only wring out our socks and moccasins when we left the flood water. We were cold! And it wasn't going to be any warmer out here in the middle of the river.

We were drifting in smooth water now, for the most part, and I could have enjoyed this section of the ride through the Second Canyon, had I not been wet and cold. There was big game in this part of the country; on a straight stretch of the river we saw a cow moose standing among some spruce on the north side of the river. And in the same area I spotted two Dall's sheep looking down on us from a talus slope on the side of a mountain.

An hour or so later I heard the welcome words from the stern: "We're coming to the east entrance of the canyon. It's just around that bend at the upper end of Dead Men's Valley," Harry announced. "After we make the turn, we'll work the raft over to the left bank and tie up as soon as we can get into slower water. There are good camping spots on the north side."

Shortly after, we were drying ourselves out alongside of a big fire, mighty glad to be on a *genuine* shore for a change. As for the dogs, they were racing and romping around in the trees, enjoying the good life while it lasted.

We were gathering more dry firewood when we spotted an old cabin back in the spruce. It was missing its door and both windows, and obviously had been deserted for a number of years. Harry thought it might have been built by Poole Field or by one of the Lafferty boys.

"Perhaps it's one of Faille's," I offered.

Harry shook his head. "No, this cabin was built long before Faille's time. Faille came into the country in 1927. He built his first cabins up the Flat River, as I mentioned earlier."

A musty smell issued from the interior as we entered the doorway. The first thing that caught my eyes was the roof jack, lying up against one of the walls. It was twisted completely out of shape and the metal was full of teeth marks—every square inch of it. The hole through the roof looked like it had been made by a beaver instead of by a man with a saw or axe. I showed it to Harry. "Now I remember!" he exclaimed. "A couple of trappers down on the Liard last summer, were talking about a cabin in Dead Men's Valley, that had been broken into by a wolverine and completely ransacked. Apparently the owner had left a quarter of moose meat in the cabin during the latter part of the winter, and the meat had spoiled before he returned. I don't remember who they said owned the cabin."

This was a shining example of what a wolverine can do when it sets its mind to something. It must have been this shaggy scavenger of the north woods that inspired the old adage: "The difficult, I do at once; the impossible will take me a little longer."

Harry's big Three-Star eiderdown was still damp, and while he continued to work on it, I proceeded to get dinner. It was then that I discovered part of our meat was flyblown. Apparently my meat-roasting operation back on the knoll hadn't been so successful.

That settled the matter. What we needed was fresh meat. We would camp here for the present and hunt for sheep. "A couple of rams should see us through to Nahanni Village—with any luck," Harry said. "It's about two days' travel."

Still having the bigger part of the afternoon left, I decided to head up the forest slope to the north cliffs. If there were as many sheep in this area as Harry claimed, I just might be able to find one. The possibility of having something other than flyblown meat for supper was something to look forward to. I wasn't overly enthusiastic about hunting Dall's sheep; I still hadn't forgotten that "siesta affair" back on the mountain at the Rabbitkettle. But we needed meat, and I might as well be sensible about it. Killing a moose (even if I had the chance) would be a waste of far too much good meat.

My best procedure, as near as I could determine, was to climb to the north cliff and find out what lay beyond. I had to be where I could scan an open area, or at least find a used game trail—which was unlikely until I reached the cliff.

I spent nearly two hours reaching that cliff, and when I scanned the narrow gorge, I saw no movement of any kind. The rock walls were too steep for even a mountain goat to scale. This didn't mean there weren't sheep somewhere in the gorge, but I couldn't see any way of getting down to it. This afternoon jaunt had turned out to be nothing more than a physical fitness session—wading through more of that Nahanni moss, clambering over fallen trees, and lichen-covered boulders sprinkled generously over the terrain. It wasn't what one would call a garden path.

Well, enough of this! I simply reversed directions and headed back to the river, using the same route down.

The dogs were waiting expectantly when they saw me coming through the trees. But when they couldn't detect the smell of fresh meat, their tails drooped and they went back to where they had been resting under a tree.

Harry had finished his supper and was doing some clothes-mending when I came in. I asked him if he enjoyed the fly nits in the dried meat and he said, "Well, not really. The eggs need another day or two to mature sufficiently to make a difference to the flavour." I couldn't see any humour in his comment. But I was hungry. That little ramble up to the cliff had produced that well-known growl in my stomach.

While I was away, Harry had found a game trail along the north shore, and prudently hung the dried meat up in a tree, out of reach of the bears. "I should have remembered," he said. "The bears come down to Prairie Creek to feed off the berries in the area. We must keep that in mind."

I corralled all the courage I could muster, and brought down one of the sacks, and put several pieces into the large billy pot. My theory was: if I can't roast the damned blows, I'll drown the buggers out at 212 degrees Fahrenheit.

Harry put the tea billy over the fire and remarked as how the Turret tin of tea was nearing empty—an observation that I had made back at the overflow camp. "Well, we won't worry about it, Friday. When the tea is finished, it's finished. What we need is meat, and I know where we can find it. Tomorrow morning we'll raft on down past Prairie Creek and camp just beyond the delta. I know that area down there. Milt and I camped there several times, and we found sheep up in the canyon [now known as Dry Canyon]. Milt named it the Sheep Pasture. I can almost guarantee mutton in the pan tomorrow night."

These were precisely the words to make a young man's stomach muscles stretch out and be prepared.

The sun had just dropped behind the mountain at the entrance to the Second Canyon, and the purple alpenglow shed its sheen of light across the tips of the limestone peaks in a blaze of colour. It was a sunset to see—one that I could have watched until the long, June twilight faded into the dusk of evening.

But it was mosquito time now, and the determined devils were after their supper in a hurry. We pondered the idea of setting up our mosquito bars out on the pole platform of the raft out on the water, where the cold breeze off the river might discourage the pests, but finally decided against it. It wouldn't be a very comfortable place to sleep. We ended up putting the night camp as close to the shore as possible, lit up by a blazing fire that would make those little blood-suckers pay for every drop of blood they got.

There was something to talk about here on this evening, as we sat on our eiderdowns, enjoying the warmth of the fire. For we were now in the Valley of Silent Men. Dead Men's Valley—the valley that spawned "The Legend." It turned out to be a legend of many versions.

We talked about this valley, and how it came by its name, and tried to sift the chaff from the grain, the truth from fantasy. For it was on this north shore, somewhere near where we were now camped, that Willie and Frank McLeod's bones were found. And so the story of the "lost" gold and its legend began.

I had read (and heard) different accounts of the story of the McLeod brothers. And always there were so many things missing in the telling. There were some accounts so utterly fantastic (even to a layman's mind) that I often wondered how they ever reached the printed page.

And so I said to Harry, "You've been here on the Liard and Nahanni all this time—what do you know about the McLeod brothers? What is one to believe?"

"As I understand it, there were four McLeod brothers. They were a Metis family and their dad, Murdoch, was the Hudson's Bay factor at the turn of the century at Fort Liard. In 1904 three of the brothers, Frank, Willie, and Charlie went into the Flat River country, looking for gold. The following year, 1905, Willie and Frank were supposed to have gone back up the Flat to the same area. They never returned. Their bones were found in 1907 or 1908." This was Harry's account.

"Well who found their remains?"

"Their brother Charlie and several others—as I understand."

"You say their bones were found in 1907 or 1908. Well if there were several in the party, surely somebody must have known the *exact* year. I'm a bit confused," I said.

"So are a lot of other people," Harry retorted. "There is even a difference of opinion as to who all were in the party that did find the remains."

"Well did the three brothers find gold in 1904, or did they not?" At my tender age of twenty-two, I suppose I was trying to get at something concrete—something definite.

"Who knows?" was Harry's answer. "You talk to a dozen people, you get a dozen answers. Everybody down on the Liard seemed to think so. As I said before, everybody and his brother prospected McLeod Creek. I have to admit Milt and I bought the newspaper stories—along with a hundred others."

"What about this other man—Weir, who was supposed to have been with Willie and Frank in 1905?"

"That's pure crap, Al. I don't believe there was any such person. I tried to get to the bottom of that story up at Fort Liard from men who should have known. Some of the stories circulated were downright weird. I was told at Fort Simpson that the Mounted Police did make an investigation in 1909. They concluded that the McLeods died of starvation—and that's my belief."

As for my opinion, there were a number of questions that should have been asked—and answered—regarding the fate of the two men. Were rifles or axes found near the skeletons? Were there cuttings near the death site? If not, this would indicate that the two men had met with a mishap on the river and had lost the keys to their means of survival. If their remains were found in 1907, there would have been a three-year period involved, and of course any accurate investigation after that length of time would have been impossible. But at least the search party should have been able to come to some fairly reasonable conclusions. After all, bears and wolves don't eat axes and rifles. But as Harry said, "One could point to a dozen different reasons why they died and still be wrong." And so we let it rest at that. The only part of the McLeod saga that we could be certain about was how Dead Men's Valley got its name.

Even though we were close to the river, and under the protection of the mosquito bars, the mosquitoes were really on the warpath. And when we looked through the evening dusk, towards the mountains in the west, we knew why: a storm was brewing back there and it was heading our way. Well, we might not be able to keep dry on the river, but there was no reason to spend the night soaking wet on the shore.

We got busy in a hurry and moved the big tarp into the timber and quickly shaped it into a lean-to. Everything was put under the shelter, including the dried meat. As far as the fur was concerned, it didn't really matter. Most of it was already gone.

It was sometime before midnight when a "Dead Men's Valley cloud-buster" (as Harry put it) hit our camp and down came the rain. In a torrent! A bright sheet of lightning, then a crash of thunder brought Nigger and Liza under the lean-to in a hurry, which left men and dogs jockeying for the driest spot under the tarp. But the heavy downpour was welcome in one sense—it put an end to the mosquitoes. They were really giving the dogs a working over before the cloud burst.

Despite a bad night, we were loaded and ready to move camp at eight in the morning. A heavy wind later in the night, had carried the storm down into the First Canyon, which we were glad to see. One of our major problems of late, seemed to be the difficulty of keeping our belongings dry, whether on or off the river.

During the way downstream, we were keeping in close to the left shore, out of the main current. The river was much wider here, and suddenly the entire valley seemed to open into a vast lake, studded with several islands. Fresh driftwood had been piling up on the upstream end of some of these islands, giving an indication of the amount of flood water rolling down out of Second Canyon.

Over to our right, across the valley, Harry pointed out the Meilleur River emerging out of a cleft in the high ridge below the mountains to the southwest—another main tributary dumping its tons of rain and meltwater into the Nahanni. In a matter of minutes we were drifting in a fast current that seemed to be cutting off a half dozen fast-flowing creeks, each running through a water-ploughed channel of rocks and gravel, gouged out by past years of spring floods. We were passing the delta of Prairie Creek—another tributary flowing into Dead Men's Valley. I could plainly see the cleft in the canyon ridge to the north, out of which the creek flowed.

"Would you believe that Milt and I walked across that delta in the fall of '35 and barely got our knees wet?" Harry called out.

"Well, you sure as hell wouldn't wade across some of those creeks now," I called back. "A man would be swept off his feet."

Just past the last gravel ridge of the delta, we pulled the raft into an eddy, then paddled and poled our way to a small cove where we could make a decent camp and put up a lean-to in a hurry if we had to. The weather looked to be very unsettled. We also wanted to be close to the ridge, to use it as a retreat if the mosquitoes drove us out of the wooded cove.

Harry was anxious to set out after meat while the threat of more rain held off. He pointed to a canyon rising into the north cliffs to the east, just above the entrance to the First Canyon. "There are sheep up there, Al. It's a high climb but it's not that far from here— just a nice jaunt."

Harry took my rifle and left immediately, and I set to work unloading the raft and making camp. The weather in the west threatened more rain, even this early in the day, so I put the big tarp up again, to be ready for another deluge if it came. It was warm here in the cove and by noon I knew I would have the unwelcome hordes of mosquitoes for company. Then I would head for the delta, into the cool breeze coming off the river.

Every sign pointed to a rising flood. Out near the centre of the river, I watched two balsam poplar trees drifting downstream—and they were moving. Their green, leafy branches were still intact, which meant that not far upstream the angry Nahanni was tearing its banks out along the outside curves, and with more and more water to handle, and with no room to put it, it simply *made* room. And by the time these two balsams found a resting place up against some island log jam, it's a safe bet they would have lost all of their spring finery, and most of their branches. Clearly, this river was not in a pleasant mood.

But as one came down the river and took note of all the wooded islands, it was plain that this ancient waterway could build as well as destroy, and perform both tasks in the same effort. For as one island or a strip of shoreline was being rooted out, the flood water would be depositing the resulting aggregate in another spot farther downstream. And thus a new island would be born to raise a new crop of forest plants.

Feeling certain Harry wouldn't be coming back empty-handed, I spent part of the morning building a small drying rack. There was no way fresh meat would be kept very long in this temperature, and I wasn't keen on having any more sheep meat spoil.

Later, I took Harry's .22 Hornet, and leaving the dogs to guard camp, I set off into the timber to see what I could find. Fifteen minutes later, I flushed two ruffed grouse into a tree and managed to pick the heads off both. With a Hornet bullet one had to be careful about hitting these birds in the body.

I had just returned to camp when I heard the first rifle shot. Not long after, I heard the second. The dogs also heard the shots and were instantly on their feet, staring through the timber to the east.

Early in the afternoon I heard stones rattle on the gravel ridge. I knew Harry was carrying a heavy load by the careful manner in which he was picking his way into camp.

"Two rams," Harry announced. "But the other one is in a bad place. He is lying in the bottom of a rock basement about ten feet deep. I managed to bleed it by using a cache pole to get down to it. I'm hungry, let's get some of this meat in the pan. We'll have a quick meal and hike back to the hill."

"That's easier done than said," I replied, reaching for my axe. In nothing flat, the ram chops were on the fire. After many meals of dried meat, this one was another to remember.

As yet, the threatening rain hadn't materialized, which must have made Harry's hunt much easier, but the heat of the day did bring out the mosquito legions in full force. It seemed to take double the time to do the simplest chores, having to spend part of one's energy fighting the devils off.

Harry had noticed the drying rack I had set up, and remarked that perhaps we would not need to dry the meat. He suggested we quarter the meat when we got it all in camp and store it on the water—on the raft.

"The temperature out there will be a lot cooler than here in the cove. Then tomorrow morning, bright and early, we'll have a quick breakfast, load the *Queen* and head for the village. It's about sixty miles from here. If things work out we could make it in one stop. We could even stop over at the hot springs. The meat wouldn't have time to spoil—not out there on the water. How does that sound to you, Friday?" He had used my assumed name, which went a long way to relieve certain misgivings that I seemed to have had of late.

"It's like music to my ears," I replied. I had done some rapid calculation: in an eight-mile-an-hour current it would take less than eight hours to reach the village—in constant travel on the river. Let's say we spent two hours at the hot springs (I didn't really have any idea just where these hot springs were) we could still be on the Liard in ten hours. Why hell's fire, we could make two stops and still be at the village in daylight. The idea of being off this river in one more day—without daydreaming about it—appealed to me in more ways than one. It wasn't just the bother we'd save by not having to dry the meat: I sensed that Harry had a more important reason for wanting to leave camp as soon as possible. Several times I had caught him eyeing the river with more than a little concern. I knew he didn't like the looks of that current out there. It had been raining upriver for the past two days, and by the looks of it there was more on the way. He had been in the country long enough to know that a twenty-one carat flood could pin us down in this valley for another week or more. An extra day could make a lot of difference.

Four p.m. found us heading up the North Canyon (now called the Dry Canyon) and shortly after, Harry turned up a rocky draw that led out of the main gorge, upward into the queerest looking place I had ever seen.

Actually, we had ascended a well-used sheep trail that led to a ridge overlooking a series of rocky, wall-like structures that lay across a small gorge beneath the ridge. These walls varied in width and in one section they had divided part of the gorge into roomlike compartments. One or two of the walls were in a state of disintegration and appeared to be about ready to crumble. The entire affair looked as if the ancient Greeks had been trying to erect a stone dormitory for their gladiators at this spot, and had made a proper mess of it. But this was no manmade job. It had taken nature a couple of aeons of time, perhaps, to create this wonderment, and would likely take the same amount of time wearing it down. I found myself wishing I were a geologist who knew something about the kinds of rock and their formations. I could spend a lifetime wandering around in this country.

"One couldn't imagine a better playground for wild sheep," Harry remarked.

"Perhaps that's what it is," I said. "They've made a trail up here for some reason."

"There's likely a salt lick around here somewhere close," Harry suggested. "That could be the main reason they've been congregating in this area."

We tied the dogs up on the ridge and I followed Harry out onto one of the walls where he had made the kill. I looked into the rock chamber and saw the ram lying at the bottom. It looked all of ten feet deep to me and I could see why Harry had called it "a bad place," and why we would need the three-eighths rope.

"I would have thought that a man of Crusoe's intelligence should have picked a better place to hunt. Did you choose this area on purpose?"

"Honestly Friday—I'm not a mean man. The ram was standing on the wall and this is where he dropped."

Harry's pole "ladder" that he had cut to get down to bleed the ram was still in the chamber, and while he was performing this job another ram had apparently come up the sheep trail, either to join his comrade or to investigate the explosion in his own backyard. In any case, it was a mistake: the ram was standing on the ridge when Harry climbed out of the rock chamber. He had left the .30-.30 on the top of the wall, and his second shot was the one that killed the ram that he had partially carried back to camp.

Getting the animal out of this cramped cubicle was going to be tricker than it looked. I wanted to cut another pole, notch the steps, and combine it with the one we had, into some semblance of a proper ladder (we had plenty of rope) so that we could steady the ram while we hoisted him up the wall. Harry saw my point. This was no place for either of us to be hurt for the want of a bit of extra work.

We began the butchering job at the top of the draw, and Harry reminded me to keep my eyes peeled for bear. "We could easily meet one up here."

An hour later we were making our way slowly down the draw with smallish packs of mutton. Harry was right about the bears: in several places we saw their claw marks on the aspen trees.

Part way down we heard water running in a side gully. We shed our packs by the rivulet and stopped long enough to have a smoke and a cool drink of water. I could always tell when Harry was thinking deeply about something—as if it was a problem that had to be solved one way or another. And finally he broke the silence. "There is a place on the river which might give us a little trouble at this stage of water. Perhaps we should go over and have a look at the Snyder Gate while we're up here. They say it can be a rough place in high water."

The Snyder Gate! The name sounded familiar; I had read about the place—likely in the *Calgary Herald*. It was named after Harry Snyder, a naturalist who conducted aerial flights into the Nahanni in the early Thirties. (It was also called George's Riffle.)

"Is that near the entrance to the First Canyon?"

"Yes," Harry said. "It's just below us and to our left a bit. We can leave our packs here and take the dogs with us. I don't like to leave them tied up with bears around. We won't be gone long, anyhow."

Fifteen minutes later we were standing at the bottom of a narrow gully that ended abruptly at the edge of a cliff overlooking the river. Directly below us was an island in the canyon, with the main part of the river flowing between it and the south wall. It was one wicked-looking place around that island.

"Good God! How did you and Milt get through that hell hole? You came through there *four* times!"

"It's not the same river now, Al."

A determined and turbulent mass of swirling water was pushing transient, evergreen trees intermingled with large balsam poplars into an old log jam at the upper end of the island near the centre of the river. Rejected by the massive pile-up of trees already occupying the point, these newcomers were being rolled back into the main force of the waves, only to be overtaken by more driftwood. Some of these trees had been tossed around so that they were heading *downstream* with their root-ends in the "bow" position. A weird looking sight to behold!

I reached for my tobacco pouch and rolled a smoke. I needed one to steady my nerves. One look at that wild procession down there was enough for me.

"There's a lot of water going through there," Harry admitted. He kept staring down at the churning foam. I could see he was trying to analyse the situation—trying to find a possible way to conquer this place that had defied more than one experienced river man in lower water than we were looking at. This was my partner's nature; he hated to be beaten—to admit defeat. He was born that way, and would remain that way. I had known this man as long as I had known anyone.

"Now if we could keep the raft over to the left of that island—over at the left wall of the canyon—I think we might have a chance to get through." He kept studying the scene below.

"I don't think we would have a hope in hell of ever getting through that place—not and be alive to tell about it," I said. "Look at all those trees—the driftwood—all that stuff is being funnelled through those rapids on the right-hand side of the island. That's where all the water is. And that's where we'd be—mixed up with a bunch of timber. I think it's suicide to try to run that place." That was the way I saw it.

"Well Al, let's not stand here swatting mosquitoes. We'll pick up the meat and head back to camp. Then we can decide what to do."

It was after nine when we got back to camp. The mosquitoes had been giving us trouble on the way down the canyon, with the packs to carry, but their numbers dwindled somewhat when we reached the river. As Harry remarked: "There are only two ways you can beat the devils—either stay on the river, or climb the highest mountain."

There had been some strenuous climbing and packing that afternoon and we four were hungry. The mutton chops hit the big fry pan once again, and the dogs, meanwhile, were given the entire rib cage of the first ram Harry had brought into camp earlier. It took us an hour to finish that meal. And I know we were both doing a lot of thinking during that time. For a decision had to be made promptly about running the Snyder Gate through the First Canyon.

There were three options open to us. We could camp here in the valley and wait for the river to drop—and only God knew when that would be. That might take us into July. And by that time, our relatives would be getting a bit perturbed. There could be a search plane sent in to look for us—something that neither of us wanted to have happen. The Great Depression was still very much alive back home; our folks would be hard pressed to finance an aerial search—or any other kind for that matter. This left us with the remaining two: we could run the First Canyon and take our chances, or portage around the canyon on an old Indian trail. Harry explained that the Indians had blazed a trail through the bush that they used mostly after freeze-up when their sleds could be pulled over the frozen creeks.

"The trail starts at Sheep Creek [now Ram Creek] just across the river. The mouth of the creek is right this side of the canyon entrance. It follows the creek for a ways, then heads east to Clausen Creek which empties into the Nahanni at the eastern end of the canyon."

"How long is this portage trail?"

"It's about eighteen miles, so I've been told," Harry said.

I knew what I wanted to do: I was all for making the portage. We had already been through two sizable skirmishes with the river, and I wasn't fussy about having a third. The law of averages strongly suggested that we couldn't win them all. I think my preference was based on what I knew I could do (or at least what I *thought* I knew) on terra firma. A twenty mile hike didn't seem like much of an undertaking to me—if there was any trail at all. I was a smaller man than average, perhaps by Northern standards, weighing just over 140 pounds, and providing I didn't pack more than I was built to pack, I knew from my foothill excursions back in Alberta that I could outwalk most men in heavy terrain. I said I thought we could reach the end of the trail in one day if we had to. Harry didn't agree. "Listen Al. This makes my fourth spring in this country. There is no way we will make that portage in one day."

"Well why not—if there's a trail and we have light packs?" I asked.

"Because the mosquitoes will stop us! That's why. As soon as we get away from the river, those little bastards will be plain hell. You'd better believe it! I know. I would rather drown in the river than be eaten alive back in the bush."

I took a long look at the man I had known since childhood, and I knew he meant it. The last thing I wanted was a disagreement with an old pal, and likely the best friend I would ever know.

"But twenty miles, Harry—suppose it takes us two days to reach this Clausen Creek you're talking about. Surely we can cope with the mosquitoes that long. We do have our mosquito bars."

"We are not under our bars while we are plodding through the bush, and face nets aren't worth a damn in this country in June. Milt and I found that out. It's just that I don't know much about this old Indian trail. I've never been over it. It can't be well-travelled. The Indians only use it during the winter months. We are not going to be following a well-marked trail which would easily be followed in winter. This is springtime. An Indian can follow a blazed trail in summer where a white man would be lost in half an hour. Especially if it's been blazed by an Indian. We have to understand that. Of course if we kept travelling *east* we'd be bound to hit Clausen Creek."

As if by a prearranged signal we reached for our pouches and each rolled a well-shaped cigarette. Perhaps a pause in troubled thoughts might help to steady the situation.

Finally I decided to put things straight. We weren't playing a game of poker now; all cards had to be face up on the table. And so I said, "Listen Harry, I don't want to run that Snyder Gate! But it's not my decision to make. We will go with your experience, because that's the way it should be. We will do whatever you think best."

I squeezed the last two cups of tea out of the billy and handed one to Harry. I didn't mention that that was the last of the Blue Ribbon, he probably knew anyway.

Harry pondered for a moment, then said, "I won't ask you to, Al. It's a bad place down by that island. I wouldn't wish it on my worst enemy. There's too much water going through! Too much wood! There's another place near the lower end of the canyon that could give us trouble also. I guess it's best to make the portage. But I can promise you—it won't be any picnic."

And so it was settled. Tomorrow we would deal with the job of drying the sheep meat, in preparation for the portage. Meanwhile it would keep cool out on the raft. We just had to hope that a bear wouldn't wander into the cove. The dogs were having the feast of their lives, as we were feeding them all the rib meat they could eat. And why not—while the opportunity was at hand?

We spent ten hours the next day turning the meat over and over on the drying rack I had built. That evening Harry rendered a short discourse on how the natives operated, which seemed to make a lot of sense to me. "They are never in a hurry when they travel—especially when the conditions are favourable. They don't have to be. They camp wherever they make a kill, and take their time about this business of drying meat. Home to them is wherever they happen to be at the end of the day. It's not the same with us. We never have enough hours in the day—or enough days in the week, for that matter, to accomplish what we deem to be necessary. This seems to be the white man's trouble."

It was getting late and there was no more time to spare. We sacked the meat and hung it up in a tree, then crawled under the mosquito bars and went to sleep—minus the usual cup of tea in the evening.

At eight the next morning, under a cloudy sky, we poled out of the cove and headed the raft across the river to the south shore. We were trying to keep the Queen at a slight upstream angle through this flood-watered north channel, but we suddenly received a bad shock— the raft was refusing to face the oncoming volume of water. At mid-channel, the current caught the bow in a single sweep, pushing it back downstream without the least bit of effort. Despite all the strength we could put into the paddles, the bow would not come around. And in the meantime the channel was turning towards the north shore.

It couldn't possibly be! But it was: we were heading right for a sweeper! It was as though we were bent on challenging this lifelong enemy of all river men.

"We're going to hit that tree!" Harry shouted. "We can't go under!"

That was only too evident from where I was, kneeling in the bow. It was plain to see what was going to happen—I would either be pinned against that tree or swept into the water. The trunk of the tree was lying about a foot above the surface of the water.

I did the only thing I could think of: I grabbed the coiled mooring rope, got to my feet, and at the last moment I jumped off the bow. I landed between two upright branches, having the wind knocked out of me for a moment. I recalled hearing a snap as I struggled to get my hands back on the rope.

The raft must have struck something underneath, for it momentarily halted, then began lurching ahead again just as I was able to wrap the rope around one of the limbs that I had fallen against. I heard something tearing loose and then I saw the current sweeping the stern around. But Harry wasn't sleeping—he was up on his feet and swiftly jammed his paddle between the tree trunk and the outside log of the raft before the stern was swept under.

"For God's sake bring the rope and snub the stern. I don't know if I can hold it!"

But I was already there, and swiftly tied the end of the rope to the end of the outside log, then over the tree trunk. Now the nightmare part of the thing was over. Now to put our possessions on shore!

First, I turned the dogs loose and they didn't need to be shown the way to shore. Up the tree they went. Harry wasn't wasting any time: he came forward holding his axe and .22 Hornet in his hands. "Take these and get them on the shore," he said. These were two of our key possessions and I watched each step I took as I made my way through the branches of that over-hanging spruce tree until I reached the riverbank.

I seemed to be so unsteady on my feet and I couldn't figure out why—until I turned to go back and suddenly noticed the tree was gently weaving back and forth, undulating in unison with the ebb and swell of the current.

I didn't waste any time getting back; I wanted to get my axe and Winchester. Harry greeted me with the news: "Your rifle is gone—along with the sack of meat. The forward crosspiece was pushed back when we hit." And then I remembered that I always tied the rifle to the crosspiece so I could reach the gun in a hurry. My axe was in its usual position beneath the poles. I cut it loose and flung it onto the shore. I shouted to Harry, "Give me your ammunition—the pack containing your ammunition!"

"I can't," he shouted back. "I have to give you the packs as they come off the line. There is no other way."

Then I could see why. Instead of tying the packs separately, we had run a length of the three-eighths rope from the stern to the bow. Then each pack had been threaded onto the rope through its handle. But the crosspiece had been torn loose and the loop in the rope had slipped off its end. Fortunately for all of us, Harry had gotten hold of the end of the rope before any more items were lost.

So it was one bag at a time—take them as they come. Trip after trip I made over that damned tree and it was taking forever.

To make matters worse, the constant rush of water hitting the raft tended to push the lower side deeper into the water, causing the *Queen* to be lying at an angle against the tree. In fact the current would have pushed the raft upside down had the opposite or "upper" side not been tied to the tree in the manner it was. Part of our gear was now partially under water and was only held against the raft by the big tarp and the force of the water behind it. Harry's job was both tricky and dangerous.

"Hurry it, Al!" he beckoned. "I'm afraid this bloody sweeper may break loose from shore. If it does we're goners!"

Well, I had to watch what the hell I was doing too. Running up and down the trunk of a tree swaying back and forth in the river, grabbing tree branches with one hand and a bag in the other, was a gymnastic exercise with which I was not familiar. I never did have any inclination to be a high-wire performer in a circus.

I know we both began breathing easier when I finally had Harry's packboard onto the shore. What use would the Hornet be without ammunition? Finally the last items, the big axe, the bucksaw, and the big tarp were also on the bank.

But our ordeal wasn't over yet. There was the mooring rope to think about—and the *Queen* itself. Harry kept looking at the roots holding the spruce tree to the bank. "I think it's still safe enough. Let's try and save the raft."

I was in complete accord. For I had now lost all the fear I possessed, and had committed myself to "the life hereafter," anyway. So if our luck finally *did* give out, I was ready, and prepared—and waiting.

But pulling the raft *out* of this mess was going to be harder than it was to get into it. Obviously we had to release the stern first. When this happened, most of the raft would be swept under the tree. This might mean that the pole platform, already partially torn apart, would be caught up underneath the trunk. Harry soon solved that potential hazard: "We'll cut the platform loose. To hell with it!" And that's what we did. Off came the rope from the outside log, which turned the raft downstream, stern first, just as nice as could be, and only held by the bow.

Now we had about thirty-five feet of free rope. It just reached to one of the tree roots on shore, with only a couple of feet to spare. Had the rope been short, it wouldn't have mattered; we could have used one of the branches on the upper end of the trunk, from which to make a pull.

Finally the last maneuver: Harry held the half-hitch at the bank while I went out on the trunk for the last time and used the bucksaw to cut off the limb that I had used as a snubbing post. Now the bow was released. It was the most wonderful sight in the world to see the *Queen* floating free of that tree.

Twenty minutes later we had our vessel safely to shore, moored to another tree that was firmly in the ground—*and still growing*. We weren't trusting that sweeper any longer than we had to.

We built a fire to ward off the mosquitoes, then sat down to try to determine what went wrong. During the next fifteen minutes we consumed a considerable amount of tobacco.

We had made our first "avoidable" mistake—aside from knowing that we shouldn't have been on the river at flood stage, to begin with—by misjudging the volume of water out there, and the force behind it. We were trying to move an outfit that weighed close to fifteen hundred pounds against this force. But what was our alternative? We still had to get across the river.

The Portage Trail

We stood there by the tree and took stock of our situation, thankful that neither of us had gotten hurt during this affair. Two important items were missing—my rifle, and the sack of meat, which meant another waste of wild mutton. At least we four had been well fed over the past two days. Thank God we still had the mosquito bars and our axes. Without them we would have had to run the Snyder Gate or stayed in Dead Men's Valley, shooting more sheep until the river dropped.

There was no point in further discussion; the thing to do was hit that portage trail without any further delays. "If we have to hunt we may as well do it on our way to Clausen Creek than spend more time here," I said. "I just want to be rid of this place."

Harry agreed. "We'll put another platform on the raft and pole it back past the cove. We need all the room we can get to make it across the river. I'm going to saw that goddamn sweeper off right now."

The platform didn't take long; I only had to replace the front crossbar and the poles, and we were ready to reload. At 11 a.m. by Harry's watch, we pushed off from the gravel ridge past the cove.

This time we faced the raft at an angle *with* the current, gaining the crossing a foot at a time. And we didn't have much room to spare. Twice we urged each other to paddle harder as we saw the entrance looming closer and closer. Then the river widened out, providing a slower current, and we were able to bring the *Queen* to shore east of the mouth of Sheep Creek. It was a close call—too close for comfort.

Now came the job of sorting the stuff out—what to leave here at the creek, and what to take on the portage. We knew we had to ditch the heavy items. It didn't prove to be that difficult to decide.

The big tarp, the double-bitted axe, the large, cast-iron billy pot, my .30-.30 ammunition, and Harry's Three-Star eiderdown were left behind. We debated about the paddles—they would be awkward to carry. We decided to take them; it would save time at Clausen Creek. "Milt and I will likely be trapping somewhere in the Yukon next winter, and we can pick these items up in our boat later on this summer when the river is back to normal." So up a tree the articles went, wrapped solidly in the tarp. Harry then blazed the tree and left a short message—the date (June 15) and our names and destination.

The dogs carried the two small tarps, our few utensils, the two axes, and a few items of clothing to round off their panniers. The remaining articles—mostly clothing and the three beaver pelts—went into our dunnage bags, which were strapped to our packboards. The mooring rope was one of our heavier items (when wet) but there was no way we could leave it behind. I elected to carry Mrs. Mulholland's packsack while Harry packed the rope. All in all, we four would be toting heavy loads.

Shortly after noontime we set off up Sheep Creek, and I never bothered to look back. I just wanted out of Dead Men's Valley.

The mosquitoes were bad! I think at the time, had we not had the mosquito bars, I would have been willing to run the Snyder Gate. It was obvious these pests were going to deal us some punishment before we hit the river again. The object was to move ourselves over this portage as fast as possible; the sooner we were back on the water, the less grief we would endure.

We were gaining altitude each step of the way as we proceeded up the creek but we weren't covering much ground. Judging the distance travelled seemed to be a hazy problem since we couldn't concentrate on our rate of movement for having to swipe at the countless numbers of these winged devils.

We finally arrived at an old winter campground near the creek, which Harry concluded must have been the western end of the portage, where the Indians camped before sledding on down to the Nahanni after freeze-up.

There was plenty of dry wood lying on the ground, so we quickly built a fire and had a hot water drink, taking a brief respite from the hordes of insects. The hot water idea came from me, as I had once read an article about the Klondike gold rush where this prospector, on running out of tea, continued to boil a pot of water at mealtime, and sipped a cup or two while eating. It was merely a psychological thing on my part I suppose, but Harry sipped right along with me and never passed any remarks. Perhaps it did create an illusion of having the real thing.

But there was another reality that wasn't going to be dispelled by drinking hot water. And that was the fact that we hadn't eaten since 7 a.m. this morning.

It was an effort for us to leave the fire, for we knew the mosquitoes would be worse as the afternoon wore on, but we shouldered our loads and headed east towards the timbered ridge that lay ahead.

We fought myriads of the winged devils for two more hours when Harry called a halt beside a small stream that was flowing northwest either into Sheep Creek or the Nahanni. This stream would have normally been dry had it not been for late rains.

Here we decided to camp for the night, and I didn't waste any time in gathering wood. We had soon learned that you couldn't combat these swarming hordes with a smudge fire like one would build in the backyard; you had to have a thirty below zero fire, and you had to keep the flames shoulder high to stop the devils. Gathering dry wood, we realized, was both time-consuming and extra work but there seemed to be nothing else for it.

We drank more hot water, then set our bars up on our tarps spread out on the moss. It was only 6 p.m. but we were two tired boys. This could be described as our "longest day" in the South Nahanni.

We chained Nigger and Liza close to our beds so that they would crawl under our tarps, which gave them a certain amount of protection. It was sad to see the amount of punishment they had been taking. We had our hands to partially ward off the hordes while on the move, but our dogs had to struggle forward and suffer the torment.

We had probably travelled five miles in as many hours—a paltry mile in each hour. Of course our estimate of distance was likely inaccurate, but at this rate it would take us at least two more days to reach the river. Then another day to build a raft. And another day to reach Nahanni Village. This would translate into *five* days without food if something didn't turn up. It was a chilling thought, and one that we would be better off not to dwell on.

We broke camp at 3 a.m. the next morning. It took less than ten minutes to put the panniers on the dogs and the packboards on our backs. We knew we had to get over this portage in the coolest part of the day when these hellish insects wouldn't be so blood-thirsty.

We were steadily gaining altitude and there were some parts of the trail that were hard to follow. Indians do not mark a trail as clearly as white men do. They don't need to. They are expert trackers and can detect a trail no matter how faint the outline. It's a natural instinct; they were born and bred in the forests. On this portage their tree blazes were small and some were old and easily missed by the inexperienced. Of course the natives would never have been on this portage at this time of year anyway.

At 8 a.m. we had been moving for five hours and we needed a rest. We stopped at a small spring and boiled some water. The pests weren't a bother as yet but it wouldn't be long. Again it was an effort to leave the fire. We were still gaining altitude and the crest of the ridge appeared to be still some distance to the east. As we slowly plodded on our packs seemed to be heavier. My paddle was a frustrating article to carry—mainly because of its length, not its weight. We had debated about leaving the paddles in the valley, but as Harry said, "We'd have to make new ones at Clausen Creek, which would take up more time."

I had thought by now we should have seen at least one rabbit or a single partridge, but the only sign of life that we saw were the squirrels and the odd raven. I hated those bloody ravens—they always seemed to be following a person and waiting for something to happen—like the vultures in the desert.

At noon the trail seemed to level off and we hoped we had reached the summit of the ridge. If so, the portage would descend from here to Clausen Creek, which would be a welcome change. Farther on, the faint track divided into two branches and we took the one to the right leading into heavy timber. This proved to be an old Indian night camp. So we had to retrace our steps back to the left branch, which meant we had covered an extra mile for nothing.

We noticed that clouds were beginning to build up in the west and there was a dead stillness in the air around us—sultry and hot. There was a rainstorm brewing not far behind, bringing with it the main requisite for another batch of mosquitoes—moisture. And half an hour later, down they came from tree-top height—a funnel-shaped mass through the timber. This was the first time we had seen anything like this. Now they were attacking us from below and *above*. Was this what one called a pincers movement? Well, they sure as hell had declared total war! These clouds of mosquitoes seemed to gather behind us in the form of a large funnel as we moved along. We could clearly see the mass descending, then dispersing at ground level. It was scary! There was only one way to handle this situation and that was with fire. Now! A man could lose a lot of blood in an hour of this torture.

Harry immediately began setting up our two, eight by ten tarps in tent fashion, while I proceeded to swing the axe. It was going to rain before the hour was out and it wouldn't amount to a mere drizzle; it had all the makings of a downpour. We had to keep our belongings dry or we wouldn't be able to pack the extra weight. I solved the dry wood shortage by felling two five-inch birches. Harry had the toughest job, tying the ridge poles up to hold the tarps, trying to swat the damned insects off while I was making the fire. And it *was* a fire. One would have thought it was a winter siwash fire, but it was the only answer to the pests. As Harry stated while we were standing beside the flames, "The more these hordes come, the bigger fire we shall build." But we both knew this wasn't the main answer to our situation: we had to be on the move to reach the river.

The dogs wanted to explore the area—likely with the intention of scrounging something to eat. We didn't want to keep them tied up at every stop we made, but there was some hesitation about turning them loose. We needn't have worried; they weren't away from the fire more than five minutes.

At 2 p.m. the rain came down, and the enemy retreated. Wet wings impede an insect's flight. What a relief! We could now leave the fire and get under the tarp tents and rest in peace. We were tired and thirsty. The rain had filled our billy pail and we soon had hot water. Neither of us mentioned food. It was better not to dwell on such things.

We wondered about the storm. It could turn out to be a mixed blessing if it kept up for any length of time. Harry suggested that we hit the trail at the first streak of light in the morning—whether it was still raining or not. If our outfit got wet—well, it got wet. We simply had to keep moving. And so we put the mosquito bars up and went to bed.

We both were awake around midnight. We had slept soundly for nine hours. I got up and rekindled the fire, mainly to get some light in the area. It had stopped raining, and all we could do was wait until we could see to travel. At 2 a.m. we hit the trail. It was barely light enough to see where we were headed, but we had to cover as much ground as possible—before the hordes arrived.

At seven o'clock we waded across a small stream that was flowing almost due south, then appeared to swing back towards the east farther on ahead. Harry felt certain this stream flowed into Clausen Creek not far distant. Five long hours in one stretch was a morning's work on this portage and we all needed a break. The boggy sections between the hills were the toughest to navigate. Each step seemed to require a greater effort than the one before. The dogs were noticeably tired as they struggled through the moss-covered terrain, because of the added weight of the tarps from the previous rain.

We had no clear idea how far we had come. We had put in the hours but had not covered the proportionate amount of ground, we realized that. It had been forty-eight hours since we had eaten anything—except a couple of gallons of mosquitoes along the way, and this fact didn't contribute anything to our rate of travel. But even this short stop for the hot water was something to look forward to.

Less than an hour later, as we were preparing to leave the stream, I removed my dunnage bag from the packboard to get a new pair of peccary suede gloves that I had been saving since I left home. These hog leather gloves had been given to me as a going away present from an old school friend, and I dearly cherished having them among my possessions. But I needed the gloves now to protect my hands from the mosquitoes. My old horsehide pullovers were long since worn out and were full of holes.

Finally I found one of the gloves but not the other. I searched and searched to no avail. Finally in exasperation I lifted the bag and dumped the total contents out on the ground. Still no glove.

I blew my top! That pair of gloves had meant a lot to me—and doubly so in my present situation. It was as though all earthly elements were conspiring against me. I sounded forth with a string of freshly-created epithets that would have astounded even the likes of Webster, citing the South Nahanni country as the most godforsaken piece of real estate this side of Mars. It was a clearly-expressed, vocal enunciation designed to reveal all the evil aspects of the most mosquito-ridden haven on earth.

Harry knew when to keep his silence. Under different circumstances I am sure it would have evoked a suitable comment from the high sultan, but neither of us at the moment, was in the mood for humour. He could understand my concern because he was wearing an inside pair of woollen mitts that were also full of holes, and was fully aware of my problem of trying to cover two hands with one glove.

I finally managed to calm down sufficiently to regain my composure. Without another word I walked over to the willow bush where I had tossed the worn-out pullovers and retrieved them. I cut the back side off the left mitt and fitted it inside the other. It wasn't a smooth fit but at least the demons couldn't penetrate the horsehide.

The stretches of rough terrain after we left the fire soon began to slow us down, even though we were moving into lower country. I noticed that Harry's movements were more awkward than usual. He always did have an ungainly stride but up to now it had never lost its usual vigour. These moss jungles were harder on him than me, simply because he was a heavier man and sank deeper into the bog with each step. I was worried about myself as well; I had learned long ago to watch where I stepped when negotiating rough terrain. Stepping on small rocks or pieces of wood when these impediments could be avoided, tended to sap one's strength. But I was tired and was no longer watching the trail closely. Like Harry I was just plodding ahead, trying to move faster than I was able.

Being without food was not the main cause of our loss of energy. Many men have gone a week or more in the bush and are still able to navigate on an empty stomach. It was the loss of blood that was getting us down. I only had to observe a single mosquito bloat itself on my arm to realize there was more than one drop of blood in that meal. Now multiply that single bit by a thousand or more in a short afternoon! How much would one lose in that time?

At 10 a.m. the heat of the morning brought the demons out and we were forced to stop. We were spending more time gathering dry wood than we were on the trail. By the looks of the area Harry felt that we must be nearing Clausen Creek. "I sure as hell hope so," he said.

"And so do I," I replied. "We don't cover much ground sitting by a fire." I was thinking that at best it would be at least two more days before we ate again—unless we were lucky.

After a brief stop, we managed to pull ourselves away from the fire once again and plodded on. I noticed that Harry had ceased to swipe at the mosquitoes as we trudged along. He seemed to be growing indifferent to their presence. This was a bad sign. Well, as long as I was able to lift a hand, I'd fight the little bastards every step of the way. One had to or be smothered by the devils. A single smack on the side of one's face would wipe a dozen off. Even the steady drone of the hungry droves was enough to drive a man crazy. We seemed to attract these winged battalions like steel to a magnet. They must have been endowed with some sort of a super-sensory system that enabled them to seek out warm-blooded animals. Always they seemed to be following us from above and behind.

We had been keeping our berets pulled well down over our ears, and once in awhile one of the little demons would find its way underneath. Once when I removed my beret I thought I heard the sound of running water. I was in the lead at the time and some distance ahead of Harry and the dogs. I stopped and listened. I did hear water! I looked through the trees to the left and could see the outline of a bank. Harry came up behind and stopped. "I can smell flood water," he announced. "We've reached Clausen!"

Off with our packs and to the axes. We put this fire within two feet of the west bank of the creek so that we now had both flame and cold water to protect us from further punishment. It was a godsend to remove our footwear and let our bare feet dangle in the brown, murky water that was running from bank to bank, and to be able to roll a cigarette and have a smoke in peace for a change.

The fire was also a mixed blessing, for it would stop any game from passing near our camp. But we had to have one until we could get our bars up, which we placed side by side on one of our tarps. We covered our belongings with the other in case of rain.

It was 1 p.m. when we turned in. It was going to be more than twelve hours before we could make our way to the river, unless we were willing to travel when the mosquitoes were at their worst. And that would be foolish.

The sun was still above the ridge in the west when I awoke. Something must have wakened me, I thought. And then I heard Nigger growl. I glanced over in the direction the dog was looking: a cow moose was standing on the other side of the creek! I tugged at Harry's bar and he suddenly came to life. I pointed! He slowly pushed one side of the netting up and reached for his Hornet. He fired the first shot from a sitting position, and the cow dropped. Her little calf had been standing behind her when she fell. When the dogs started barking the calf disappeared into the willows. Harry quickly got to his feet and let go another head shot—just to make sure.

In the space of a few seconds, our entire situation changed, except for the mosquitoes—8 p.m. was prime time for them.

For the first time in two days, Nigger and Liza showed some desire for living. When we turned them loose they began patrolling our side of the swollen creek. It was still in flood, busy moving recent rain and meltwater down out of the mountains in the southwest.

Here was one stream that we weren't going to be able to ford, and the only way to reach that moose was to fell a tree across this flood water. There were plenty of these along the bank. Harry selected a fair-sized one, then grabbed his axe and went to work. I felt ten years younger when I eyed all that meat on the other bank, and after a few minutes I suggested he let me spell him off while he light a fire and boil some water. He consented without argument and added a note of caution: "Make sure that you fall this tree in the right direction, Friday."

"You have my word, Crusoe," I replied.

It was a great feeling to hear our designated names once again.

Later, Harry took another turn at the tree while I had my drink of Clausen "tea" water. It was beginning to be a psychological thing at this stage of our journey—perhaps even a necessity. Presently I heard a sharp, crackling sound and looked up just in time to watch the tree topple. It was obviously going to fall in the right direction—but something was terribly wrong: when the tree hit the water, the current picked up the top end of the spruce and swung it downstream. Our tree had been about three feet short of reaching the far bank. I could have cried. It was Harry's turn to blow his top. His verbal response wasn't near as lengthy as mine had been about the missing glove, but it was just as expressive. He simply said, "Well I'll bet you two-bits to a pinch of coon shit that I *will* find a tree that shall reach to the other side of this damned creek." And up the bank he strode, with me following. He stopped at one senior citizen that was about eighteen inches in diameter and he never even bothered to glance up at its length. His determination would have put Paul Bunyan's to shame as the chips began to fly. I took one look at this monster and thought, "God! We'll starve to death before we ever get it down!"

I don't remember the length of time we spent at that tree before we finally reached that moose. Nigger was the first to reach the kill. He crouched down flat on the ground in front of the dead animal, as if he expected it to rise at any moment and get away from us.

Another fire had to be built beside the kill to ward off our legions of enemies. We were the next thing to being played out before we finally had the moose gutted and part of the meat cut up. As hungry as the dogs were, they made no attempt to get at the meat. They waited by the fire until they were fed.

I was worried about the little calf. I wanted to see if I could find it and put it out of its misery. It would slowly starve to death without its mother. And while Harry was preparing a long-awaited meal of heart and liver in the two little skillets, I set out into the mosquito jungle with the Hornet. I searched the area for nearly an hour as best I could, but I never found the calf. Under the circumstances, I probably could have walked within ten feet of the calf and never spotted it. God! How I hated mosquitoes!

After sixty-three hours without food, we had to watch how much meat we ate at one sitting. We also made sure the dogs wouldn't gorge themselves; we all had to remain in shape to do the work that lay ahead.

"I'd sure like to know how far we are from the river," Harry remarked, after we had called a halt to our supper. I knew what he was hinting at. I walked over to a tree nearby as big as the last one we had felled, and climbed to the top. Between a couple of wooded ridges, I caught sight of a stretch of blue water. It had to be the Nahanni!

"How far from here, Friday?"

"Could be two miles or less," I said.

"Well, we'll have at it early in the morning," the high sultan said. We cut about fifty pounds of meat off the hindquarters and wrapped it in the small green tarp we had found near the Rabbitkettle River while waiting for breakup that Harry thought might belong to Mulholland or Eppler, and hung the bag from a willow into the cold water of the creek. It was nearly 10 p.m. when we crawled under our bars and fell asleep.

At 8 a.m. the next morning we set out for the river. We were a bit sluggish after eating a heavy breakfast and were late in leaving camp. We reached the Nahanni shortly before noon and dropped our packs near the mouth of the creek. One of us had to go back to the kill to fetch the meat, and I volunteered. Meanwhile Harry would seek out the logs for our third raft.

When Nigger and I reached the camp, we saw that nothing had been near the kill nor was there any sign of the calf. With only fifty pounds of meat to carry, we had light loads going back. We left considerable meat behind but there was nothing to be done about that. It was a relief for me to realize that we had finally slogged over the last few miles of this hellish portage. Now we were near water, where we could get protection and some rest when it most was needed.

Harry had found good timber on the slope and there were five logs lying on the bank of the creek when we returned. Although part of the afternoon still remained, we were tired—very tired—so we decided to call it a day.

We finished the raft late the next day, and that last evening at the creek was a happy one. I asked Harry where the hot springs were that he had mentioned back before the portage. He said the two main ones were south of the river a short distance. "There are one or two small ones here on the beach but they're buried now in flood water." (Later they were named Kraus Hot Springs after Gus and Mary Kraus, who lived there off and on between 1940 and 1971.)

What I remembered most about this area were the number of hummingbirds; they seemed to be everywhere. And the wild roses— the emblem of the province where I was born.

The four of us were on the river at nine the next morning, and even the dogs seemed to be willing to be back on the new raft. We didn't lose any time going through The Splits, a multi-channeled, low-lying area of dozens of wooded islands jammed high with log piles at their upper end. It was a vast, open flood-way of swiftly moving water. No effort was required with our paddles. It was only necessary to keep in the centre of the channels, well away from numerous sweepers jutting out from the islands.

Just after 4 p.m. we drifted down the last mile and tied the raft up to the little dock below the village. Dogs began to bark up on the bank, and as we were moving our outfit off the raft, Mrs. Mulholland came running down to the dock.

"My God! You chaps are back! We've been wondering. Come up to the cabin. These mosquitoes are terrible!"

We brought the moose meat up with us, and the first thing I smelt when I entered the cabin was newly baked bread. Now I knew we were in civilization.

Mrs. Mulholland was glad to have her clothes back. "I thought I'd never see them again," she said. She never mentioned the flour and I never asked. It was all water under the bridge as far as I was concerned.

At the moment, Nahanni Village was deserted except for Mrs. Mulholland and a number of husky dogs. Jack Mulholland and several other residents had gone down to Fort Simpson, along with part of the Indian population. The others were fishing at a lake, including Boo Joda and the Indians at Netla.

Nigger and Liza were glad to find refuge in a couple of vacant dog kennels that were equipped with mosquito netting. After we removed the mooring rope from the raft and brought the rest of our belongings up to the cabin, we were also thankful to be away from the swarming hordes. They were even worse here than on the portage.

Our supper that night at the mouth of the Nahanni was beyond description. Fresh meat and freshly-baked bread! Butter! Strawberry jam! All with thanks to Mrs. Mulholland's hospitality.

Gold Is Where You Find It

Mrs. Mulholland made our day the next morning when she treated us to a pancake breakfast, complete with Roger's syrup and plenty of hot coffee. It had been almost ten months since Harry had tasted java. And it was here in this same cabin since I had mine. How could I possibly forget the occasion that cost me our precious flour? And I am sure Mrs. Mulholland remembered that morning also.

She said that we were welcome to take Jack's small canoe to the Netla. "Milt has been worried about you fellows and he will be waiting."

We didn't know how Milt was fixed for food at Boo Jodah's place, so Harry purchased a small sack of oatmeal, twenty-four pounds of flour, and a pound of tea as we were making ready to leave. We left one of the beaver pelts in return. Considering the shape it was in, it likely wasn't worth much more than the items.

At 10 a.m. we were paddling the sixteen-foot canoe close to the west shore of the Liard, managing to keep out of the current and making good time upstream to the Netla River, fourteen miles away. I asked Harry if it was proper for me to sit down in the canoe while paddling. "The last time I was in one was the summer of 1935 at Sylvan Lake in Alberta," I said. "Is it permissible? I don't like to look foolish. I never did find out where to sit on our rafts—as you know."

"Well log rafts are more complicated, Friday, me lad. You don't learn where to sit on them overnight. Now when I was your age I was full of energy. Where to sit never entered my mind; I never sat. But if you feel comfortable in the bow seat, I'd use it. You have my permission."

And so I sat, and was enjoying every minute of it, even if it was upstream travel. This Liard—she was one big stream!

At noon we put the canoe into shore and made tea. The mosquitoes were terrible. We drank our tea holding our heads almost over the small flame of the birch fire. Harry admitted they were just as bad—or even worse—here in the Liard River country as anywhere he had been. We didn't tarry long at this break. And the dogs couldn't get back in the canoe fast enough.

At three in the afternoon, Harry pointed to the mouth of the Netla across the river. We ran the canoe a bit farther upstream, then began the crossing to the east shore. We dug in with the paddles to counteract the Liard current, and after more than half a mile of it, I learned how big this Northern river really was.

As we paddled the mile up Netla River to Jodah's place, Milt must have seen us coming for he was standing in the doorway of the cabin when we tied up at the landing. He did look relieved, as one well could imagine.

The first thing I noticed was a pan of baking powder biscuits that looked like they had just come out of the oven. And Milt was just as glad to see the roast of moose meat that Mrs. Mulholland had prepared. We were soon sitting down to what might be described as an afternoon supper—and I didn't have to rustle a single piece of firewood in the making. Not one of Milt's biscuits survived the onslaught. The only thing that marred that meal was the constant drone of mosquitoes determined to fight their way into the cabin.

We talked the remainder of the day about the nineteen-day trip down the Nahanni—and of the latest news from home. A great thrill for me was the old gramaphone sitting on a small table by the window. I had been a country music fan since I was eleven years old, and presently "The Wreck of the Old 97" and "There's an Old Spinning Wheel in the Parlour" were resounding throughout the cabin. There was also a small mantel radio, belonging to Milt, which served to remind me that I really was back in civilization.

After breakfast the next morning, we asked Milt if he would cut our hair. After a quick appraisal he said, "I'm not sure it can be done with just a pair of scissors. What's needed is a brush-cutting machine like they use for clearing land, but I'll try." And try he did for the rest of the forenoon.

Harry and Milt were anxious to get on down to Fort Simpson to purchase supplies for the coming winter's trapping season. This time they would be together, running a trapline in the proper manner—having a main cabin and adequate out-camps, and with at least one dog team. As the regulations in the Northwest Territories required four years of residence (they only had three) it meant that the boys would be heading for the Yukon where there were still no regulations.

According to the news from Alberta (or any of the other provinces) the Depression was still flourishing as strong as ever, so it seemed to be the best move for them to make. As for me, I also wanted to be in Simpson as soon as possible. I had no idea what I would do when I got there. With me it was a case of "seek and ye *may* find."

As it turned out, we spent more than a week at the Netla. Jodah and all the Indians were away fishing and Milt didn't want to leave the cabin unattended while Boo was away. There was also one or two other matters to be attended to.

I wanted to make use of myself, doing something constructive and so I spent most of the mornings, when the mosquitoes weren't so bad, hoeing Boo's big potato garden or splitting wood. Harry was right: these head nets might have been of some protection back home, but they sure as hell weren't much good here on the Liard.

Finally one evening, an Indian family returned, and the next morning, July 1, we loaded our belongings into Harry and Milt's eighteen-foot canoe and set out on the 120 mile (193 km) trip to Fort Simpson. And we didn't need to paddle; the five-horsepower Johnson outboard motor supplied the labour. And the six-mile-an-hour current helped us on our way.

About twenty-five miles (forty kilometres) past Nahanni Village, Milt, who was handling the kicker, turned the canoe into the right shore where we tied up on the beach below a large cabin overlooking the river. I remembered what Harry had said when we were building our first raft at the Rabbitkettle: "We won't go by the Lindberg place without stopping in to see them."

It wasn't just another cabin on the Liard that one might find anywhere along this great river. It was a well-kept homestead in every sense of the word—complete with a nice garden and even a deep well where perishables could be kept over a period of time.

We were invited to coffee in their spotless cabin where I was introduced to Ole and Anna, his Plains Cree wife, and their little boy. We spent an hour or more at their home, talking about the Nahanni and trapping in general. We could have talked longer but we had to go.

We arrived at Fort Simpson at noon the next day, and beached the canoe at the boat landing beneath the high bank of the island. Milt went ahead with the axes and began setting up his ten by twelve tent on the flats, just south of the village. Meanwhile Harry and I began packing our belongings up the hill.

There were at least a dozen tents pitched at random along the length of the flats. "We will have plenty of company, Al, these next few days. It's Treaty time and the Indians will be here in full force."

"How much are they paid?" I asked.

"Five dollars per person," Harry said.

"I sure wish I was an Indian, I don't even have five cents, let alone five dollars."

Harry laughed and sort of passed it off as a joke—as if it was quite natural for one to be financially impoverished. I saw it in a different light.

Nigger and Liza were the last of the outfit to be brought up from the beach. When they saw about fifty of their kind staked out among the tents, and each one howling to its heart's content, our dogs drew back on their chains, cowering on the ground, and refused to advance an inch farther. They knew their own species out there, but they wanted no part of those long-haired huskies. We almost had to pack both dogs up to the tent.

Tiny Gifford was the man I wanted to see. The mail plane had arrived that morning from points south and I found Tiny sorting letters at his table. He was glad to see me and wanted to know about my trip. I told him. He said, "Well, I'm sorry to hear that—but you're back, and that's all that really matters. That Nahanni is a bad river in

222

the late spring . . . just find yourself a chair while I put the coffee on. Do you like raisin muffins? I made a batch yesterday."

Tiny was full of questions. He asked if we had found any trace of Mulholland and Eppler, and I told him we hadn't. I mentioned about finding the green tarp at a trapper's apparent trail stop near the mouth of the Rabbitkettle, but that it hadn't provided any clues. "We left the tarp with Mrs. Mulholland," I said.

"I knew both men well—especially Eppler, and I have been concerned about them ever since they didn't come back. One hates to believe that old friends are suddenly gone."

I told Tiny that he would never know how much his toboggan meant to me out on the trapline and why we had to leave it in Dead Men's Valley. "It's tied up in a tree, along with some other stuff, at the mouth of Sheep Creek."

"Well any time I can be of help, just ask," the big man said.

And he was. He told me that the Indian agency had four acres of brush adjacent to the Dominion Experimental Farm that they wanted cleared. He said that it was his understanding the Agency would pay seventy-five dollars per acre for the job. Would I be interested? Tiny knew my answer before he asked. "The land in question is little more than a stone's throw from my cabin. Let's go have a look at it."

A single glance at the area told me that I could make some real money at this clearing job.

That afternoon Tiny went with me to see Fort Simpson's resident doctor, a Dr. Truesdell, who was also the Indian agent at the time. The doctor sized me up reasonably closely and decided I was the man for the job. Tiny explained that I had seen the acreage to be cleared and knew the exact location. The only stipulation the doctor made concerned four large trees: he wanted them set aside for firewood.

I said that I would measure out the area to be cleared (the four acres) and have Tiny and the doctor verify it.

"One acre of land covers a piece of ground 69 1/2 yards square," I said. "And I will put the brush in reasonably high piles, but I won't pack any of the stuff more than forty feet. And at the end of a week I'd want you to come out and inspect my work."

The doctor looked at Tiny and Tiny looked at the doctor, and smiled. "I take it that you have cleared land before," Truesdell said.

"I have," I said. "I was born and raised on a farm in Alberta, and

I've seen more than one brush-clearing dispute. It's better to have things understood at the start."

And so it was agreed. I opened an account at the Bay store that evening and bought a large axe and food items: beans, rolled oats, flour, rice, and some cured bacon and tea. I decided I would live like a king as long as the work lasted.

The next morning I moved my belongings down to the south end of the acreage and set up a fly-camp, similar to a lean-to, but not as elaborate. Harry remarked that he had never heard of anyone getting a job in Fort Simpson on the first day of his arrival—especially when he knew only one person in the village.

When I thought about the roundabout route it took me to get here to work, and the many months since that January boxcar ride to Dawson Creek, I answered, "Yes, I suppose I am lucky. But a man's luck has to change for the better sooner or later—thanks to Tiny Gifford."

A few days later, Tiny came down to see how I was making out. The first thing he saw was my fly-camp. "Good God, man—you must be sleeping on the bare ground! You need a cot and a tent! Come with me!"

"I really don't need a tent, Tiny. If I get cold [I laughed] any time this summer, I can always build a fire. There's no shortage of wood close at hand."

"You can't just leave your stuff under a fly. Come with me—I have an eight by ten tent up at the cabin."

He made me stop and have coffee with him, and while we were waiting, he asked me if I ever attended the Calgary Exhibition and Stampede.

"At least every other year since I was knee-high to a grasshopper. Where could I see entertainment like that for fifty cents each day? Grandstand seats were only a dollar."

"Did you know Pete Knight?"

"Only to see him," I said.

"Well, he was killed by a bucking horse at a rodeo in the States a few days ago. And there's more bad news: Amelia Earhardt and her navigator, Noonan, have disappeared somewhere over the Pacific. I got the news from the Wireless boys. My radio isn't working at the moment."

These were tidings that no one across North America wanted to hear. But Tiny also had welcome news. Any day now, the paddle-wheeler *The Distributor* would be arriving on its first trip of the year down the Mackenzie to Aklavik. "It's quite an event for all of us here at Simpson. You make sure you don't miss it."

And sure enough—about two days later, I heard a boat whistle. I dropped my axe in a hurry and headed for the path leading down to the road above the river. *The Distributor* was just tying up at the small dock built out a few yards from the beach. The RCMP and other important people, including the doctor and Hudson's Bay manager, were already down on the beach, forming the welcoming committee, for there were some highly regarded dignitaries aboard this vessel. Standing on the high bank overlooking the beach, was every remaining person in Fort Simpson—Indians and whites.

There was a second welcoming committee, also. About 200 sleigh dogs sensed that something was afoot, and when the entourage appeared at the top of the hill, it was greeted by 200 different wailing howls. Everyone in the group must have realized they were now in the True North.

First to arrive on the road was a small man flanked by two Mounties. Everyone recognized him. He was Sir John Buchan, governor general of Canada—a modest man admired by all. He struck me as a man who wanted to see as much as possible while time permitted. *The Distributor* had a schedule to keep.

And in the troupe was a woman who wanted to see *everything* at once, and to record it at once on film. She was Margaret Bourke White, the famed photographer from *Life Magazine*. To watch her trying to get just the *right* picture of that three-year-old Indian girl was something to see. And she did—for I saw the picture months later. She reminded me of a hummingbird as she flitted from one place to another.

That evening I decided to splurge. I had received ten dollars in advance on my brush cutting account, so after the boat had left, I made off to Andy Whittington's small "hotel" where people passing through or staying for a short time, could bunk for the night or have a good meal for the sum of *one* dollar. Everybody liked Andy—a man who had trod many a forest trail and seen many streams of the Liard and Mackenzie country in his time.

And a sumptuous meal it was. He too, had heard a thing or two about our trip down the Nahanni. He had one comment: "A log raft on the Nahanni in high water—you boys must have been on the right side of the angels."

"We were," I said. I handed him the ten and he pushed it away. "It's already paid for," he said. "Harry came in to see me yesterday and brought in two beaver pelts. He said that one of them was yours. I'm sorry I couldn't offer more than eight dollars apiece. They were in pretty bad shape."

I had completely forgotten about the pelts, but Harry hadn't. He wanted me to have my share—no matter how small. Andy was about to pay me the seven dollars owing on the pelt, but I told him I'd take it in future meals.

A couple of days later, Harry came to the tent and said that he and Milt were leaving for Nahanni Village that morning. I walked back to the beach with him to say goodbye and wish them well. I gave each dog a pat on the head and a shake of the paw as they were led onto the boat. And that was the last time I saw Nigger and Liza. I felt a bit lonely as I made my way back to the tent.

I always worked in the early mornings and later in the day to avoid the extreme July heat. And one evening just at sundown, I thought I heard an unusual amount of activity in the village so I went down to investigate. All the Indians in Simpson were gathered around a large tent on the flats. They were milling about, laughing and joking—one family with another, and they all seemed to know one another. Tiny Gifford was standing in his doorway when I came by and I asked him what was going on.

"They've received their Treaty money and they are having their annual celebration. It's a genuine powwow. It's something to see."

"How long does it last?"

"Till the sun rises in the morning," Tiny said.

It *was* quite a show. The dance began about 10 p.m. and everyone formed a large circle. It was not a dance in our sense of the word, but rather a continuous shuffle, whereby the participants grasped hands and moved sideways in a unique, sliding motion while always keeping in perfect tempo with the three of four drummers who sat in the centre of the circle. The steady *pong pong* of the beat never changed, nor

226

did the rate of movement. When someone in the circle grew tired, another would step in to take his or her place. The children shuffled too—and every single one was chewing gum. Most of the elderly Indians were sitting inside the tent, smoking their pipes—women as well as men. The other men were all smoking Turret tailor-made cigarettes extracted from a ten-cent package. A young Slavey saw me watching the circle. He came over and held out his package. I took one. I learned later that the Indian would have been offended had I not accepted. He, like all the natives I was to meet while in the North, was only trying to be friendly to a white person and to be considered his equal.

It was the ten-cent package of cigarettes that brought back memories to me of home. Why, I was no different than this chap—except in colour! At the dances back home, did I not make a big thing about flashing that little ten-cent package among my friends? Of course—and for the same reason, almost. I was trying to pretend that I was *affluent* and was above having to "roll my own." Yes, those tiny packs were symbolic of the Great Depression—whether in the provinces of Canada or here on the bank of the Mackenzie.

It was truly a night for the natives and one for me to remember. The circle never stopped moving and it must have been after one in the morning when I returned to the clearing.

The first week of August was passed and I now had more than half the acreage cleared and the brush piled. I knew that I could complete the contract in early September and would soon have to think about the winter. Tiny came out to the area one day and I asked him what he thought my chances were of getting a cordwood contract from the Hudson's Bay Company.

"I don't see why not. Anybody that can swing an axe like you do ought to be able to make a winter's stake-out there along the river. You will need a tent in any event. I have a proposition to make. If you will give me a week's work digging potatoes, I will give you the tent."

The wages rate for day-labour along the Mackenzie at that time was five dollars. I knew the tent was worth more than a week's work and told Tiny so. "That may be," he said, "but I need a man I can depend on. My potatoes must be loaded on the scow by September 10th and no later."

I told Tiny I would be there with bells on. He was the last man in the world I would have turned down—even if I hadn't needed the tent.

September 1 found me with a six-tine fork in my hand, making the spuds fly, and on the due date Tiny Gifford was plying his scow northward down the broad Mackenzie. I went back to the clearing. I figured that two more days would finish the job.

At noon on the twelfth, I heard a place overhead. I was expecting mail from home, but when I watched the aircraft make the U-turn to come in for a landing, I knew it wasn't a Norseman or the Bellanca, which were the designated mail planes, but I wanted to make sure.

You can imagine my surprise when I reached the beach. There was Dalziel. The Flying Trapper. He had just finished heeling in his Fairchild (I think it was) to the shore. We shook hands. He mentioned that he had seen Harry and Milt in late July at Nahanni Village, so he obviously knew all about our sojourn in the Nahanni. He seemed anxious to know what I was up to, and I told him.

"I have a better idea," he said. "Gold has been discovered at Yellowknife and I'm on my way there now. Why don't you come along?"

During the past month it had been rumoured at Simpson there was a gold strike at that place but nobody seemed to be very interested—rumours had existed for two years about gold being found on the north arm of Great Slave Lake. And rumours are cheap, as we all knew.

And so I said—a bit testily perhaps, "Listen Dal! There was supposed to be all that gold up the Flat River. And there was supposed to be all the beaver in the world up at the Rabbitkettle. Well there wasn't."

"You can take my word for it, Al. There are going to be two mines at Yellowknife—the Consolidated and the Negus. Consolidated is building the head frame now, and mill machinery has already arrived at the camp dock. Part of the camp—cookhouse and one bunkhouse—is already built. The Negus is doing groundwork at the moment. If you still want to cut wood, I'll guarantee there will be lots of that to do."

I could picture myself sleeping in a snow-bound tent along the Mackenzie River somewhere, eating frozen bannock and talking to myself night after night, and so I said, "How much will the flight cost me?"

"How would sixty dollars suit you?"

"I'll go," I said. "But I need about two hours to get ready."

"I'll wait," Dal said, "but please don't dally around." That was George Dalziel—always the man in a hurry.

At the doctor's residence, I learned that Truesdell would be away for several days downriver. "I could give you $200 now, and the doctor will send you the remainder after he checks the area," Mrs. Truesdell said. That sounded fair enough to me. I explained to her that there was about a half day's work left to do on the north side of the clearing.

We took off at 1:30, and when we reached the Gros Cap at the junction of the two great rivers, Dalziel headed the plane up the Mackenzie into the east, then followed the northwest shore of Great Slave Lake until it reached the long north arm. There Dal flew directly across the arm to Yellowknife Bay. We were barely over the Bay when I saw the new buildings going up on and near the west shore. Farther along we passed over a group of tents and several cabins clustered around a big rock outcrop. Along the middle of the Bay, near the north shore, Dal brought the plane down and taxied to a small island near the mainland. When the pontoons touched bottom in the shallows near the narrows between the island (Latham Island) and the mainland, Dal cut the motor, and immediately we both waded to shore and secured the plane to the nearest tree.

Over on the mainland, I saw two planes tied up to a large dock on the south side of the Bay near the main settlement. I asked Dal why he hadn't moored his plane there and he said, "That dock belongs to Canadian Airways, and they can go to hell! I don't need any help from them." Dal didn't elaborate and I didn't ask questions.

A very capable, teen-aged girl, Bertha Watt, rowed us across the narrows in her small skiff, to the settlement surrounding the Rock, on the mainland. Here we had coffee and sandwiches at Pete Racine's log hotel.

I spent several hours that evening exploring the tent and cabin village (now known as Old Town). Dalziel hadn't exaggerated: this place was really humming—humming with the drone of aircraft overhead, coming in for a landing in the Bay and taking off for unknown lakes to the north and east that held the promise of more gold. Yellowknife was not a pretense; it was the real thing.

Pete Racine, the jovial Frenchman, a true northerner and everybody's friend, introduced me to Ted Cinnamon, another man of the North, who had obtained a large wood-cutting contract to supply wood for the boiler house at the Consolidated camp.

The next morning I joined his crew, engaged in cutting logs on the east side of the Bay. There was a great demand for log cabins and Ted was just the man for that type of job. He was a hustler and he ran a good camp.

Late in September, I received a cheque for fifty dollars, "in payment for the balance owing you," the statement read. It was signed by Dr. Truesdell of Fort Simpson. According to my arithmetic the cheque was short by thirty-five dollars—assuming that a day's pay should be sufficient to cover the half day's work left on the clearing site. Truesdell never replied to my caustic letter stating that I expected to be paid the money still owing me.

After the cabins were built, I cut cordwood for Ted from the beginning of the winter until the following April. It was tough work, as the trees were small and it took a lot of axe-work and sawing to make a cord. But I still cleared more than six hundred dollars for the winter's work, besides meeting some fine friends.

In early June, after the spring breakup began, the real rush for gold was on in earnest. One of the men who had been at the wood camp, a carpenter by trade, asked me if I would help him set up a tent camp for a small mining outfit that was locating at a lake east of Yellowknife. There was a week's work involved, he said.

The next day found me loading rough lumber into a Canadian Airways Junkers plane, and an hour later the pilot had put us down in a small cove on the shore of an unnamed lake. We worked long hours and the camp was completed in five days. Henry paid me forty dollars for my help in setting up the camp. I decided that I would stay in the Yellowknife vicinity forever.

When the plane was due in, the manager of the mining company, who had been living in a small tent at the site, asked me if I cared to stay another week and help him put up a small log building that would be used to store dynamite. "Henry tells me you have helped build log cabins," he stated. I said I had. And the next day I began cutting logs for the eight by eight foot structure.

During the second day we became better acquainted and he asked me to call him Amos J. and said that he would appreciate it if I wouldn't divulge where this campsite was situated. "There are a lot of secrets connected with this mining business—and in any event they will find out sooner or later what's going on out here."

On the fifth day the building was finished, complete with an air vent on the gable roof. Now I'd have two days to wait for the scheduled plane.

"How would you like to stake a couple of claims for yourself while you are waiting? We have ours registered. You could tie onto ours if you want."

"I don't know the first thing about staking claims," I said.

"I'll come out and show you. You only need to swing an axe—and you sure know how to do that. We'll be starting our assessment work on our claims as soon as the men arrive. Until that's finished we won't know what we have out there—if anything."

By mid-afternoon that job was finished—with my name on the corner posts. Two days later, I was back in Yellowknife at the mine-recording office.

I found Henry, the carpenter, working for another contractor from Edmonton, who was building a warehouse for the Yellowknife Supplies store that had been built in the late summer of 1937. I went to work at the helper's rate of seventy-five cents an hour, pretending that I knew something about carpenter work and fooling no one.

One day the contractor asked me to build a small table, suitable to put a typewriter on. He quickly drew a sketch, telling me to use four short lengths of two-by-fours for the legs. "It doesn't have to be very elaborate," he said.

While I was busy working on this job, an important looking chap, dressed in khaki shirt, whipcord pants, and genuine, Yellowknife prospector's boots, kept coming over to my work place, intently inspecting my workmanship. Finally, the crude-looking specimen was finished and I gave it to the foreman. Later I happened to be packing a length of lumber through the store, and spotted the chap at his typewriter, about twenty feet away. He held his arm out and crooked his index finger in my direction. I laid the length of lumber down on the floor and walked over to the table. "Say keed," he said, "How's about you cutting an inch off these legs. They are a little long."

I stared at him a moment, then asked, "Are you usually in the habit of summoning your underlings in this manner?" He just looked at me and grinned.

"Well how's about you cutting the damned legs down yourself, chum," I said, and walked away. Later the foreman asked me if I knew who this guy was. I said I didn't. "He's Gordon Sinclair, the roving reporter for *The Toronto Star*," he said.

"Well, if he is King Tut's greatest grandson I couldn't care less," I replied. I was told some months later that he had written an account of his stay in the North, in which he described Yellowknife as the town of "cream puff" gold miners—a very endearing remark indeed, if true.

In August we had another visitor from the east. An amphibian plane landed in the Bay, bringing Premier Hepburn from Ontario. Vic Ingraham, the man who lost both legs in a boat accident at Great Bear Lake in the fall of 1932, and who now had Yellowknife's first frame hotel almost completed except for the steps leading up the slope to the entrance, was trying in every way possible to have the building ready for the premier's party. Two men from our crew were sent over to help out.

On September 7, two days after the first gold brick was poured at the Consolidated Mine, I and most of the helpers around the Rock were laid off. The building activity was coming to a close due to the shortage of lumber and other material.

I had seen some muskeg timber in a long draw (where School Road is now) north of the Con camp that I thought might be worth cutting, so I went to see George Carter, the surface foreman at Consolidated. I had known George during the past winter when I was working at Cinnamon's camp. "Why that draw can't be more than fifteen minutes from our woodpile by the cookhouse. We'll buy every cord you can find. Just make sure we can get a sleigh into the piles."

That afternoon I made preparations to move my tent over to the draw. I was busy packing when Henry came over and told me that someone wanted to see me at the Ingraham Hotel. Who should it be but Amos J. from the lake east of town. They had been trenching, he said, and found good indications but diamond drilling would be required before any major activity could take place. "However, there is a man upstairs who will buy your two claims if you care to sell. I thought you should know. I am not advising you one way or the other."

"How much will he pay for them?" I asked.

"Two hundred apiece."

"Send him down," I said. I was having a hard time trying to conceal my enthusiasm. An hour later, the two claims had changed hands. Now I was *certain* I would stay in Yellowknife forever.

To celebrate, I went over to the Wildcat Cafe to have a meal before moving camp. And there I received the surprise of my life—a shock might be a better word: there in a booth sat Harry Vandaele.

We talked for nearly two hours, eating raisin pie and drinking coffee. I gathered that he and Milt had had an unsuccessful winter's trapping season in the Yukon, and had decided to seek a different occupation. Harry had arrived in Yellowknife the week before and had gotten a job with Boyle's Diamond Drilling Company, which had its camp just across the Bay on the north shore. It was his day off and he had come to look me up.

"I finally decided to visit Yellowknife, Al, and I'm not sorry. I've seen more gold in the past week than all that time I spent in the Nahanni or on the Liard."

Willie Wylie, the owner of the Wildcat, brought us more coffee and asked, "Are you the two guys who came down the South Nahanni on a raft?" We said we were. "Well, the next time you two chaps come in, your dinner will be on me."

From mid-September to November 10, I had cut forty-two cords of wood and I earned every stick of it. The trees were small and some of them had to be packed down off the rock slopes bordering the draw. But I was not about to complain. George Carter seemed to be impressed by what he saw. "We need another man to work on the wood haul this winter. Would you be interested? The job pays five dollars per day but some of them may be long ones, due to sleigh trouble and such," he said.

"Are you kidding? When do I start?"

"Tomorrow morning," Carter said.

That evening I began a three year and two month's stint with Consolidated Mining and Smelting, and never regretted it.

In late November Harry came into my room at the Con bunkhouse. He looked haggard and worn out. "My back is giving me trouble, Al. I've just been over to see Dr. Stanton [the resident doctor for many years after whom the hospital was named]. He says I need an operation and it may have to be done in the States."

I didn't know what to say. Finally it came out. "That's the last thing I wanted to hear, Harry."

"Well Al, that's the way the ball bounces." It was one of his favourite expressions when things went wrong.

"When will you leave for Edmonton?"

"Just as soon as the planes can use skis. It should be any day now."

I walked with my old pal down to the dock where Bob Guck would take Harry back to Yellowknife town with his dogteam. It was not a happy parting.

"Goodbye Crusoe," was all I could manage.

"Take care, Friday," he replied, "and don't take any wooden nickels."

It took me a long time that night finally to fall asleep.

On Christmas Eve I was to have another stroke of luck in earning money the easy way. During those first Depression years at our house in Alberta we played poker instead of bridge. It was mostly penny-ante stuff; the most anyone could lose would be two or three dollars during an evening. But here in the back room of Pete Racine's Corrona Inn, the bets were slightly higher. The play was for "table stakes," meaning that you sat into the game with the amount of money you intended to wager during the evening placed directly in front of you on the table. In other words it could not be replenished from one's pocketbook.

During the first couple of hours, I was ahead of the game by about forty dollars, and then the play began to get a bit rough. These guys proceeded to raise the price of poker by raising each other's bets—a not uncommon practice in most places.

At 1 a.m. it happened. There were five of us playing seven-card stud. The first and second cards were dealt face down and the third one up. One fellow opened the pot for ten dollars. Everybody anteed up. I had the jack of hearts showing, and when I peeked at the under cards I noted that I had the three and four of hearts. Three hearts—just like that—and four more cards to come. On the next card dealt, the chap on my right drew the king of spades. He now had the ace and king of spades showing and he placed a ten dollar bet. Everyone called. I hadn't helped my hand with the queen of clubs. On the next card up, the fellow on my right drew another king and I drew the six of hearts. Another ten dollar bet was made. On the following card I drew the five of hearts. The fellow on my right was dealt another king and he now placed a twenty-five dollar bet. The other three gamblers dropped out. I couldn't see how I could fold; I had a flush and he definitely had three kings. I should have raised his bet, but I just called.

Now cometh the last card. The appointed dealer for the evening wet his thumb and forefinger and deal the seventh card face down. The man on my right didn't hesitate: he made a table stakes bet, which meant that I could call but could not raise.

I pondered the situation. This chap likely figured that I had a flush. I thought that he could have four kings or perhaps a full house. Either hand would have my flush beat.

I gently raised my seventh card and stole a peek. It was the seven of hearts! I couldn't believe it. I pushed the ninety-five dollars in front of me, into the centre of the table. There was a noticeable hush in the small room. The guy on my right turned his under cards up. He held a full house—three kings and a pair of tens. My opponent couldn't believe it either, when he saw my *straight* flush in hearts.

My total winnings on this Christmas Eve were $180. The lights were on in the Con cookhouse when I returned to camp. I had a couple of sandwiches and some coffee. Although I was a long way from home on this festive evening, I did not feel lonely.

I was to spend three more memorable years at the Consolidated mine. Dalziel had not been spoofing when he said they had found gold at Yellowknife.

I was married in the fall of 1939 and built a small frame house near the lakeshore the following spring. In '41 it was rumoured that the mine might shut down because of the war in Europe, and that summer a number of workers left Yellowknife. I sold the house that fall and on New Year's Day of 1942 I flew out to Edmonton.

The Great Depression was alive and well in that city. I had three different jobs in less than three months. One consisted of candling eggs at thirty-four cents an hour. Candling eggs? Decisions, decisions! Was this one a grade B or a C? And just a few months earlier I had been earning $5.60 a day, running a stoper underground at the Con.

In April I had the reunion of a lifetime: Harry Vandaele had had a successful operation in Rochester, Minn., and was now operating his own mink ranch just south of Calgary. I spent a happy week with Crusoe, helping him dig a well at his acreage.

A month later I began working for the Canadian National Railways at their shipyard in Prince Rupert, B.C. We were building Liberty ships for the Navy. Here I joined the pipe-fitting department and through hard work and diligence, earned my Marine Ticket before being called into the Army in October of 1944. I had received two deferments previous to this.

My stay in the Infantry was short. Our battalion was sent from advanced training at Petawawa to Debert, N.S., when the war in Europe ended and we were sent west to Dundurn, Sask., in June of 1945. That fall I was given another deferment to work in the Black Diamond Coal Mine east of Edmonton. This was a dangerous pathway to take but in many ways was the most rewarding: those coal miners were *real* men—men whom I soon came to respect. Being a coal miner never held a stigma for me.

I received my Army discharge in September of '46, whereupon I acquired an acreage in Edmonton. From then on I followed heavy construction jobs until my retirement in 1971. I was most fortunate to have been a part of the oil refinery days during the boom years from 1947 into the early Fifties. During that time I also built three houses on the acreage. My working hours in those days never ended at 4:30 p.m.

In 1954 I moved to B.C. where I continued in construction work, taking part in building a total of five pulp and paper mills throughout the province. A couple of years were also spent in the shipyards in Victoria. My last move was made to Seattle, Wash., where I installed piping systems in destroyer escorts that were being built for the Navy in the shipyards there. It was demanding work and required a certain degree of efficiency. Those five years in Seattle were among the most gratifying of any I spent in the construction industry. When the contract was finished I returned to my home in Victoria where I was to enjoy semi-retirement.

Then came 1984 and the sentimental journey.

Epilogue

One March evening in 1984, I was sitting in my den, sorting out the day's mail. There was an outdoor magazine in the lot and one advertisement caught my eye. It read: Nahanni Two Week National Park Canoe Trip. August 14–August 27. The ad was from Trail Head/Black Feather, a wilderness outfitting group based in Ottawa, Ont.

Now this was something to think about! Just imagine—drifting down a calm and contented Nahanni at one's leisure, gazing up at all that scenery while actually *sitting* in a specified seat. And never a mosquito to bother—not in August.

On further thought, I decided that I deserved this trip: I hadn't even been through the First Canyon, and as for the others, all I remembered seeing was a lot of angry water.

There was just one catch to this contemplated venture: my age. Forty-seven years had gone by since the February day that Stan McMillan had set me down by Harry's little tent near the Rabbitkettle River. And it didn't require a mathematical wizard to determine my age, since I was born in 1914. Seventy might be a trifle old to be cruising down the Nahanni in a two-man canoe. But after a short period of meditation, it suddenly became obvious to me that the only one to suffer from my inabilities would be my paddling partner during the trip. And so the decision was made.

On August 13, my son and I flew from Victoria, B.C., to the Edmonton airport in Alberta, and the next day—after boarding three different airlines—we found ourselves flying south over the Liard River, bound for Nahanni Butte, N.W.T. Six of our party, including the trip leader, Paul Mason, son of Bill Mason, were aboard the Twin-Otter aircraft that afternoon when we took off from Simpson Island and landed at the small airstrip at the Butte. Here at Park Headquarters, three aluminum canoes were loaded on one side of the plane while we passengers occupied the removable seats on the other.

Once again in the air, our destination was the Glacier Lake gravel bar, several miles west of the lake of that name, approximately 215 canoe miles (345 km) up the South Nahanni River. I was hoping that my picture of a gravel bar—as seen from a log raft—would be different from the one we were about to land on. But my apprehension was unfounded; we touched down as though there had been a tarmac strip below. We all helped to unload the canoes and camping equipment, and the pilot immediately took off back to Fort Simpson. In the morning he would return with the other half of our party and the remaining canoes.

While we were pitching our tents, Paul Mason was busy arranging his "kitchen" atop the nineteen-foot, overturned freight canoe. Its flat bottom served as an excellent table, while various items could be stored underneath.

Just before dusk, I walked over to the water's edge and gazed across the river into the east. Somewhere along that wooded slope, my part of *that* long-ago trapline must have run. I did have a faint recollection of the foothill ridge to the south, which rose on the right-hand side of the river. But no individual landmark stood out in my memory.

Early morning brought the remainder of our party into camp, and among them was Martyn Williams from Whitehorse, Y.T., a wilderness wanderer indeed. He was to be our back-up leader. He also knew a thing or two about geology, as we discovered later.

Our destination this first day was to an island near the western entrance to the Park (Nahanni National Park was established in 1972)—a short afternoon's run of about ten or twelve miles (sixteen or nineteen kilometres). Here we made camp. Everyone in our party was looking forward to this stop, for tomorrow we would be visiting

Rabbitkettle Hot Springs, which had acquired a scenic status second only to Virginia Falls over the years since my mammoth snow-covered rock that Harry had identified for me in 1937. Truly one of the Park's famous landmarks.

The next morning we beached our canoes on the south shore of the Nahanni and hiked the half mile into Rabbitkettle Lake to the warden's cabin. From there we set out on the trail, eastward, to Rabbitkettle River, here ferrying ourselves across the river by means of a small skiff attached to an overhead cable, and pulleys. A short walk brought us to the foot of the North Mound (my "Big Rock") on the south side of the river.

This flat-topped mound, as explained by the park warden, consists of a soft, rocklike matter called tufa, a porous limestone formed by minerals deposited by the radiating water arising from the hot springs. This emerges from an opening at the top of the mound, spreading to create a series of terraces. The mound is nearly 90 feet (27 m) in height and measures more than 200 feet (61 m) in diameter—a sizable work of nature.

After spending a lengthy time at the top around the orfice, most of the group began making its way back down the tricky incline. I tarried awhile at the summit, and as I chanced to gaze out into the spruce that lined the south bank of the river, I suddenly saw a picture. It was so amazingly clear in every detail: I saw a young man in a fur-trimmed parka, slowly making his way along a narrow snow trail—each snowshoe moving forward of the other in measured strides—followed by a grey, short-haired dog with the handle of an axe sticking up from one of her panniers. I stood there for a few moments with my thoughts on another day long past. But it was time to break from the reverie and join the others.

We had returned across the ferry and most of our group were already part way back to the lake. It had been a steep climb to the ridge and I was tired. I stopped at a vantage point and was looking into the Rabbitkettle Valley, when a young lady from the other party caught up to me. "It's a beautiful valley, isn't it?" she offered. I agreed. "It doesn't look a bit different than it did in 1937," I said.

"You must be the trapper that Jim Kievit [one of another party, who had preceded us to the island] was talking to last night! And you were here that long ago! It must bring back memories."

"It does," I said. And the lady's questions followed in quick succession. I could have mentioned Mulholland and Eppler, but there wasn't time. "We had both best get back to the lake, before the others have eaten all the lunch."

That evening, back on the island, the guides were discussing the next day's itinerary with our group. I knew what I wanted to do—I wanted to find those old campsites of 1937. That was what my sentimental journey was all about.

"By all means!" Paul said. "Where was your camp?"

"It's about two miles past the mouth of the Rabbitkettle—on the right-hand side of the Nahanni."

"If you think we can find the site, we'll sure try—things can change a lot over all that time," Paul said.

"That high cut-bank hasn't changed," I said. I'd recognize it in a second."

"Then we'll be at your old camp in less than an hour tomorrow," Paul said.

And we were. Paul and I were in the lead in the freight canoe when we glided past the Rabbitkettle. Less than a mile downstream I saw a bend in the river that looked familiar. We pulled over to the right and followed the shore for another mile, and suddenly across the river I saw the high bank. We tied up and scrambled through the willows onto the bank and waited for the other canoes to follow.

I was looking for certain stumps. There were many cuttings here of different ages, which was understandable as Dalziel likely had used this base camp for several years after Harry and I left the scene. There were a number of old stumps in the area where our tent had been, which may have been examples of our handiwork, but I couldn't be sure. I touched one of the stumps with my toe; I could have pushed it over.

Where was the old cache that Dalziel had built? I saw no sign of it. And the forest cover had changed. The area back of where the cache had been was covered with balsam poplars in 1937, and now time had replaced them with white spruce.

Martyn Williams made the clinching discovery. He beckoned me over to where he was standing and pointed to two, ten-gallon fuel drums and one four-gallon oil can lying in a willow thicket. We pulled the drums onto open ground for closer inspection. Martyn saw

241

me staring closely at the galvanized one, and asked me if I recognized it. I nodded and pointed to the top of the drum. "See those three capital letters—DAL—which are painted in red. Look closely. The paint is almost worn off but the outlines are still visible. The Flying Trapper always went by his nickname—Dal. He flew my partner into his camp in the fall of '36 and I joined him later in February. We used to cut up meat on that drum. Dal died at Fulford Harbour on Saltspring Island two years ago. My old pal died young—at the age of forty-eight, in Calgary in 1956. I wish he were here now." The memories were surging back and the tears came. Our group walked back to the old tent site and left me, momentarily, to my thoughts.

After pictures were taken, we all paddled across the river to the high cut-bank where the spring camp had been. Nothing had changed down through the years—except that the steep climb up the bank had gotten steeper. Was it just my imagination? Even the game trail was there, running past where our tent had been. "Looks like it has been used recently," Martyn exclaimed, pointing to bear dung. On examining the feces with a stick we found traces of caribou hair present, which indicated the presence of these animals in the area.

What I really wanted to find was some object that I could remember using (or having) that I might take back with me as a souvenir. I thought for sure that Paul had found it when he handed me a rusty tin plate that had been lying in the duff under a tree. But it hadn't belonged to either Harry or me. I would have remembered if we had left one of these behind (we only had three).

One object at the site did arouse my interest: it was a lone-standing cache tree. There was no trace of its mate. It could have blown over and been used for firewood. The top of the standing tree had been sawn off about one foot above the notch, as Harry and I had done when we built our cache here, but that was not positive proof that we were looking at the remains of ours. There are times when it becomes too easy to assume. It was obvious that other men had also camped here in the past.

Although there was nothing of special interest to the other canoe trippers at either of these old camps, I am sure they all understood what this visit meant to me, and they also were aware of how much I appreciated their undivided attention.

Later that day, Paul brought us to another stop which was definitely of everyone's interest. It was one of Albert Faille's old cabins that he had likely built above the Falls shortly after Harry and I had been in the country. The cabin was in bad shape, as is evident in the picture. One or two more June floods would have completely claimed it.

One of the boys helped me climb through an open window. There was a battered-up stove lying on the dirt floor, but Faille's bunk was still in position against the north wall. It boasted an old, ragged straw mattress that had been a maternity ward for God knows how many mice. There were several pages from a July 1941 issue of the *Edmonton Journal* fastened on the wall above the bunk.

That evening in camp this grand old man of the Nahanni was the main topic of interest, and well he should have been. Never did he cease trying to find the gold he was sure was there, until age forced him to stop.

The following day, in the afternoon, our canoes reached that long, straight stretch of water leading to the bend in the river, above Virginia Falls. A few minutes later we were pitching our tents in the Park campground on the south side of the river.

We had arrived at one of the most famous spots in North America and the excitement showed on everyone's faces. Paul took our group around a footpath that overlooked the main chutes leading to the Big Drop. A lot of scenery was recorded on film before the last of the sunlight finally faded into dusk.

Morning brought another busy day. Most of our party took the two-mile hike to Maringo Falls, which lay to the southwest of our camp. I wanted to locate the old Klondike portage trail Harry and I had taken and use it to reach the foot of the Falls. I followed the Park boardwalk over the bog area, then walked north into the bush for a short distance to where I thought the summit of the ravine should be, but I couldn't find it. No problem: I would use the Park trail down to the Falls. I knew I could find the ravine from below, then I would make the ascent back up to the boardwalk at the bog.

On the cobble beach, where we had built our second raft on that sultry June day, nothing looked the same as it was back then. The pinnacle rock near the centre of the main drop looked huge. As I remembered, it was just a small, triangular-shaped pinnacle, jutting into a cloud of fog. But the main difference was in sound: the rumble and thunder was missing until one reached the bottom of the drop. And the river! What a beautiful sight to see! There wasn't a ripple on the surface of that water. Not a single wave to be seen. One part of the landscape hadn't changed—the mountain rising back of the Falls, on the left side of the river, Sunblood Mountain.

I couldn't miss the bottom of the ravine. The short logs Faille had laid across the old trail were there to be seen. The first fifty yards of the climb was bad enough, and then time had made a genuine job of blockading that forty-five degree incline, and I was forced to back down, and take the easy way back to camp. One would have thought that I might have remembered that it was always easier to go from the top *down* than from the bottom *up*.

We were all busy the next morning moving the outfit down to the beach by the river. The younger men transported the canoes and I didn't have any objection to that.

I shuddered when I saw the loads Martyn Williams was packing down the lower part of the Park trail. Putting the spray covers on the canoes was the next job, and it kept both Martyn and Paul busy showing us how it is done. Finally, after several mistakes we were ready to board and leave the Falls behind.

My ride with Paul through the Five Mile (or Fourth) Canyon was a bit different than the one on the raft in '37. What few waves we encountered, were in a playful mood and it was a joy to glide through the multi-coloured walls under different circumstances.

A short run brought us to our next stop of interest: the notorious Hell's Gate. Our party had all heard of this place—the place that had stopped more than a few river men in its day. Almost everyone went up the portage trail to the top of the cliff to take pictures of the view that Harry and I had contemplated when he decided we could run Hell's Gate. Paul and I stayed behind to make sure the splash covers were in place.

But we needn't have worried. At this low stage of water there was no problem, and the other canoes followed us through the gorge without difficulty. But it was not for me to disparage the dangers of Hell's Gate; I had a long memory. It was the volume of water that had made the difference forty-seven years ago.

We camped that evening at Wrigley Creek, if I remember correctly, and quite early the next morning, a young caribou almost ran over me as I was walking around a bend on the gravel beach. It was the first wildlife I had seen since the start of our trip.

This day brought us down to the mouth of the Flat River (about twenty miles from the Falls), which was my partner's old stomping grounds, past Mary's River (where the young Indian girl was lost) and thence into the Third Canyon where we made camp at The Gate, where stood that famous pinnacle, Pulpit Rock. Aside from the Falls, this is probably the most photographed site on the river. For me, it was as if I had never been through this place before—except perhaps in some long-ago dream.

We were well into the Second Canyon the following morning when I was trying to determine where Harry and I had tipped over our raft that unlucky day, but I wasn't sure. On today's map it was likely at a bend in the river about six or seven miles below Pulpit Rock, while still in Third Canyon.

Early that afternoon, we drifted around the last bend in the Second Canyon and entered into the wide stretch of water in Dead Men's Valley.

Immediately I was able to recognize the surrounding terrain—the heavily-wooded shoreline on the north side of the river, and farther down the valley, the cleft in the canyon walls where Prairie Creek emerged down out of the mountains in the north to spread its fan-shaped delta over a wide area. I remembered when the western part of that delta was covered in water.

Directly across from the delta, we beached the canoes at the camp-site on the south shore and did the evening chores. Part of the group spent the night across the river near the delta.

Martyn took the group the next morning on a hiking trip up the Dry Canyon. They were gone most of the day. Paul stayed in camp, catching up on his art work and other essential activities. I spent several hours walking an old game trail down to the mouth of Sheep Creek (now Ram Creek) where Harry and I had begun our mosquito-infested portage around the First Canyon in 1937. I could have walked across that creek without getting my feet wet!

We spent the late afternoon taking pictures of the remains of old cabin sites along the south shore, and later, much of the history of Dead Men's Valley was bandied back and forth among us before the long evening finally ended.

Our first stop after leaving the valley was at the cobble island at George's Riffle—first known to me as the Snyder Gate—near the entrance to the First Canyon.

The route was obvious—as it had not been to us in that spring of '37 when we chose the mosquito-misery of portaging instead. We took the right channel and there was no problem in avoiding the standing waves; we simply skirted them by keeping to the left. And this time there were no balsam poplar trees competing with us for the right-of-way.

Several places drew our interest as we drifted through the First Canyon, where one could gaze forever at those awesome walls and cliffs. Someone in our party described the waterway as Canada's scenic wonderway. This wasn't an overstatement.

My biggest thrill of the trip was at the Lafferty's Riffle, where the alluvial deposits emitted at the mouth of Lafferty Creek have re- stricted the river's course, resulting in high, rolling waves on its right side. These can easily be avoided by keeping to one's left. Paul, however, wanted to make my sentimental journey as enchanting as possible, and with a single, subtle movement, he put our canoe through one of the waves, which dumped a few gallons of water over the bow onto my chest.

This particular spot on the river provided a sensational interlude between the areas of calm water. It was a section of the river where everyone could indulge in a bit of white water maneuvering in com- parative safety.

Mid-afternoon brought us to the Kraus Hot Springs at the eastern entrance of the Canyon. While the group lost no time in taking a long-awaited dip in one of the riverside pools, I spent some time in locating the mouth of Clausen Creek. I couldn't believe the water was that low. It was difficult for me—even now—to fathom what I clearly remembered: did Harry and I *really* fell that tree across the swollen creek that humid afternoon, desperate to get to the moose we'd shot?

We made our last river camp that evening in the area known as The Splits. I will always remember that Nahanni sunset. Words escape me to describe it. I give thanks that we could capture it on film.

The following afternoon, August 26th, we beached the canoes below the Park Warden's cabin at Nahanni Butte. An hour later we heard the drone of the Twin Otter, then watched it come in to land back of the Park buildings.

Too soon it seemed, we were bidding the Nahanni goodbye. My sentimental journey was over, but it will not soon be forgotten. Nor will those ten new friends I made during our short time together.

A. C. Lewis in 1984 on his return trip to the Nahanni area at age 70.